Dress and Cultural Difference in Early Moderr

European History Yearbook
Jahrbuch für Europäische Geschichte

———

Edited by
Johannes Paulmann in cooperation with Markus
Friedrich and Nick Stargardt

Volume 20

Dress and Cultural Difference in Early Modern Europe

Edited by
Cornelia Aust, Denise Klein, and Thomas Weller

DE GRUYTER
OLDENBOURG

Edited at Leibniz-Institut für Europäische Geschichte by Johannes Paulmann in cooperation with Markus Friedrich and Nick Stargardt

Founding Editor: Heinz Duchhardt

ISBN 978-3-11-063204-0
e-ISBN (PDF) 978-3-11-063594-2
e-ISBN (EPUB) 978-3-11-063238-5
ISSN 1616-6485

Library of Congress Control Number:2019944682

Bibliographic information published by the Deutsche Nationalbibliothek
The Deutsche Nationalbibliothek lists this publication in the Deutsche Nationalbibliografie; detailed bibliographic data are available on the Internet at http://dnb.dnb.de.

© 2019 Walter de Gruyter GmbH, Berlin/Boston
The book is published in open access at www.degruyter.com.

Typesetting: Integra Software Services Pvt. Ltd.
Printing and Binding: CPI books GmbH, Leck
Cover image: Eustaţie Altini: Portrait of a woman, 1813–1815 © National Museum of Art, Bucharest

www.degruyter.com

MIX
Papier aus verantwor-
tungsvollen Quellen
FSC
www.fsc.org   FSC® C083411

Contents

Forum

Cornelia Aust, Denise Klein, and Thomas Weller
Introduction

Dress has always been one of the most obvious markers of difference. Very close to the body, "vestimentary signs" become part of the daily habitus and an unavoidable means of communication.[1] Whereas most material objects of symbolic communication and social distinction are distant from the body, dress constitutes a "second skin" and is thus more likely than any other item to be identified with its wearer.[2] Many languages capture this relationship in the proverbial expression "clothes make the man".[3] And many cultures have folktales in which the motif appears. For instance, there is that of Nasreddin Hoca, the witty and wise hero of hundreds of stories told for half a millennium from the Balkans to the Middle East and Central Asia, who once went to a banquet where nobody took notice of him. On the next occasion, he put on his best clothes and found himself being treated with the utmost respect, whereupon he fed his soup to what had earned him this honor, his coat, telling it, "Eat, my fur coat, eat!"[4]

---

1 Roland Barthes: *The Language of Fashion*. London 2005 [*Système de la mode*. Paris 1967]; Joanne Entwistle: *The Fashioned Body. Fashion, Dress, and Modern Social Theory*. 2nd ed. Cambridge 2015; Odile Blanc: Historiographie du vêtement. Un bilan, in: Michel Pastoureau (ed.): *Le vêtement. Histoire, archéologie et symbolique vestimentaire au Moyen-Âge*. Paris 1989, 7–33; Roland Eckert and Stefanie Würtz: Kleidung als Kommunikation, in: Dorothea Lüddeckens, Christoph Uehlinger, and Rafael Walthert (eds.): *Die Sichtbarkeit religiöser Identität. Repräsentation – Differenz – Konflikt*. Zurich 2013, 77–84. For an anthropological view of dress, see Terence S. Turner: The Social Skin, in: *Journal of Ethnographic Theory* 2:2 (2012), 486–504 [reprint of 1980].
2 André Holenstein et al. (eds.): *Zweite Haut. Zur Kulturgeschichte der Kleidung*. Bern 2010; Monika Glavac, Anna-Katharina Höpflinger, and Daria Pezzoli-Olgiati (eds.): *Second skin. Körper, Kleidung, Religion*. Göttingen 2013; Joanne Entwistle: Fashion and the Fleshy Body. Dress as Embodied Practice, in: *Fashion Theory* 4 (2000), 323–347.
3 Harold D. Cordry: *The Multicultural Dictionary of Proverbs*. Jefferson 1997, 41; Martin Dinges: Von der "Lesbarkeit der Welt" zum universalisierten Wandel durch individuelle Strategien. Die soziale Funktion der Kleidung in der höfischen Gesellschaft, in: *Saeculum* 44 (1993), 90–112, here 90; id.: Der "feine Unterschied". Die soziale Funktion der Kleidung in der höfischen Gesellschaft, in: *Zeitschrift für Historische Forschung* 19 (1992), 49–76, here 51.
4 Nasreddin Hoca is his Turkish name, in other regions he is known as Molla Nasreddin, Juha, or by different names. On this literary figure and his tales, including the one cited above, see Pertev Naili Boratav: *Nasreddin Hoca*, 5th ed. Istanbul 2007, 168. For this and similar folktales from Western and Eastern Europe, see Hans-Jörg Uther: *The Types of International Folktales. A Classification and Bibliography Based on the System of Antti Aarne and Stith*

Dress tells stories about identity and belonging as well as about exclusion and stigmatization.[5] An expensive fur coat allows for the display of its wearer's status and wealth, yet old and patched clothes also mercilessly display his or her poverty and indigence. Clothes, moreover, make it possible for people to play with identities and affiliations. For instance, donning certain forms of dress enables individuals to claim higher social status, experiment with gender roles, and display or disguise their religion. It is this ambiguity of dress that makes it open to manipulation by the wearer and misinterpretation by the observer. This issue of the *European History Yearbook* investigates the intricate character of dress in society, focusing on a number of different European regions and their global entanglements in the early modern period.

The way people dressed acquired a new significance but also became more deceptive amid the early modern world's increasing social complexity. The growth of urban populations in most of Europe led to a higher degree of social differentiation, a process that went hand in hand with new perceptions of the self and of the place of the individual in society. Since the Middle Ages people across the continent had come to consider themselves – and everyone else – to be part of a strictly hierarchical order in which everybody occupied a specific place according to his or her social status, gender, ethnic belonging, and religion.[6] As symbolic communication and ritual were essential for the

---

Thompson, vol. 2. Helsinki 2004, 295–296; id.: Kleider machen Leute (AaTh 1558), Welcome to the Clothes (ATU 1558), in: *Enzyklopädie des Märchens*, vol. 7. Berlin 1993, 1425–1429.

5 Social theory has questioned the concept of identity as too static to describe an increasingly dynamic and complex social reality in which individuals often develop multiple belongings. See Rogers Brubaker and Frederick Cooper: Beyond "Identity", in: *Theory and Society* 29 (2000), 1–47; Floya Anthias: Identity and Belonging. Conceptualisations and Political Framings, in: *KLA Working Paper Series* 8 (2013). URL: http://www.kompetenzla.uni-koeln.de/sites/fileadmin2/WP_Anthias.pdf (6 Feb. 2019); Joanna Pfaff-Czarnecka: *Zugehörigkeit in der mobilen Welt. Politiken der Verortung*. Göttingen 2012, 10–12; Valentin Groebner: Identität. Anmerkungen zu einem politischen Schlagwort, in: *Zeitschrift für Ideengeschichte* 12 (2018), 109–115.

6 Barbara Stollberg-Rilinger: Die Wissenschaft der feinen Unterschiede. Das Präzedenzrecht und die europäischen Monarchien vom 16. bis zum 18. Jahrhundert, in: *Majestas* 10 (2002), 125–150; Peter Burke: The Language of Orders in Early Modern Europe, in: Michael L. Bush (ed.): *Social Orders and Social Classes in Europe since 1500. Studies in Social Stratification*. London 1992, 1–12; Dror Wahrmann: *The Making of the Modern Self. Identity and Culture in Eighteenth-Century England*. New Haven 2004. For the Ottoman context, see Gottfried Hagen: Legitimacy and World Order, in: Hakan T. Karateke and Maurus Reinkowski (eds.): *Legitimizing the Order. The Ottoman Rhetoric of State Power*. Leiden 2005, 55–83; Rhoads Murphey: Forms of Differentiation and Expression of Individuality in Ottoman Society, in: *Turcica* 34 (2002), 135–170.

legitimation and confirmation of this social and political order, and as social relations depended to a much greater extent than today on face-to-face communication, the particular place of the individual in society had to be visually apparent to the external observer at first sight.[7] Against this background, and with the growing wealth of early modern urban elites and the intensification of global trade, which brought new materials for making clothes and accessories, it comes as no surprise that dress and fashion became increasingly important means of social distinction and self-fashioning.[8] For Western Europe, where this process began during the late Middle Ages and intensified during the Renaissance, a striking example is provided by the sixteenth-century Augsburg patrician Matthäus Schwarz, who had himself portrayed more than 130 times wearing different attire.[9] In Ottoman Europe, the new significance of dress is evident, for instance, in the growing number of political treatises and social satires that discuss the clothing choices of the elite and mock the sartorial attempts of social climbers and the nouveau riche, from the second half of the sixteenth through the eighteenth century.[10]

In reaction to economic and socio-cultural transformations and in an effort to bring order to the increasingly complex social universe, religious and secular authorities on all levels and across Europe enacted an ever-growing number of

---

7 Barbara Stollberg-Rilinger: Much Ado About Nothing? Rituals of Politics in Early Modern Europe and Today, in: *Bulletin of the German Historical Institute* 48 (2011), 9–25; Rudolf Schlögl: Kommunikation und Vergesellschaftung unter Anwesenden. Formen des Sozialen und ihre Transformation in der Frühen Neuzeit, in: *Geschichte und Gesellschaft* 34 (2008), 155–224; Wim Blockmans and Antheun Janse (eds.): *Showing Status. Representation of Social Positions in the Late Middle Ages.* Turnhout 1999; Marian Füssel and Thomas Weller (eds.): *Ordnung und Distinktion. Praktiken sozialer Repräsentation in der ständischen Gesellschaft.* Münster 2005.

8 Stephen Greenblatt: *Renaissance Self-Fashioning. From More to Shakespeare.* Chicago 1980; Ulinka Rublack: *Dressing Up. Cultural Identity in Renaissance Europe.* New York 2010; Carol Collier Frick: *Dressing Renaissance Florence. Families, Fortunes, and Fine Clothing.* Baltimore 2005; Claudia Ulbrich and Richard Wittmann (eds.): *Fashioning the Self in Transcultural Settings. The Uses and Significance of Dress in Self-Narratives.* Würzburg 2015; Daniel Roche: *The Culture of Clothing. Dress and Fashion in the "Ancien Régime".* Cambridge 1996 [*La Culture des apparences. Une histoire du vêtement (XVIIe–XVIIIe siècle).* Paris 1990]; Catherine Richardson (ed.): *Clothing Culture, 1350–1650.* Aldershot 2004.

9 Ulinka Rublack and Maria Hayward (eds.): *The First Book of Fashion. The Book of Clothes of Matthäus and Veit Konrad Schwarz of Augsburg.* London 2015; Valentin Groebner: Insides Out. Clothes, Dissimulation and the Arts of Accounting in the Autobiography of Matthaeus Schwarz (1498–1574), in: *Representations* 66 (1999), 52–72.

10 See for instance Andreas Tietze: Mustafa ʿĀlī on Luxury and the Status Symbols of Ottoman Gentlemen, in: Alessio Bombaci, Aldo Gallotta, and Ugo Marazzi (eds.): *Studia turcologica memoriae Alexii Bombaci dicata.* Naples 1982, 577–590; [Anonymous]: *XVIII. Yüzyıl İstanbul Hayatına Dair Risâle-i Garîbe,* ed. by Hayati Develi. Istanbul 1998.

sumptuary laws. In the Holy Roman Empire alone, sumptuary legislation produced more than 1,300 regulations between 1244 and 1816.[11] However, the timing of authorities' heightened interference in how people dressed differed significantly from region to region. In some Italian cities, regulations on dress were already common in the thirteenth century.[12] In England, the sixteenth century was the heyday of sumptuary legislation, whereas in most other parts of Western Europe regulations peaked in the seventeenth and tailed off in the eighteenth century.[13] In Ottoman Istanbul, clothing legislation had existed for centuries but gained momentum only in the early eighteenth century with the development of a new middle class, urban culture, and heightened consciousness of fashion.[14] In certain south-eastern European regions under Ottoman rule, by contrast, clothing regulations appeared only in the late eighteenth century, as Constanța Vintilă-Ghițulescu shows in her contribution to this issue. Internal Jewish sumptuary laws, as Cornelia Aust describes, existed in Renaissance Italy and again in seventeenth- and eighteenth-century central and east-central Europe. The effectiveness of sumptuary legislation is debatable,[15] and other sources, such as inventories, provide only a limited corrective.[16] Yet the mere existence of these

---

11 Neithard Bulst: Zum Problem städtischer und territorialer Kleider-, Aufwands- und Luxusgesetzgebung in Deutschland (13. bis Mitte 16. Jahrhundert), in: André Gouron and Albert Rigaudière (eds.): *Renaissance du pouvoir législatif et genèse de l'Etat*. Montpellier 1988, 29–57; id.: Kleidung als sozialer Konfliktstoff. Probleme kleidergesetzlicher Normierung im sozialen Gefüge, in: *Saeculum* 44 (1993), 32–46; Ulinka Rublack: The Right to Dress. Sartorial Politics in Germany, c. 1300–1750, in: Giorgio Riello and ead. (eds.): *The Right to Dress. Sumptuary Laws in a Global Perspective, c. 1200–1800*. Cambridge 2019, 37–73.
12 Catherine Kovesi Killerby: *Sumptuary Law in Italy 1200–1500*. Oxford 2002.
13 Alan Hunt: *Governance of the Consuming Passions. A History of Sumptuary Law*. New York 1996, 36; Catherine Richardson: Status, in: Elizabeth Currie (ed.): *A History of Dress and Fashion in the Renaissance*. London 2017, 117–134, here 117–118.
14 Donald Quataert: Clothing Laws, State, and Society in the Ottoman Empire, 1720–1829, in: *International Journal of Middle East Studies* 29 (1997), 403–425; Shirine Hamadeh: *The City's Pleasures. Istanbul in the Eighteenth Century*. Seattle 2008.
15 Martin Dinges: Normsetzung als Praxis? Oder: Warum werden die Normen zur Sachkultur und zum Verhalten so häufig wiederholt und was bedeutet dies für den Prozess der "Sozialdisziplinierung"?, in: *Norm und Praxis im Alltag des Mittelalters und der Frühen Neuzeit. Internationales Round-Table-Gespräch, Krems an der Donau, 7. Oktober 1996*. Vienna 1997, 39–53; Achim Landwehr: "Normdurchsetzung" in der Frühen Neuzeit? Kritik eines Begriffs, in: *Zeitschrift für Geschichtswissenschaft* 48 (2000), 146–162.
16 Giorgio Riello: Things Seen and Unseen. The Material Culture of Early Modern Inventories and Their Representation of Domestic Interiors, in: Paula Findlen (ed.): *Modern Things. Objects and Their History, 1500–1800*. Basingstoke 2013, 125–150. For the Ottoman context, see Yvonne J. Seng: *The Üsküdar Estates (tereke) as Records of Daily Life in an Ottoman Town, 1521–1524*, unpubl. Ph.D. diss. University of Chicago 1991.

numerous regulations highlights the fact that the visual representation of difference by dress was a key concern of early modern European societies.[17]

The primary goals of sumptuary legislation varied from period to period and from region to region, but across Europe throughout the early modern period "hierarchic dress codes" definitely constituted its "classic form".[18] This legislation aimed at marking social difference first and foremost by restricting the use of certain extravagant clothes and luxury items to members of certain social strata. In the Holy Roman Empire, for instance, an imperial ordinance of 1530 allowed only noblemen to wear golden chains of up to 200 florins, whereas wealthy burghers had to abstain from these expensive pieces of jewelry even though they could afford them.[19] In the Ottoman Empire, an imperial decree of 1727 enjoined commoners from wearing ermine fur.[20] Some of these regulations made only very rough social distinctions, but others were extremely detailed. An ordinance issued by the city of Strasbourg in 1660, for instance, listed what members of no less than 256 professions divided into six status groups were – and were not – allowed to wear.[21] Clothing laws of that kind were promulgated over and over again, indicating that dress codes were not necessarily closely adhered to and were, in practice, continuously renegotiated. For instance, Constanţa Vintilă-Ghiţulescu highlights in her article that Romanian boyars in the eighteenth century tended to maintain the public display of luxurious clothes and accessories regardless of the law, in order both to outdo their peers and to display their sense of superiority vis-à-vis their Greek overlords from Istanbul. While commonly concerned with the appearance of both men and women, some

17 Gerhard Jaritz: Kleidung und Prestige-Konkurrenz. Unterschiedliche Identitäten in der städtischen Gesellschaft unter Normierungszwängen, in: Saeculum 44 (1993), 8–31; Katharina Simon-Muscheid: Standesgemässe Kleidung. Repräsentation und Abgrenzung durch Kleiderordnungen (12.–16. Jahrhundert), in: Holenstein, Zweite Haut, 91–115; Thomas Weller: "Von ihrer schändlichen und teuffelischen Hoffart sich nicht abwenden lassen wollen ... " Kleider- und Aufwandsordnungen als Spiegel "guter Ordnung", in: Irene Dingel and Armin Kohnle (eds.): Gute Ordnung. Ordnungsmodelle und Ordnungsvorstellungen in der Reformationszeit. Leipzig 2014, 203–219.
18 Hunt, Governance, 393. For a broader perspective on this subject see Riello and Rublack, Right to Dress.
19 Matthias Weber: Die Reichspolizeiordnungen von 1530, 1548 und 1577. Historische Einführung und Edition. Frankfurt am Main 2002, 147.
20 Quataert, Clothing Laws, 409.
21 Lieselotte Constanze Eisenbart: Kleiderordnungen der deutschen Städte zwischen 1350 und 1700. Ein Beitrag zur Kulturgeschichte des deutschen Bürgertums. Göttingen 1962, 60; Rublack, Right to Dress, 62.

clothing regulations pertained predominantly or even exclusively to women, who were seen as especially prone to expensive fashion and immoral behavior.[22]

Across Europe, women typically faced more scrutiny than men when it came to their appearance, a fact that is closely related to religious norms and ideas of sexual morality and appropriate clothing, the most prominent example of which is the veil. Today, the veil is exclusively associated with conservative Muslim women, but in the early modern era Christian women in Europe also covered their hair and face from the male gaze in order to exhibit their chastity and virtue. Yet, at times, the veil also became a fashionable item.[23] The *almalafa*, for instance, a white veil that covered the head and upper body, was used in sixteenth-century Granada by both Muslim and Christian women, until the practice was prohibited by the Christian authorities.[24] In other parts of Spain, moralists at first encouraged women to go covered and then later condemned the practice, fearing that women would escape their male relatives' control.[25]

Clothes were expected not only to cover the body, especially the female body, but also to define a person's gender more broadly.[26] A number of garments and accessories were clearly associated with the gendered body, such as the female veil or the male suit or turban, but there also existed items whose meaning was not fixed and which allowed at times for different interpretations. For instance, Thomas Weller in his article discusses male earrings, which became fashionable at the English court in the sixteenth century, but which were regarded as marker of heresy in contemporary Catholic Spain. Another clothing item that was originally designed to cover the female body but allowed for contrary appropriations was the farthingale. As Gabriel Guarino notes in his article, moralists in seventeenth-century Spain claimed that women often used the

---

22 Barbara Vinken: *Angezogen. Das Geheimnis der Mode*. Stuttgart 2013. For the Ottoman case, see Betül İ. Argıt: An Evaluation of the Tulip Period and the Period of Selim III in the Light of Clothing Regulations, in: *Osmanlı Araştırmaları* 24 (2004), 11–28; Madeline C. Zilfi: Whose Laws? Gendering the Ottoman Sumptuary Regime, in: Suraiya Faroqhi and Christoph Neumann (eds.): *Ottoman Costumes. From Textile to Identity*. Istanbul 2004, 125–141.
23 Susanna Burghartz: Covered Women? Veiling in Early Modern Europe, in: *History Workshop Journal* 80 (2015), 1–32.
24 David Coleman: *Creating Christian Granada. Society and Religious Culture in an Old-World Frontier City, 1492–1600*. Ithaca, NY 2003, 63; see also the contribution by Thomas Weller to this issue.
25 Laura R. Bass and Amanda Wunder: The Veiled Ladies of the Early Modern Spanish World. Seduction and Scandal in Seville, Madrid and Lima, in: *Hispanic Review* 77 (2009), 97–144; see also the contribution by Gabriel Guarino to this issue.
26 Odile Blanc: Vêtements féminins, vêtements masculins à la fin du Moyen Âge. Le point de vue des moralistes, in: Pastoureau, Le vêtement, 243–253.

farthingale to hide illegitimate pregnancies – or even their lovers. Of course, gendered clothing was also used to play with feminine and masculine bodily features, for instance by wearing accessories specific to the opposite gender or by cross-dressing in order to disguise one's gender.[27]

Dress also marked, and to some extent created, religious belonging. Believers across Europe were required to wear specific clothing on certain occasions, on Shabbat or to Sunday mass, for example, and there were different traditions of clothing for the members of Europe's different religious communities in their daily lives in general. This often included, in addition to specific clothing items, other features of outward appearance, such as a certain haircut, a beard, or particular accessories.[28] Religious and secular authorities across Europe watched over their peoples' appearance and tried to ensure that members of different religious communities were distinguishable from each other as part of their efforts to limit excessive social interaction and, most of all, sexual intercourse with the religious other. Among the best known examples of this practice are the regulations of the Fourth Lateran Council of 1215 regarding the visual distinction of Christians from Jews and Muslims, which paved the way for more detailed stipulations, including the compulsory wearing of yellow signs (or those of other colors) or special hats for Jews in most of Christian Europe.[29] Similar restrictions on specific colors and pieces of clothing, especially hats and luxury items, existed in Ottoman Europe, in this case targeting the many Christians and Jews living in the sultan's realm.[30]

In practice, however, we can assume that neighbors, at least, were well aware of each other's religious belonging. Specific pieces of clothing and symbols, thus, were often a means of degradation and discrimination as much as a feature of distinction. It was no coincidence that similar signs were used to stigmatize other social outsiders, such as prostitutes, beggars, or lepers, and that, in many cases, the religious other also had to abstain from overly luxurious

---

27 Valerie R. Hotchkiss: *Clothes Make the Man. Female Cross-dressing in Medieval Europe.* New York 1996; Rudolf M. Dekker and Lotte Constance van de Pol: *The Tradition of Female Transvestism in Early Modern Europe.* New York 1997.

28 Dorothea Lüddeckens: Relevanz in der Interaktion. Kleidung und Religion, in: ead., Uehlinger, and Walthert, Sichtbarkeit religiöser Identität, 37–76, here 39.

29 Solomon Grayzel: *The Church and the Jews in the XIIIth Century: 1198–1254.* 2nd ed. New York 1966, 308–309; Sarah Lipton: *Dark Mirror. The Medieval Origins of Anti-Jewish Iconography.* New York 2014.

30 Matthew Elliot: Dress Codes in the Ottoman Empire: The Case of the Franks, in: Faroqhi and Neumann, Ottoman Costumes, 103–123, here 104–108. On the religious underpinning of such dress codes, see İrvin Cemil Schick: Some Islamic Determinants of Dress and Personal Appearance in Southwest Asia, in: *Khilʿa* 3 (2007–2009), 25–53.

dress in order to mark his or her inferiority.[31] Flora Cassen, in her contribution, shows not only how these mechanisms of stigmatization and exclusion worked in Italian cities of the Renaissance but also the strategies Jewish men and women developed to retain power over their own identities. Moreover, certain members of religious minorities who were subjected to discriminatory dress codes ignored or intentionally disregarded these stipulations, in order to blend in with the majority or to avoid assault.

Social status, gender, and religion were, of course, not the only qualities expressed by dress. Regional and ethnic belonging was equally important. The first European costume books, which appeared in the sixteenth century, divided the social world first and foremost into regional and ethnic groups.[32] It is probably no coincidence that these illustrated volumes, which represented other peoples in their traditional costumes, first appeared when many European regions experienced a first formation of "national" self-consciousness. Although most historians agree that the modern nation was a product of the eighteenth century, earlier roots of national thinking can be traced back to the fifteenth and sixteenth centuries. The idea of competing "nations" was widespread among European humanists and also shaped, to some extent, the depiction of foreign dress styles in early modern costume books and travel accounts.[33]

Supposedly clear-cut differences between national dress styles were hardly straightforward in practice. Instead, we often find the selective use and combination of different styles. Certain presumably national styles spread across Europe, assuming different meanings in different contexts and times. As Thomas Weller shows for Dutch and German immigrants in sixteenth- and seventeenth-century Spain, and Maria Hayward for Scottish travelers from the mid-sixteenth to the mid-eighteenth century, the predilection for black clothes, often associated with the so-called Spanish dress, was by no means exclusively Spanish and had different connotations in different cultural settings. By the eighteenth century, similar attire consisting of a long black cloak and a white ruff was worn, at least occasionally, by Jews in Frankfurt and Fürth and was regarded as distinctly Jewish,

---

31 Robert Jütte: Stigma-Symbole. Kleidung als identitätsstiftendes Merkmal bei spätmittelalterlichen und frühneuzeitlichen Randgruppen (Juden, Dirnen, Aussätzige, Bettler), in: *Saeculum* 44 (1993), 65–89.

32 Rublack, Dressing Up, 146–163; Ulrike Ilg: The Cultural Significance of Costume Books in Sixteenth-Century Europe, in: Richardson, Clothing Culture, 29–48; Leslie Schick: The Place of Dress in Pre-modern Costumes Albums, in: Faroqhi and Neumann, Ottoman Costumes, 93–102.

33 Rublack, Dressing Up, 121–175. On the idea of "nations" in early modern Europe, see Caspar Hirschi: *The Origins of Nationalism. An Alternative History from Ancient Rome to Early Modern Germany.* Cambridge 2012.

as Cornelia Aust demonstrates. Beata Biedrońska-Słota's and Maria Molenda's contribution traces how certain garments of Eastern European and Ottoman origin constituted what would later be known as Polish "national" dress.

National ascriptions of both people and their clothes became particularly important in situations of cultural contact. Europe's courts, of course, attracted many foreigners and were major places of conspicuous consumption and sartorial display; as such, they often took the lead in cross-cultural exchange and in the spread of costumes and fashion across geographic and political boundaries.[34] Dynastic marriages among members of the high nobility, for instance, helped introduce Spanish and French courtly fashion to the court of Naples in the seventeenth and eighteenth centuries, as Gabriel Guarino shows in his article. Constanța Vintilă-Ghițulescu discusses how members of the Greek community of Istanbul who were appointed princes of Moldavia and Wallachia brought Ottoman imperial fashion to the Romanian provinces, and how the local elites soon appropriated and modified these new clothes for their own ends.

It was not only Europe's princely rulers and royal families who introduced people to foreign dress and style; diplomats, elite travelers, merchants, sailors, soldiers, and many others traveling or living abroad also did so. It is no coincidence that European fashion started influencing Istanbul's elite and middle class in the eighteenth century, when the first Ottoman diplomatic missions traveled to Paris and other European capitals, culminating, following a century of vivid cultural exchange, in 1829, when state officials were obliged to abandon their traditional costume and wear the *fez* and European-style clothes instead. At the same time, but in the opposite direction, upper-class women like Lady Montague and Elisabeth Craven, writing about their experiences in Istanbul, familiarized British high society with Ottoman costumes and fashion, contributing to the trend of *Turquerie* at the court of London and other European capitals.[35] Maria Hayward demonstrates in her contribution how young male aristocrats stimulated fashion exchange across Europe, focusing on Scottish noblemen who came to continental Europe on the Grand Tour, for trade, or as exiles, between the

---

34 Isabelle Paresys and Natacha Coquery (eds.): *Se vêtir à la Cour en Europe (1400–1815)*. Villeneuve d'Ascq 2011; Philip Mansel: *Dressed to Rule. Royal and Court Costume from Louis XIV to Elizabeth II*. New Haven 2005; Dinges, Unterschied; Kirsten O. Frieling: *Sehen und gesehen werden. Kleidung an Fürstenhöfen an der Schwelle vom Mittelalter zur Neuzeit (ca. 1450–1530)*. Ostfildern 2013.

35 Onur İnal: Women's Fashions in Transition. Ottoman Borderlands and the Anglo-Ottoman Exchange of Costumes, in: *Journal of World History* 22 (2011), 243–272; Joachim Gierlichs: Europeans in "Turkish" Dress, in: Ulbrich and Wittmann, Fashioning the Self, 151–186.

sixteenth and eighteenth century. Increasing mobility and migration during the early modern period, however, also heightened authorities' concern about how to distinguish and control foreigners. Flora Cassen and Thomas Weller emphasize in their contributions that Jews and foreign merchants were especially subject to distrust and monitoring.

Due to intensified long distance trade and technological developments since the sixteenth century, new textiles, costumes, and accessories entered the European market. Giulia Calvi describes in her article how an exotic commodity such as the cashmere shawl turned into a fashionable good all across Europe. For most of history, such luxury imports from far away were the reserve of the elite, although there had always been members of lower echelons of society who were able to afford luxurious items and fabrics (or at least their imitations).[36] But it was only with the emergence of a consumer culture in the eighteenth century that the number of such non-elite buyers increased significantly.[37] New media like fashion journals took a leading role in popularizing the latest fashion and foreign dress to a wider European public, as they spoke to and could be afforded by many, unlike the costume books and early prints of the sixteenth and seventeenth centuries.[38] However, this popularization of fashion during the eighteenth century meant that it became even more difficult to distinguish people by their dress. Indeed, by the end of the century, European societies started abandoning the utopian ideal of a self-explanatory vestimentary code mirroring a strictly hierarchical social order and gave in to the increasingly complex universe of vestimentary signs characterized by the coexistence of individual styles, transcultural influences, and rapidly changing fashions.

The eight articles assembled in this issue contribute to the growing literature on early modern dress in a truly European perspective. As the foregoing

---

36 Rublack, Right to Dress, 37; Maureen Fennell Mazzaoui (ed.): *Textiles. Production, Trade and Demand.* Aldershot 1998; Giorgio Riello and Prasannan Parthasarathi (eds.): *The Spinning World. A Global History of Cotton Textiles, 1200–1850.* Oxford 2009; Sven Beckert: *Empire of Cotton. A Global History.* New York 2015.

37 Karin Wurst: *Fabricating Pleasure. Fashion, Entertainment, and Cultural Consumption in Germany, 1780–1830.* Detroit 2005; Beverly Lemire: Production and Distribution, in: Peter McNeil (ed.): *A Cultural History of Dress and Fashion in the Age of Enlightenment.* London 2017, 45–62. On consumer culture more broadly, see eadem: *Global Trade and the Transformation of Consumer Cultures. The Material World Remade, c. 1500–1820.* Cambridge 2018.

38 Angela Borchert and Ralf Dressel (eds.): *Das Journal des Luxus und der Moden. Kultur um 1800.* Heidelberg 2004; Astrid Ackermann: *Paris, London und die europäische Provinz. Die frühen Modejournale 1770–1830.* Frankfurt am Main 2005; Karin A. Wurst: Fashioning a Nation. Fashion and National Costume in Bertuch's "Journal des Luxus und der Moden" (1786–1827), in: *German Studies Review* 28 (2005), 367–386.

outline indicates, there exist a number of studies discussing a variety of areas related to dress and appearance in the context of the political, socio-economic, and cultural transformations in Europe as well as Europe's entanglement with other parts of the world during the early modern period. Yet these studies tend to focus on one specific difference, most often social status or religion, and its expression by dress, rather than examining the intersection of various differences and their visual display. The research is also fragmented, with a large number of case studies on certain cities and regions and only a few studies with a comparative or broader European geographic scope. Modern national boundaries and ideas of separate cultural spheres, in fact, still dominate much of the scholarship.

This bias in the existing research prompted us to bring together leading scholars in the field to discuss dress as a marker of cultural difference in early modern Europe from a transcultural perspective.[39] The authors demonstrate how early modern Europeans used dress to express their various and overlapping senses of social, political, gender, religious, ethnic, and "national" belonging. They, moreover, point to the fact that dress was not only a means to make cultural differences visible but also in many cases literally produced these differences. The contributions provide many examples of how clothes actually "made" the man or woman. Yet they emphasize that it was rarely a specific garment, accessory, material, or color alone that produced meaning. The meaning of a vestimentary sign depended not only on the material object itself but also on the person who used it, the circumstances in which it was used, and the way it was perceived by others.[40] Thus, in many cases, the identification of specific garments with the wearer's social status, gender, religion, or ethnicity lay only in the eyes of the beholder. Even though authorities felt the need to define the meaning of vestimentary signs and control sartorial practices, the studies in this issue demonstrate that dress in practice always remained ambiguous and a subject of continuous negotiation. However, the articles also indicate that the actual negotiation, appropriation, and interpretation of sartorial practices differed significantly from time to time and from place to place.

---

39 A two-day conference took place at the Leibniz Institute of European History in Mainz, Germany, in October 2017, and the present issue publishes some of the papers presented on that occasion. Conference Report: Clothes Make the (Wo)man: Dress and Cultural Difference in Early Modern Europe, 26.10.2017 –28.10.2017 Mainz, in: *H-Soz-Kult* (31 Jan. 2018). URL: www.hsozkult.de/conferencereport/id/tagungsberichte-7527 (6 Feb. 2019).
40 In this regard, sartorial practices seem a case in point for actor-network-theory. See Joanne Entwistle: Fashion, Latour and actor-network-theory, in: Agnes Rocamora and Anneke Smelik (eds.): *Thinking through Fashion*. London 2016, 269–284.

Indeed, looking at dress as a marker of difference in this broader European perspective – from Scotland to Italy and from the Iberian Peninsula to Eastern Europe and the Ottoman Balkans, including marginalized regions and regions commonly regarded as belonging to separate cultural spheres – reveals a number of previously unnoticed differences, similarities, and connections across early modern Europe. Dress was definitely a key concern to all early modern Europeans and played a similar role across the continent in marking the individual's place in society, irrespective of the dominant faith and culture. Authorities also handled the issue in surprisingly similar ways and, whether Christian, Muslim, or Jewish, invoked similar concepts of morality and order to legitimize their interference in people's clothing choices. In the end, the contributions to this issue suggest that there were many more similarities among the various regions of Europe than there were differences, and that the latter often concerned merely details in form, practice, and chronology.[41] While at times concerned with independent developments, the articles also propose that common features of dress and cultural difference in early modern Europe were, more often than one might think, the result of interaction and appropriation. The vibrant transcultural exchange within Europe of the period was not restricted to textiles and technologies but also extended to ideas and practices related to dress and appearance.

---

[41] As recent research has shown, similar patterns and processes can also be found in other regions of the world: Riello and Rublack, The Right to Dress; Lemire, Global Trade.

Gabriel Guarino

"The Antipathy between French and Spaniards": Dress, Gender, and Identity in the Court Society of Early Modern Naples, 1501–1799

Abstract: *The present article explores the inter-linkage between social and cultural values, related comportments, and dress in the courts of early modern Europe. More specifically, it examines the two competing cultural models of Spanish and French fashion, and the values and historical processes that determined their respective success in the contemporary courts of Europe in general and of Naples in particular. Owing to the importance of dress in the construction of gender roles, the article assesses the influence of dress among Neapolitan men and women separately. The findings show that men's fashions in Naples grosso modo followed European trends regarding both Spanish and French fashion from the sixteenth to the eighteenth century. Comparatively, female French fashions and their related forms of sociability would only be able to flourish from the reign of Charles of Bourbon onward.*

> If we ask a Spaniard what he thinks of French clothes and their fancy, he will not only hold them to be ill-favored, but will be scandalized at something that causes such joy and lifts the heart; for to see a troop of French upon a festive day dressed in such variety of colors, with a thousand variations of feathers and cameos, embroideries, fringes, ornaments and gold laces, with so many hundreds of jewels, diamonds, pearls, rubies, emeralds and topazes that one would think the whole of India was landed on them [...] Yet the Spaniard will say that it is the greatest folly in the world [...] because in Spain the grave style is so much in use, and the colored habit so abhorred, that they force the hangman to wear a red or yellow livery to mark his shame and infamy. And if we hear the judgment of a Frenchman concerning the dress and style of a Spaniard, he will say that to go always in black is a sign of despair, the mark of a widow, or of a person gone bankrupt, even though black is one of the most honorable colors and argues modesty, reputation, authority and understanding.[1]

This Manichean categorization of the joyous, colorful, and extravagant French clothes, on one side, versus the grave, dark, and modest garments of the

---

1 I am indebted to the British Academy (grant number SG102076) for the generous funding of this article. Carlos García: *La oposición y conjunción de los dos luminares de la tierra o Antipatía de Franceses y Españoles*, ed. by Michel Bareau. Edmonton 1979, 200–202.

Spaniards, on the other, fully conforms to the dichotomic thesis of its author, the physician Carlos García, aptly titled *The opposition and conjunctions of the two planets of earth or the Antipathy between Frenchmen and Spaniards.* First published in 1617, García's original agenda was to overcome the differences between the two nations in the wake of the recent double marriage of Philip III of Spain's daughter, Anna (1601–1666), to Louis XIII of France (1601–1643), and Philip of Spain (1605–1665) (the future Philip IV) to Isabel of France (1602–1644). Nevertheless, the book's various chapters emphasized precisely an "opposition" of character – roughly speaking, between extroverted Frenchmen and introverted Spaniards – which determined the way that Frenchmen and Spaniards, respectively, talked, ate, moved, and, of course, dressed. Accordingly, García postulated that the best definition of a Frenchman is "a reversed Spaniard, because the Spaniard ends where the French begins".[2] Despite the apparent fancifulness of such a notion, the cultural animosity between the two was a common early modern trope, constantly fueled by the recurrent tide of military hostilities between France and Spain.[3]

The rivalry between these two styles will be a thread that runs throughout this article, as its aim is to trace the correlation between dress, power, and identity in early modern Naples, where Habsburgs and Bourbons reigned at different times. Specifically, the death of Charles II of Spain (1661–1700) in 1700 marked the end of the Habsburg dynastic rule of the Kingdom of Naples, which had begun in the sixteenth century. With the ascendancy to the throne of Charles II's successor, Philip V of Bourbon (1683–1746), the Neapolitan subjects of the Spanish Monarchy continued to be governed by a Spanish viceroy, albeit one that now represented the new dynasty. July 1707 marked yet another change of regime, as the Austrian Habsburgs took over the Kingdom of Naples from their Bourbon rivals as part of the War of the Spanish Succession, ushering in 27 years of Austrian viceregal rule. In 1734 Charles of Bourbon (1716–1788) reclaimed the Neapolitan Kingdom for Spain and was nominated by his father, Philip V, as King of the Two Sicilies, thus starting a new cadet branch of the Bourbon dynasty. During these shifts of power, dress interacted with various sources of identity, including an individual's dynastic allegiance, nation, gender, social status, religious confession, and so on. Indeed, according to Daniel Roche,

2 Ibid., 222.
3 See a recent collection of essays on this vast topic. Anne Dubet and José Javier Ruiz Ibáñez (eds.): *Las monarquías española y francesa (siglos XVI-XVIII). Dos modelos políticos?* Madrid 2010.

connected with religious convictions, faith and powerful symbolic expressions, clothing is a prop to beliefs and observances, as it is to social representations. At every moment clothing expresses links with authority, suggests the sexual hierarchy of roles in the family, points to the power of beliefs both in its details and in its totality.[4]

Accordingly, looking separately at men's and women's fashions, this article will identify the national origins of these clothes, the values they inspired, their means of diffusion in Naples, and their change through time.

Between Habsburgs and Bourbons: Men's Fashions in Spain and Naples

Some of the cultural differences between Spanish and French men's outfits in the early modern period have been attributed to the divergent visions of ideal image-making cultivated by the two leading European courts of the time. Political and cultural historians have juxtaposed a Habsburg Spanish tradition of "private kingship", also known as "hidden monarchy", initiated by Charles V (1500–1558) and continuing throughout the rule of his Habsburg heirs, with one of "public kingship" offered by the French Bourbons, best exemplified by Louis XIV's (1638–1715) Versailles. According to this argument, Spanish kings chose to remain remote and inaccessible to most of their courtiers, rarely appearing in public and even then only behind a curtain. Those hidden monarchs who best played this role, like Philip II (1527–1598) and Philip IV, acquired an aura of mystery and awe.[5] The Habsburgs' physical withdrawal and personal modesty was also reflected in their preferred garments, faithfully depicted in their official portraits. From Charles V to Charles II, these included the same unassuming black clothes described by García.[6] Moreover, the portraits usually rejected the visible signs of royalty – a scepter, a crown, a canopy – that typically identified and exalted royal persons. Elliott explains this choice of the

---

4 Daniel Roche: *A History of Everyday Things. The Birth of Consumption in France, 1600–1800*, transl. by Brian Pearce. Cambridge 2000, 195.
5 See for example: John H. Elliott: The Court of the Spanish Habsburgs. A Peculiar Institution?, in: id.: *Spain and its World. Collected Essays*. New Haven, CT 1989, 142–161; and Carmelo Lisón Tolosana: *La imagen del rey. Monarquía, realeza y poder ritual en la Casa de los Austrias*. Madrid 1991.
6 Fernando Checa Cremades: Monarchic Liturgies and the "Hidden King". The Function and Meaning of Spanish Royal Portraiture in the Sixteenth and Seventeenth Centuries, in: Allan Ellenius (ed.): *Iconography, Propaganda, and Legitimation*. Oxford 1998, 89–104.

Habsburg monarchs as the epitome of political sophistication, whereby a purpose-fully understated execution of royal portraiture reflected the unquestioned assurance of Spain's claim to European supremacy.[7] The French ideal, on the other hand, best explained in Burke's masterful analysis of Louis XIV's management of his image, espoused an ever-present, attention-seeking monarch, whose court revolved around his daily movements. Accordingly, Louis' iconography abounds precisely in the hyperbole, allegorical imagery, and typical accessories of monarchical power that the Habsburgs chose to omit. His portraits depicted him in the flamboyant and colorful clothes that would become the standard of European fashion from the last decades of the seventeenth century through the end of the eighteenth.[8]

From the middle of the sixteenth century to the middle of the seventeenth, in concordance with wider European trends, Neapolitan aristocrats appear to have assiduously followed the example presented at court by the resident Spanish viceroys. The viceroys, in turn, belonging invariably to the titled nobility of Spain, followed men's court fashions of Madrid.[9] The Neapolitan nobility's adherence to the fashion of Spain conformed to its general loyalty to the Habsburgs; but it also ought to have come quite naturally, as male black outfits were already fashionable during the fifteenth-century Aragonese rule of the Kingdom of Naples.[10] This also made sense in terms of the nobility's corporate calculations, as fealty to the Spanish crown granted the titled nobility access to military posts, state offices, and pensions, as well as honorific privileges like admission to chivalric orders, titles, and various ceremonial honors displayed at court.[11] Contemporary assessments of the Spanish influence on Neapolitan dress are also confirmed by the archival findings of Scognamiglio Cestaro and Musella Guida, whose examinations of sixteenth-century Neapolitan inventories corroborate the predominant use of black clothes among the Neapolitan nobility.[12]

---

7 John H. Elliott: Power and Propaganda in the Spain of Philip IV, in: id., Spain and its World, 162–188, here 167.

8 Peter Burke: *The Fabrication of Louis XIV*. New Haven, CT 1992.

9 For fashions in Naples during this period see Adelaide Cirillo Mastrocinque: Cinquecento napoletano, in: Ernesto Pontieri (ed.): *Storia di Napoli*, vol. 4. Naples 1976, 515–575.

10 Lina Montalto: *La corte di Alfonso I di Aragona: vesti e gale*. Naples 1922, 86, 88.

11 Angelantonio Spagnoletti: *Principi italiani e Spagna nell'età barocca*. Milan 1996, esp. 51–128. For recent studies dealing with the Neapolitan court see John A. Marino: *Becoming Neapolitan. Citizen Culture in Baroque Naples*. Baltimore, MD 2010; and Gabriel Guarino: *Representing the King's Splendour. Communication and Reception of Symbolic Forms of Power in Viceregal Naples*. Manchester 2010.

12 Silvana Musella Guida and Sonia Scognamiglio Cestaro: Le origini della moda napoletana, in: *Proceedings of the XIII International Congress TICCIH: Industrial heritage and urban*

A more detailed look at the constitutive elements of the Spanish dress of the period shows that it reflected the severe and morally strict values of the Catholic Reformation shared by both Spaniards and Neapolitans. Spanish men's fashions abandoned the soft and sexually effeminate elements typical of the Italian Renaissance, like skirts and long haircuts. They included, instead, mid-thigh-length breeches and a long-sleeve blouse topped by a padded doublet. Men sported full beards and short-trimmed haircuts. The predominant color of these garments was black, with the exception of the white ruff and white cuffs that completed the outfit. According to John Harvey, the values associated with the color black – "self-effacement and uniformity, impersonality and authority, discipline and self-discipline, a willingness to be strict and a willingness to die"[13] – were conducive to the maintenance of an imperial order. For this reason black was the color of choice not only for Spain but also for various other nations at the peak of their power, including fifteenth-century Burgundy, early modern Venice and Holland, and England in the nineteenth century. Nevertheless, this did not come at the expense of a sumptuous appearance at court. The expensive process of achieving black dye, significantly improved during this time with the novel use of logwood, became a status marker *per se*, especially when used on such expensive textiles as silk and velvet.[14] Accordingly, when Baldassare Castiglione advised in his handbook for the ideal courtier (first published in 1528) that the most befitting clothes at court were the black and austere garments of Spain, he was preaching to the choir.[15] By 1590, as depicted in the contemporary fashion plates of Cesare Vecellio, the nobles of Naples and Milan were wearing the dress of their Spanish rulers; but so were the politically independent Genoese, Romans and Florentines.[16]

After the middle of the seventeenth century, the plot thickens. The portraits both of Spanish viceroys of Naples and of the contemporary Neapolitan nobility,

---

landscape, *Terni-Rome, 14–18 September 2006*, 1–28. URL: *http://works.bepress.com/theinterna tionalcommitteefortheconservationoftheindustrialheritage/12/* (11 Sep. 2018).

13 John Harvey: *Men in Black*. London 1995, 156.

14 For the influence of black in Spanish and Italian male dress see: Amedeo Quondam: Tutti i colori del nero. Moda "alla spagnola" e "migliore forma italiana", in: Annalisa Zanni and Andrea di Lorenzo (eds.): *Giovanni Battista Moroni. Il cavaliere in nero. Immagine del genti-luomo nel Cinquecento*. Milan 2005, 25–45; and José Luis Colomer: Black and the Royal Image, in: id. and Amalia Descalzo (eds.): *Spanish Fashion in Early Modern Europe. The Prevalence and Prestige of Spanish Attire in the Courts of the 16th and 17th Centuries*, vol. 1. London 2014, 77–112.

15 Baldassare Castiglione: *Il libro del Cortegiano*, ed. by Luigi Preti. Turin 1965, book II, ch.27.

16 Indeed, the author asserted that this was the fashion of "most Italian gentlemen". Cesare Vecellio: *Habiti antichi et moderni di tutto il mondo*. Paris 1859, 22.

along with literary descriptions in contemporary local memoirs, show that men's dress underwent some change.[17] Apart from the introduction of longer coiffures and the restriction of facial hair to long and curved moustaches, the main alteration was the elimination of the expensive ruff in favor of the *golilla*. This was a rigid cardboard support over which came a simple white collar, the Walloon, which was introduced by Philip IV in 1623 in his *Capítulos de Reformación* with the intention of reducing superfluous luxuries during times of economic strain. Together with the black attire the *golilla* became a pre-requisite for anyone who wished to be accepted at the court of Madrid. Although kings were exempted from sumptuary prescriptions, Philip IV made sure to regu-larly wear the rigid collar as a personal example of self-imposed austerity. Consequently, the *golilla* would turn into the quintessential symbol of the somber traditional Spanish attire, at a time when it was being challenged by French fash-ion.[18] It is precisely this paragraph from Spanish attire to French fashion that would be at the center of a vivid, long-lasting public debate in both Spain and Naples, which would prove to have significant economic, social and cultural consequences.

Crystallizing in Louis XIV's Versailles in the last two decades of the seven-teenth century and continuing throughout the eighteenth, the standard ensemble of a European gentleman dressed in the French way consisted mainly of a match-ing three-piece suit made up of a knee-length cassock known as *justeaucorps*, an under jacket, and breeches. Distinctive accessories included a silken cravat (the precursor of the modern tie), and a periwig, which changed in size and shape throughout the eighteenth-century. This was a sumptuous version of the contemporary French military habit, the adoption of which by Louis XIV, as the new court dress, marked his chauvinistic attitude and insatiable appetite for personal and dynastic glory.[19] Despite their military origin, however, the French garments were also permeated with feminine attributes. The adoption of these attributes went hand in hand with the central role acquired by women at Versailles in new, refined forms of sociability and entertainment which later dif-fused to the entire continent, bringing about the feminization of the European male courtiers enmeshed in these forms of sociability. The integration of

---

17 For the viceregal portraits in Spanish Italy see Valeria Manfrè and Ida Mauro: Rievocazione dell'immaginario asburgico. Le serie dei ritratti di viceré e governatori nelle capitali dell'Italia spagnola, in: *Ricerche sul Seicento Napoletano. Saggi e Documenti*. Napoli 2011, 107–135.
18 Ruth Matilda Anderson: The Golilla. A Spanish Collar of the Seventeenth Century, in: *Waffen und Kostümkunde* 11 (1969), 1–19.
19 For Louis XIV's dress and its success in Europe see Philip Mansel: *Dressed to Rule. Royal and Court Costume from Louis XIV to Elizabeth II*. New Haven, CT 2005, 1–15.

feminine attitudes into daily life was expressed in men's increasing concern with their appearance, spending long grooming sessions in front of the dressing table, applying cosmetics, and wearing feminine accessories.[20]

The introduction of French men's fashion in the Spanish court began with Charles II. Although this has been attributed to the influence of his French wife, Marie Louise of Orléans (1662–1689), following their wedding in 1679, already a decade earlier the young monarch was reported wearing French dress. French outfits, however, were limited to informal occasions, as the court etiquette in Madrid required the king and his court to maintain the traditional Spanish attire. In fact, the chronically infirm king, often described as a "martyr" to the strictness of Spanish ceremonial, was described during the last years of his troubled existence as unable to give audience because his ill health would not allow him to wear the cumbersome *golilla*.[21] With the accession to the Spanish throne of Philip V of Bourbon following the death of the childless Charles, in 1700, it would be logical to expect the advance of French fashions with a greater impetus than ever before. Yet, during the first years of his reign in Spain, Philip V was reported to stick to the existing court dress. This was suggested to him by none other than his grandfather Louis XIV, with an eye to achieving much-needed legitimation of the new dynasty by stressing continuity with the previous regime. This was sound advice in the light of the strong challenge mounted by the Austrian Habsburgs throughout the War of the Spanish Succession, which included the self-declaration of Archduke Charles (1685–1740) as King of the Spanish monarchy and his installation in Barcelona in 1705. Accordingly, Philip V and his court would abandon the *golilla* only after the Bourbon monarch felt safe enough in his position, following the crushing defeat inflicted on his Habsburg foe at the Battle of Almansa in 1707. From then on, and throughout the eighteenth century, French fashions would become the rule in the Spanish court. Nevertheless, the fact that its full acceptance there would take more than three decades after its adoption by most European court circles shows the strong aversion of Spaniards towards it.[22]

---

20 For the more ridiculed aspects of Italian male sociability see Roberto Bizzocchi: *Cicisbei. Morale privata e identità nazionale in Italia*. Rome 2008.

21 For men's fashions in Charles II's reign see Amalia Descalzo Lorenzo: Spanish Male Costume in the Habsburg Period, in: ead. and Colomer, Spanish Fashion, vol. 1, 28–31.

22 For eighteenth-century Spanish court dress see ead.: El traje francés en la corte de Felipe V, in: *Anales del Museo Nacional de Antropología* 4 (1997), 189–210; Arianna Giorgi: De vestidos y gala. Influencias francesas en el apariencia y el aparato de la corte de la primera mitad del siglo XVIII, in: María José Pérez Álvarez et al. (eds.): *Campo y campesinos en la España Moderna. Culturas políticas en el mundo hispano*. León 2012, 2035–2045.

Moreover, the newly adopted garments would become the object of censure for moralists and satirists throughout the eighteenth century, who objected to the sizable expenses incurred for the showy garments and accessories, and deplored their effeminacy. A contemporary critic ridiculed the spending of Spaniards *à la mode* in "powders, trimmings, beauty-marks and bracelets, and all the dissimulated cosmetics proper for a lady. They are men when naked, women when they are dressed."[23] In other words, notwithstanding the adoption of French garments in the eighteenth century, Spanish traditionalists considered them to be an attack on masculine respectability and traditional national values.

The Neapolitan case seems to present a much readier process of assimilation. The introduction of French dress among the Neapolitan nobility coincided with its acceptance in the rest of the Italian peninsula, around the middle of the seventeenth century.[24] As early as 1648, a local chronicler described French barbers in Naples buying the hair of condemned criminals from the hangman, out of which "they wove false heads of hair, which they call wigs."[25] This point is also corroborated by contemporary portraiture. Dombrowski, studying the sculptures of the Neapolitan aristocracy of the sword during the last years of the Thirty Years' War, outlines the clearly French characteristics of their dress. The best example is provided by the statue of Carlo Maria Caracciolo – completed in 1643, two years after his death – clearly documenting "his French hairdo, his French *cravate*, the *justeaucorps*, a kind of short soutane, the lace ribbon peering out from under his armour."[26] Predating the aforementioned censorious judgments of the Spanish, Neapolitan traditionalist commentators condemned the senseless extravagance and effeminacy of the French clothes. For example, Carlo Celano, writing during the last two decades of the seventeenth century, ridiculed with gusto the fashionable young nobles wearing a bounty of jolly colors, great quantities of ribbons on the arms and the neck,

---

23 Quoted in Álvaro Molina Martin and Jesusa Vega González: Vistiendo al nuevo cortesano. El impacto de la "feminización", in: Nicolás Morales and Fernando Quiles (eds.): *Sevilla y corte. Las artes y el Lustro Real (1729–1733)*. Madrid 2010, 165–178, here 173.

24 Adelaide Cirillo Mastrocinque: *Usi e costumi popolari a Napoli nel Seicento*. Rome 1978, 116–118.

25 Innocenzo Fuidoro: *Successi del governo del conte d'Oñatte MDCXLVIII–MDCLIII*, ed. by Alfredo Parente. Naples 1932, 72.

26 Damian Dombrowski: "Il Genio Bellicoso di Napoli". The Warrior Ethic of the Neapolitan Nobility and its Threats in the Mirror of Portraiture, in: Klaus Bussmann and Heinz Schilling (eds.): *1648. War and Peace in Europe. Ex Cat. Münster / Osnabrück, vol. 2: Art and Culture*. Munich 1998, 525–531. URL: *https://www.lwl.org/westfaelischer-friede-download/wfe-t/wfe-txt2-57.htm* (11 Sep. 2018).

and applying very close shaves because, in Celano's words, "aiming to look like women, they must not be hairy."[27]

This swift adoption of French fashion by the old Neapolitan nobility can be explained by various factors. The economic and political dynamics of seventeenth-century Naples favored the ascension of parvenus from mercantile extraction and the further reinforcement of the nobility of the robe at the expense of the nobility of the sword – a process that had been promoted by a monarchical project of "divide and rule". Thus, the old nobility's symbolic reaction to a substantial loss of its political and economic power was to keep up appearances by indulging more than ever before in luxurious expenses of conspicuous consumption, like the extravagant and expensive French attire.[28] The Neapolitan nobility's adherence to French dress seems to have also been encouraged by the Spanish viceroys, who started to wear it around the same time as the more fashionably inclined Spaniards in Madrid were starting to do the same. For example, according to the chronicler Antonio Bulifon, in the summer of 1672 the viceroy the Marquis of Astorga (1672– 1675) introduced the French military dress, "showing his pleasure that the gentlemen wore the same".[29] Astorga's successor, the Marquis of Los Vélez (1675–1683), started wearing a wig in April 1679. Well aware of the effect that viceroys' dress had on the local nobility, the chronicler predicted that this "will be seen as an example to confirm those who wore it before him, and it will also create a desire to wear it for those who did not wish to do so."[30] According to the philosopher Paolo Mattia Doria, the need to promote French civilization might have had a more concrete political goal. Writing with hindsight, Doria claimed that in the wake of a probable Bourbon succession to the Spanish throne, the viceroy the Count of Santisteban (1687–1696) redoubled the efforts of previous viceroys to promote French fashions in Naples in order to "extirpate from the hearts of the kingdom's peoples that old hatred towards the French nation, which has been planted meticulously by the very same Spaniards."[31]

Indeed, the Bourbon dynastic passage in 1700 did not pass seamlessly. As in the other territories involved in the War of Spanish Succession, Neapolitans were

---

27 Carlo Celano: *Degli avanzi delle poste*, vol. 1. Naples 1676, 11.

28 For this explanation see Alida Clemente: Note sulla legislazione suntuaria napoletana in età moderna, in: *Dimensioni e problemi della ricerca storica* 1 (2011), 133–162, here 143.

29 Antonio Bulifon: *Giornali di Napoli dal MDXLVII al MDCCVI*, ed. by Nino Cortese. Naples 1932, 192.

30 Innocenzo Fuidoro: *Giornali di Napoli dal MDCLX al MDCLXXX*, vol. 4, ed. by Vittoria Omodeo. Naples 1943, 257.

31 Paolo Mattia Doria: *Massime del governo spagnolo a Napoli*, ed. by Vittorio Conti. Naples 1973, 47.

split in their support between those siding with the Bourbons, locally known as the Gallispani, and their rivals, the Filoasburgici. The 1701 Conspiracy of Macchia, orchestrated by the Habsburg faction, despite its ultimate failure testifies to the weak grip of the new Bourbon dynasty on Naples. Philip V's visit to Naples on February 1702 as a result of pro-Habsburg sentiments can be interpreted as a desperate attempt to consolidate his tenuous rule there.[32] Significantly though, Philip's public appearance in Naples was unapologetically French, unlike his decision to wear the traditional Spanish dress during these same years while in the Madrid court. According to Bulifon, Philip wore "a *justeaucorps* in the color of fire, ornate by golden frills, and his hat, in addition to a white feather, was trimmed with a precious stone."[33] There is no mention of the type of collar he wore, but given the rest of his outfit it is safe to assume he was wearing a *cravat* rather than a *golilla*. This hypothesis is reinforced by the curious request made to the Spanish king, during the time of his visit, by the Neapolitan association of solicitors. They requested his permission to wear French clothes, and most importantly, to relinquish the *golilla* when presenting a case at the courts of justice. Although there was no particular law obliging them to appear in one way or another, the solicitors expressed their apprehension of being ill-regarded by the judges if they abandoned the conventional Spanish dress. The king granted the motion, although informally, given that no formal precedents were applicable.[34]

This unusual request testifies to the limits of the appeal of French fashions in Naples. The traditionalist judges who insisted on maintaining the Spanish decorum in dress effectively comprised a powerful group of legal professionals, belonging to the local nobility of the robe, who were empowered by the state to put a check on the political might and corporate privileges of the old feudal nobility of the sword. These became a veritable thorn in the side of their aristocratic rivals after the middle of the seventeenth century, and by the time of Charles' visit the majority of state councils were manned by them.[35] Thus, the corporate rivalry

---

32 For a recent study of the conspiracy see Francesca Fausta Gallo: *La congiura di Macchia. Cultura e conflitto politico a Napoli del primo Settecento*. Rome 2018.

33 Antonio Bulifon: *Giornale del Viaggio d'Italia Dell'Invittissimo e gloriosissimo Monarca Filippo V Re delle Spagne, e di Napoli, etc. Nel quale si dà ragguaglio delle cose dalla M.S. in Italia adoperate dal dì di 6 d'Aprile, nel quale approdò in Napoli, infin'al dì 16 di Novembre 1702 in cui s'imbarcò in Genova, per far ritorno in Ispagna*. Naples 1703, 14.

34 See Giuseppe Galasso: *Napoli spagnola dopo Masaniello. Politica, cultura, società*, vol. 2. Florence 1982, 647.

35 For some of these developments see Anna Maria Rao: *Napoli nel Settecento*. Naples 1983, 26–32; Raffaele Ajello: *Il problema storico del Mezzogiorno. L'anomalia socioistituzionale napoletana dal Cinquecento al Settecento*. Naples 1994, 236–238; Cinzia Cremonini: Riequilibrare il

between the two aristocratic models was also expressed in their looks. The iconographic evidence clearly shows that the robed nobility, locally known as the *ceto togato*, kept wearing a black toga and a *golilla* after the middle of the eighteenth-century Figure 1. This was in plain contrast to the ever-more extravagant French clothes of the feudal nobles Figure 2, who had been pressured to maintain a particularly grand style following the establishment of the independent monarchical court of Charles of Bourbon in 1734.[36]

This split between a group of "progressives" favoring French clothes and a group of "traditionalists" wearing the old garments became even more pronounced in Spain after the middle of the eighteenth-century, when the *afrencesados* became a stereotyped image of spendthrift, indulgent, and effeminate men who had abandoned what were regarded as long-standing national values.[37] It is in this context that we should interpret a contemporary anonymous Spanish assessment of Charles of Bourbon, King of Naples: "He dearly loves and favors the Spanish nation (which one may call his) and it is known in him an affectionate disposition to benefit her. He thinks like a Spaniard and makes decisions as a Christian. He dresses unwillingly in the French way and he carries the *golilla* in his conscience."[38] This fanciful assertion tells us more about the traditionalist values of the speaker than about the object of his remarks. In reality, it can be entirely refuted by the fabulous expenditures supporting Charles' wardrobe, much of which consisted of the expensive ceremonial versions of French outfits that he frequently wore at court. What is more, the various luxuries consumed by Charles and his Neapolitan court were produced by French artisans and imported by French and Swiss merchants, in a way that directly harmed local producers.[39]

---

sistema: mutazioni e permanenze in Italia tra 1706 e 1720. Alcune considerazioni, in: *Cuadernos de Historia Moderna* 12 (2013), 177–188.

36 Sonia Scognamiglio Cestaro: Leggi "scomode", clientele e fedeltà. Aspetti socio-istituzionali ed economici della legislazione suntuaria del Regno di Napoli in Età moderna, in: *L'économie du luxe en France et en Italie, Journées d'étude organisées par le Comité franco-italien d'histoire économique (AFHE-SISE), Lille, Ifresi 4–5 mai 2007*. URL: *http://lodel.ehess.fr/afhe/document.php?id=454* (11 Sep. 2018).

37 Martin and Vega González, Vistiendo al nuevo cortesano, 172–175.

38 Anon.: *Registro curioso de lo interior y exterior de la Corte de Napoles*, Biblioteca Nacional de España, MS. 11036, fol. 37v.

39 For these processes in Bourbon Naples see: Silvana Musella Guida and Sonia Scognamiglio Cestaro: Il 'tempo eroico' e la politica commerciale di Montealegre. La Manufacture Royale de Joseph Fleuriot et François Boucharlat, in: *Napoli Nobilissima. Rivista di arte, filologia e storia* 10 (2009), 195–206; Sonia Scognamiglio Cestaro: *Le istituzioni della moda. Dalle strutture corporative all'economia politica. Napoli e Francia (1500–1800)*. Bologna 2015, 391–418; and Alida Clemente: *Il lusso "cattivo". Dinamiche del consumo nella Napoli del Settecento*. Rome 2011.

Figure 1: Portrait of Gaetano Argento, in: *Funerali nella morte del signor duca d. Gaetano Argento: reggente della Real cancelleria, presidente del S.R.C. e gran veceprotonotario del regno di Napoli: celebrati nella Real chiesa di S. Giovanni a Carbonara, con varj componimenti in sua lode di diversi autori.* Naples 1731, frontispiece.

Challenging the Boundaries of Respectability: Women's Fashions in Spain and Naples

Recent scholarship on gender in the Iberian world from the mid-sixteenth to midseventeenth century has shown the connection between female education, women's expected gender roles and daily experiences, and their attitudes to their own bodies as reflected by their sartorial choices.[40] Spanish pedagogical texts dealing

---

[40] A good starting point is the collection of essays: Alain Saint Saëns (ed.): *Religion, Body and Gender in Early Modern Spain.* San Francisco, CA 1991.

Figure 2: Portrait of Don Antonio Miroballo, in: Antonio Bulifon: *Funerali nella morte del Signor D. Antonio Miroballo celebrati nella Real Chiesa di S. Gio: a Carbonara.* Naples 1695.

with female education written during the militant years of the Catholic Reformation reverberate with the anxieties of the age. For example, the influential *Education of a Christian Woman* (1523), by Juan Luis Vives, advised that the main purpose of female learning should be the maintenance of chastity. Specifically, in regards to appearance, Vives condemned deep cleavages, eccentric coiffures, make-up and perfumes, perceiving these as external signs of dishonorable intentions, which invited men to act upon the lascivious thoughts that they triggered.[41] Similarly, Fray Luis de León, in his *Manual for the Perfect Wife* (1583), explained

---

41 Juan Luis Vives: Formación de la mujer cristiana, in: id.: *Obras Completas*, ed. by Lorenzo Riber, vol.1. Madrid 1947, 985–1175. On proper clothes for young ladies, married women, and widows, see respectively: ibid., 1015–1026, 1116–1120, 1169–1171.

clearly that just as it was natural for men to speak and to be at the center of attention, so it was becoming for women to be enclosed and covered. He stressed the
point by endorsing the example of the Chinese, who "twist the feet of girls when
they are born, so when they grow up to become women they are not able to go
outside."[42] Significantly, these ideas prevailed among the European Catholic clergy
during the militant phase of the Tridentine Reformation, when intensified attacks
came from diverse sources, including schools for catechisms, sermons, and pamphlets. Along with these rhetorical tools, extensive use was made of Baroque imagery in churches, which stressed the simplicity of dress of Madonnas and
female saints in order to instruct women on their expected social roles.[43]

Women's court dress closely reflected these values. The effacement of the feminine body in Spanish attire from the 1550s to the 1630s, at least – not coincidentally the militant years of the Catholic Reformation – matched the deep suspicion
of religious authorities towards female sexual temptations. The garments themselves included a linen corset tightly fitted to the waist, upon which came
a confining bodice that flattened the bust. To this was added the farthingale
(known in Spanish as *verdugado*), a bulky underskirt constructed of hoops of
wood or whalebone that extended from the waist down to the feet and gave its
wearer the shape of a bell. Its sizeable volume prevented a comfortable proximity
to the table, and noble women had to be fed by their servants. Finally, the most
popular head cover, used by Spanish women of all ranks, was a long black thick
veil to be worn outdoors, known as *mantilla*, that almost entirely covered the face
and hair. Practically, owing to these garments, Spanish women were covered from
head to toe, with the aim of promoting sexual chastity and preserving family
honor.[44]

However, a deeper look at these sartorial choices shows that women were able
to fight back in subtle ways within the system. Those same garments that were
promoted by Catholic-Reformation moralists proved to be exploitable for feminine
subterfuge. Various recent studies have emphasized the ambivalence of the

---

42 Fray Luis de León: *La Perfecta Casada*. Madrid 1583, 71.

43 On Catholic Reformation imagery see Sarah F. Matthews Grieco: Pedagogical Prints.
Moralizing Broadsheets and Wayward Women in Counter Reformation Italy, in: Geraldine
A. Johnson and ead. (eds.): *Picturing Women in Renaissance and Baroque Italy*. Cambridge
1997, 61–87.

44 On these Spanish-inspired constrictive clothes in Italy see Grazietta Butazzi: Vesti di
"molta fattura". Reflections on Spanish-Influenced Fashion in the Second Half of the
Sixteenth Century, in: Annalisa Zanni (ed.): *Velluti e moda: tra XV e XVI secolo*. Milan 1999,
169–175; and Gabriel Guarino: Regulation of Appearances During the Catholic Reformation.
Dress and Morality in Spain and Italy, in: Myriam Yardeni and Ilana Zinguer (eds.): *Les deux
réformes chrétiennes. Propagation et diffusion*. Leiden 2004, 492–510.

tightly-dressed and veiled attire of Spanish women, known as *tapadas*, which was widely introduced during the reign of Philip II. After at first encouraging *tapado* attire, moralists started to condemn it, fearing that women were abusing the anonymity it offered in order to escape the control of their male relatives. Not surprisingly, then, the bans promulgated against the use of veils, beginning with Philip II in 1590 and reissued throughout the reigns of his Habsburg successors, failed, as they encountered strong female resistance.[45] The same was true for the farthingale when, towards the 1630s, it was reintroduced to Spain in its exaggerated French version known as the *guardainfante*. According to Amanda Wunder, this change in style inspired an outpouring of vitriolic criticism that stemmed in part from the garment's association with French fashion. The implication of its new appellation, *guardainfante* (loosely translatable as baby-keeper), was that women not only used it to conceal their legs but also abused it to hide illegitimate pregnancies. Moreover, various contemporary reports told of women utilizing *guardainfantes* to conceal contraband goods or to hide their lovers.[46] It seems, then, that the self-effacing qualities of Spanish fashion proved to be carriers of freedom, just as they could be symbols of oppression, and the sumptuary laws promulgated against veils and *guardainfantes* were generally ignored. This points toward a certain degree of agency that women were able to claim for themselves despite the constant attempts of oppressive vigilance and control imposed on them.

How well did these fashions do in Naples? Both iconographic and written evidence, from contemporary chroniclers, memorialists, and travel writers, shows the proliferation of Spanish fashion throughout this period. For example, in tune with post-Tridentine moralistic values, according to Cesare Vecellio, the "grave and pompous" women of Naples took great care in appearing "closed and secured in their bosoms". He also mentions their predilection for the bell-shaped farthingale, as well as the same sort of face cover – a thin black *mantilla* – favored by Spanish women, which they wore when strolling outside the confines of their homes.[47] Curiously, the sumptuary law issued by the viceroy the Duke of Alcalà (1559–1571) in 1559 reinforced the widespread use of the farthingale in Naples by sanctioning the use of the bulky skirts, although requiring that they be

---

45 See, for example: Laura R. Bass and Amanda Wunder: The Veiled Ladies of the Early Modern Spanish World. Seduction and Scandal in Seville, Madrid and Lima, in: *Hispanic Review* 77 (2009), 97–144. For a wide temporary and geographic scope of the veil see Maria Giuseppina Muzzarelli: *A capo coperto. Storie di donne e di veli*. Bologna 2016.
46 Amanda Wunder: Women's Fashions and Politics in Seventeenth-Century Spain. The Rise and Fall of the *Guardainfante*, in: *Renaissance Quarterly* 68 (2015), 133–186.
47 Vecellio, Habiti antichi, 224.

kept within prescribed limits.[48] Based on evidence from the diarist Antonio Bulifon, it seems that Neapolitan women maintained this fashion until well after the middle of the seventeenth century. Describing their garments in an entry from 1670, Bulifon reports them as wearing "a thin, black, silk mantle, called veil", which allows them to "go all covered".[49]

The enduring success of the grave and modest garments can be explained by the close affinity between Neapolitans and Spaniards regarding sexual mores, as stated above, and the resulting emphasis on maintaining the integrity of family honor. Indeed, this like-mindedness can be understood within the larger frame of a "Mediterranean code of honor and shame" identified by social anthropologists and cultural historians. In full concordance with the aforementioned prescriptions of Spanish moralists, there is a wide agreement that female honor in Mediterranean societies relied on the purity of women's sexual behavior, namely on sexual abstinence before marriage and fidelity to their husbands thereafter. The men of the family whose honor was tarnished through female sexual impropriety – either via the loss of virginity for unmarried daughters or by means of adultery in the case of wives – could avenge it with blood.[50] Spanish testimonies of honor killings abound during the early modern era. For example, two contemporary Spanish soldiers, Alonso de Contreras and Don Diego, Duke of Estrada, killed their wives and their lovers, in similar circumstances, when they caught them committing adultery.[51] Both men displayed sorrow when remembering their murderous actions, while implying that such

48 Lorenzo Giustiniani (ed.): *Nuova collezione delle prammatiche del Regno di Napoli*, vol. 7. Naples 1804, 26.

49 Bulifon, Giornali, 188.

50 Specifically, for the case of Spain, see: Julio Caro Baroja: Honor and Shame. A Historical Account of Several Conflicts, in: John George Peristiany (ed.): *Honour and Shame. The Values of Mediterranean Society*. London 1965, 79–139, and Bartolomé Bennassar: *The Spanish Character. Attitudes and Mentalities from the Sixteenth to the Eighteenth Century*, transl. by Benjamin Keen. Berkeley 1979, 213–236. For Spanish Naples see Gabriel Guarino: The Reception of Spain and its Values in Habsburg Naples. A Reassessment, in: Melissa Calaresu, Joan-Pau Rubiés and Filippo de Vivo (eds.): *Exploring Cultural History. Essays in Honour of Peter Burke*. Aldershot 2010, 93–110. For a comparative approach see the various contributions in: *Acta Histriae* 9 (2000), special issue on *Honour. Identity and ambiguity of an informal code (The Mediterranean, 12th-20th centuries)*.

51 See, respectively: Alonso de Contreras: Discurso de mi vida. Desde que salí a servir al Rey a la edad de catorce años, en el año de 1595, hasta fin del año 1630, el 1 de octubre, en que comencé esta relación, in: José Cossio (ed.): *Autobiografías de soldados (siglo XVII)*, Madrid 1956, 76–143, here 107; and Don Diego Duque de Estrada, Comentarios del desengañado de si mesmo, prueba de todos estados y elección del mejor de ellos, o sea Vida del mesmo autor, que lo es Don Diego Duque de Estrada, in: ibid., 251–484, here 268.

actions were compulsory for men wishing to salvage their honor. Indeed, a Spanish law under Habsburg rule sanctioned these forms of popular justice, proclaiming that "if a married woman commits adultery, she and her fellow adulterer shall be submitted to the power of the husband, and he may do whatever he wishes with them and their property, though he cannot kill one and spare the other."[52]

The proliferation of similar practices among Southern Italian elites is evidenced by a curious manuscript collection of accounts, titled *Tragic Stories that Took Place in the Kingdom and City of Naples*, which traces dozens of these cases throughout the sixteenth and seventeenth centuries, and wherein the authors usually place the blame for adultery on the ever-tempting nature of women. One of the most scandalous of these cases involved the viceroy Pedro Téllez-Girón, Duke of Osuna (1616–1620). Described as having a "great proclivity to lasciviousness", the viceroy abused his position of power by sending local nobles on various missions on his behalf, in a way that freed him to pursue their wives during their absence. Osuna did not always have his way, however, as illustrated by his failed pursuit of one Vittoria Scaglione. Taking advantage of the absence of Scaglione's husband, the viceroy used the help of a servant to furtively enter the house. After overcoming the initial shock of Osuna's intrusion and his indecent expectations, the Neapolitan lady firmly asserted that she would "not damage the honor of her husband in any away". The unyielding Osuna finally gave up, deterred by her strong resistance and her insistence that she "would rather die than having her reputation tarnished".[53] This should not be too surprising, as the suspicion alone of adultery could seal the fate of contemporary Neapolitan wives. The same sort of honor killings that abounded in Spain occurred also in early modern Naples, where women belonging to the highest ranks of the local aristocracy were executed by their families for adultery, as indicated by the deaths of Ippolita Carafa of Stigliano, Maria of Avalos, Princess of Venosa, and Giulia Orsino, Princess of Bisignano.[54]

Traces of such strong honorific values seem to have lasted among the Neapolitan elite well into the eighteenth century, a time by which most European courtly circles had already embraced the liberating fashions – and the related

---

52 Jon Cowans (ed.): *Early Modern Spain. A Documentary History*. Philadelphia, PA 2003, 201.
53 Silvio and Ascanio Corona: *Fatti tragici successi nella Citta e Regno di Napoli*, Biblioteca Nazionale di Napoli, MS. I. D 36, fols. 239–252.
54 Mastrocinque, Cinquecento napoletano, 552. On noble violence and sexual transgression in Naples see also Gabriel Guarino: Taming Transgression and Violence in the Carnivals of Early Modern Naples, in: *The Historical Journal* 60 (2017), 1–20.

looser relations between the sexes – present at Versailles. Indeed, as clearly evidenced by many recent studies, eighteenth-century Italians allowed for the growing role of women in higher spheres of society. This included women's learning and claiming for themselves a significant part in occasions of sociability in the public sphere, as best portrayed in the institutionalization of the salon.[55] As mentioned above, according to Paolo Mattia Doria, some of the last Spanish viceroys tried to change both the old Spanish costumes and the customs that informed them. Doria traces the change back to the viceroyalty of Gaspar Méndez de Haro, Marquis of Carpio (1683–1687), in which he sees a veritable "process of civilization", to use Norbert Elias' famous term.[56] During those years, the nobility stopped its dueling and its honorific squabbles and started to embrace the love and knowledge of arts, letters, and worldly affairs. More importantly for us, according to Doria, "most of the nobility started to dress in the French way, and one could witness the birth of a liberty of conversation between ladies and gentlemen." The abandonment of the modest and grave Spanish garments was thus coupled with the refinement of taste and style, which encouraged new, more egalitarian and interactive forms of sociability. Nevertheless, Doria claims, these changes were done only half-heartedly: men encouraged women to speak freely, but at the same time criticized them in the name of "the good old habits of modesty", causing the women to revert back to their timid behavior. Significantly, according to Doria, those responsible for this situation were none other than the Spaniards, who "implanted in the hearts of Neapolitans the principle of excessive severity towards women, which they compensate with exaggerated signs of admiration and adulation" in an attempt "to shield themselves from a taint on their honor caused by their women's sins."[57] A case in point can be seen in the censorious comments made by a contemporary chronicler, deploring the indecency of ladies who appeared in public "exposed down to their breasts and shoulders, a habit invented by the French liberality".[58]

Doria's assessment fits well with the observations of the contemporary Vincenzio Martinelli, trying to explain the allegedly Italian eighteenth-century phenomenon of *ciceisbeismo*, whereby a husband entrusted his wife's good name and reputation to the hands of a gentleman of his confidence, also

---

[55] See the various contributions in: Maria Luisa Betri and Elena Brambilla (eds.): *Salotti e ruolo femminile in Italia: tra fine Seicento e primo Novecento.* Venice 2004; and Paula Findlen et al. (eds.): *Italy's Eighteenth Century. Gender and Culture in the Age of the Grand Tour.* Palo Alto, CA 2009.

[56] Norbert Elias: *The Civilizing Process*, transl. by Edmund Jephcott. 2 vols. Oxford 1978–82.

[57] For the various quotes in this paragraph see Doria, Massime, 48–50.

[58] Fuidoro, Giornali, vol 1, ed. by Franco Schlitzer. Naples 1934, 35.

known as *cavalier servente* (gallant servant). This gentleman would be in charge of accompanying the wife in her daily pursuits when the husband was busy, safeguarding the wife's virtue and the husband's honor. Paradoxically, however, many suspicious minds perceived the relationship between wife and gallant servant as an institution of sanctioned infidelity.[59] According to Martinelli, the custom of keeping a gallant servant was diffused by way of imitation among all fashionable nobilities in the Italian peninsula. The Neapolitans, however, were the most reluctant in adopting it. Indeed, Neapolitan husbands made sure to keep all the rooms of their residence open, and to post guards, ensuring that no one could enter or leave the house unobserved. When leaving the house, every lady would be followed by a second carriage manned by various male attendants who watched her every move. This situation, which Martinelli sarcastically dubbed "a sort of Muslim custody", lasted until well into the 1740s. But twenty years later all of that had changed: "no more second carriages [but rather] conversations, dinners, and magnificent lunches with foreigners, morning visits to the toilettes where the ladies apply their make-up, [replicating] another Genoa, another Bologna."[60] Such a belated acceptance of French civilization is probably exaggerated,[61] but there is little doubt that its full reception was ushered in by the splendid court society of the independent Bourbon court. This was so much the case that by 1739 the French traveler Charles de Brosses would be forced to admit that the sumptuousness of the Neapolitan court surpassed that of Paris.[62]

Conclusion

In conclusion, our findings show that both men's and women's aristocratic fashions in Naples followed the Spanish tradition during the years of Spain's European political hegemony, which coincided with the strict values of the Catholic Reformation (roughly speaking, from 1550 to 1650). In the case of

---

59 For a particularly malicious assessment of this practice see Samuel Sharp: *Letters from Italy. Customs and manners of that country in the years 1765, and 1766.* London 1766, 18–22, 72–75, 210–211, 253–254, 266.

60 Quoted in Elisa Bianco: Le "Notturne Conversazioni". I cicisbei secondo Vincenzo Martinelli (1770 ca.), in: *Mediterranea* 8 (2011), 572.

61 The first signs of French forms of sociability are evidenced in the early eighteenth century in: Elisa Novi Chavarria: *Sacro, pubblico e privato. Donne nei secoli XV-XVIII.* Naples 2009, 132–135.

62 Quoted in Elena Papagna: *La corte di re Carlo di Borbone. Il re "proprio e nazionale".* Naples 2011, 5.

women's court dress, it appears that the strict values regarding sexual morality shared by the Spaniards and Neapolitans were paramount in delaying in both countries the success of French forms of socialization and their associated fashions, in comparison with the rest of the major European courts of the time. Things differed in the case of French men's fashions. In the court of Spain, as it had been throughout the Habsburg rule, the process was led by the king's example. However, owing to the strictness of court etiquette and the traditionalist attitudes of Spanish aristocrats, Philip V delayed the full acceptance of French men's fashions until the second decade of the eighteenth century, several decades after the rest of the continent. In Naples, the sartorial choices of men reflected internal scissions within the local elite. Guided by their expensive tastes, and encouraged by the Spanish viceroys themselves, the nobility of the sword started sporting the French habit after the middle of the seventeenth century. The nobles of the robe, by contrast, carried on wearing a black toga and *golilla* well into the eighteenth century, long after the Kingdom of Naples had become an independent monarchy governed by a Bourbon king, whose court honored the splendid fashions of Versailles.

Maria Hayward

"a sutte of black which will always be of use to you": Expressions of Difference and Similarity in the Clothing Choices of the Scottish Male Elite Travelling in Europe, 1550–1750

Abstract: *Some of the Scottish soldiers who fought for Gustavus Adolphus during the Thirty Years' War wore their national dress. While very distinctive, their clothing was not representative of that chosen by many of the Scottish men living in Europe. Having left their homeland for reasons of trade, education, leisure, or exile, their fashionable clothing was carefully selected to ensure that they integrated into the societies they visited. Taking the fashion advice of Andrew Fletcher of Saltoun and the letters and accounts of Robert, lord Kerr of Newbattle and his younger brother William as two small case studies, this article explores how elite Scottish men used black clothing, as a staple component of their travel wardrobe, because black was socially acceptable throughout Europe. Their choices abroad will be contextualized by their choices at home, those made by English men, and the guidance offered by Baldassare Castiglione that transcended national boundaries.*

Introduction

Men, dressed in black "suits", consisting of doublet, hose and gown, or coat, waistcoat and breeches, were a familiar sight throughout Western Europe in the sixteenth and seventeenth centuries.[1] Their black garments conveyed multiple meanings that were linked to the wearer's age, social status, location, disposable income, and their religion.[2] Indeed, it was the ubiquity and adaptability of the black suit that made it a staple item in the wardrobes of early modern men of means as an item of fashion as well as for mourning. Indeed, as Elizabeth Currie has shown, secular Florentine men used black as an expression of their civic, mercantile, and courtly personas, identities that ran alongside those of the lower

---

1 For a very clear analysis of seventeenth century Stuart dress, see Aileen Ribeiro: *Fashion and Fiction. Dress in Art and Literature in Stuart England*. New Haven 2005.
2 John Harvey: *The Story of Black*. London 2013.

ranks of black clad clergy.[3] However, as the Florentine example hints at, one man's desirable black suit was something in which another would not be seen out of doors. In other words, the devil was in the detail, and the subtle but very significant details of each suit included the type of fabric used, the quality of the black, the cut, and the use, or not, of trimmings. When combined, these factors made a world of difference between a fashionable suit and one that lacked distinction on all fronts. These clothes also conveyed ideas about the nationality of the wearer, or rather where the suit had been made, because to the well-trained eye there were noticeable differences in cut and underlying attitudes between a "haughty" Spanish black suit and a "civic" suit at home in one of the Italian city states, for example.[4] With this in mind, this article will consider, through three short case studies, the role of the black suit in the luggage of members of the Scottish male elite travelling in Europe. These men will be contextualized by reference to a wider circle of English men and Scots who stayed at home.

The questions explored in the case studies are drawn from the English edition of Baldassare Castiglione's *Il Cortegiano* or *The Book of the Courtier*. Born in Mantua, Castiglione (1478–1529), was a diplomat, scholar and soldier and his book of advice on how to be a courtier was highly influential throughout Europe. When Sir Thomas Hoby published his translation in 1561, he made Castiglione's ideas accessible to the English-speaking/reading world.[5] Castiglione stated that the clothing of the courtier should be:

> rather somewhat grave and auncient, than garish. Therefore me thinke a blacke colour hath a better grace in garments, than any other, and though not thoroughly blacke, yet somewhat darke, and this I mean for his ordinarie apparell.[6]

This courtly grace is evident in Castiglione's portrait. Painted by Raphael in 1514–15, Castiglione followed his own advice and was elegantly dressed in black, grey and white.[7] While not all of the men under consideration here were "courtiers", Castiglione's three key points were applicable to a much broader section of society: that black was suitable for everyday or "ordinary" wear, that it was not just black but also included "somewhat dark" shades and that its virtues were expressed in specific terms – namely "somewhat grave and auncient", meaning

---

3 Elizabeth Currie: *Fashion and Masculinity in Renaissance Florence*. London 2016, 108.

4 Ibid., 105–106.

5 Mary Partridge: Thomas Hoby's English translation of Castiglione's Book of the Courtier, in: *The Historical Journal* 50 (2007), 769–786.

6 Baldassare Castiglione: *The Book of the Courtier*, trans. by Sir Thomas Hoby, 1561, ed. by J. H. Whitfield. London 1974, 116.

7 Raphael: *Baldassare Castiglione*, 1514–1515, oil on panel, 82 x 67 cm, Louvre, Paris, no. 611.

sober, rather than "garish". This article does not follow the view presented by Michel Pastoureau that there was Protestant "chromoclasm" that reflected their wish for sobriety.[8] While many Scottish Presbyterians were painted in black, their bills and accounts indicate that they owned colored clothing too.[9] Equally, Scottish Catholics, like their European counterparts also favored black on occasion.[10] Black straddled the confessional divide and other considerations were important including being in fashion if the occasion required a particular sartorial display and looking like you were part of the society that you were living amongst.

The fashionability of the black suit was closely linked to where it was worn, and where it was scrutinized by observers. As the merchant-adventurer Marmaduke Rawdon (1583–1646) observed, when he bought new clothes for a visit to London in the early 1630s, after he had traveled abroad "he was to be clothed after the English fashion which was then blacke cloothes."[11] If black was a noticeable color choice in the 1630s, by the 1660s it was the cut that gave clothes a London look, as is evident when Sir Gideon Scott of Highchester wrote to his son William, the earl of Tarras, on 9 June 1664, saying that he was sending him clothes from London noting that "everie thing is just in fashione thoughe they may seeme strange to yow."[12] Scott's choice of the word "strange" indicates he was very conscious of a difference between London and Scotland. "Strange" was the word that the diarist Samuel Pepys used when he described the visit of the French ambassador, Jean-Baptiste Colbert (1619–1683), to London four years later in August 1668. The Frenchman was "a comely man, and in a black suit and cloak of silk; which is a strange fashion now, it hath been so long left off".[13] Here strange, or as is implied, old-fashioned, was not a desirable quality in a man's wardrobe, especially when that man was representing his country. The style in question may well have been that depicted by Claude Lefèbvre in 1666, and this example highlights the ways in which fashionable clothing did, or in this case did not, successfully cross national borders.[14]

---

8 Michel Pastoureau: *Black. The History of a Color*. Princeton 2008, 124; Hilary Larkin: *The Making of Englishmen. Debates on National Identity 1550–1650*. Leiden 2014, 96.

9 Rosalind. K. Marshall: Conscience and Costume in Seventeenth-Century Scotland, in: *Costume* 6 (1972), 33.

10 José Luis Colomer: Black and the Royal Image, in: José Luis Colomer and Amalia Descalzo (eds.): *Spanish Fashion at the Courts of Early Modern Europe*, vol. 1. London 2012, 77–112.

11 Robert Davis (ed.): *The Life of Marmaduke Rawdon of Yorke*. London 1863, 24.

12 Sir Gideon Scott to Tarras, his son, London, 9 June 1664, GD157/2123 (National Records of Scotland).

13 Robert Latham and William Matthews (eds.): *The Diary of Samuel Pepys*, 11 vols. London 1983, vol. 9, 284.

14 Claude Lefèbvre: *Jean-Baptiste Colbert*, 1666, oil on canvas, Palace of Versailles, inv. no. 2187.

Black in Scottish Society

When looked at as a group, portraits of early modern Scottish men reveal a sizeable number of black-clad men such as James Stuart, duke of Richmond and Lennox, dressed in a black doublet, breeches, and cloak (Figure 1). Other examples include George, first earl of Kinnoull, in his black full-length gown, symbol of his office as Lord Chancellor of Scotland (1633), James, third marquis of Hamilton, all in black satin in 1643, a choice that Rosalind Marshall attributes to personal grief and sorrow at the Stuarts' three kingdoms being at war and the sober black cloth of Archibald, first marquis of Argyll (1656).[15] However, while black was

Figure 1: Sir Antony van Dyck: *James Stuart, Duke of Richmond and Lennox*, c. 1633–35, oil on canvas, 215.9 × 127.6 cm, Metropolitan Museum of Art, New York, Marquand Collection, Gift of Henry G. Marquand, 1889, acc. no 89.15.16.

---

15 Rosalind Marshall: *Costume in Scottish Portraits 1560–1830*. Edinburgh 1986, 16–18.

a frequent choice, it was not the only choice made by Scottish men as the silver camlet suit selected by third marquis of Hamilton in 1629 or the coat and vest, adorned with ribbon and braid, worn proudly by John, first duke of Rothes in 1667.[16] Each portrait offers just one glimpse into the sitter's wardrobe, but what they strongly suggest is that for elite Scottish men, black clothes and robes played an important but not necessarily dominant part in their clothing choices. Indeed, as Keith Brown has observed the Scottish elite spent heavily on their clothes, with the heir of the fifth earl Marischal, Lord Keith, spending £2,448 on clothing in 1610.[17]

For those shopping for black fabric in sixteenth-century Scotland a range of different qualities were available as indicated by a list of clothing stolen by Thomas Charteris of Kinfawnis and John Charteris of Cuthilgurdy from John Moncur of Ballumy in September 1544. Their haul included a doublet of black worsted containing three ells, five pairs of black hose, a "hugtoun" coat (a short sleeveless coat) of Paris black walit (guarded) with velvet, a gown of French black lined with budge, a single gown of black, and a riding coat of Scots black lined with black gray.[18] The funeral preparations for James V of Scotland (1512–1542) reveal a similar range of choice, with the French and Paris blacks being more expensive than the Scottish versions.[19] Thus black fabrics crossed national borders, carrying with them associations of cost and quality.

These black materials were regularly incorporated into men's everyday wardrobes, as in the case of the doublet and breeks (breeches) of black satin that George Oustine, merchant and burgess of Edinburgh, made for Colin Campbell, fiar of Glenorchy, in 1606.[20] Black clothing was also valued enough to be left as bequests, and in 1623 John, second lord Madertie, discharged his brother Sir James Drummond of Machanie, of a range of items including a doublet and breeks of black satin and a two-handed sword.[21] The black was put to a range of other

16 Ibid., 15, 19.
17 Keith Brown: *Noble Society in Scotland. Wealth, Family and Culture, from Reformation to Revolution*. Edinburgh, 2004, 83.
18 Signet letters of apprising against Thomas Charteris of Kinfawnis and John Charteris of Cuthilgurdy, who have stolen goods from John Moncur of Ballumy, from his lands of Knokhill in September 1544, GD112/3/18 (National Records of Scotland).
19 Sir James Balfour Paul (ed.): *Accounts of the Lord High Treasurer of Scotland, vol. 8: 1541–1546*. Edinburgh 1908, 142–146.
20 Discharge by George Oustine, merchant, burgess of Edinburgh, to Colin Campbell, fiar of Glenurquhay, of £116 in complete payment of all accounts and merchandise furnished, 12 November 1613, GD112/23/7, no. 12 (National Records of Scotland).
21 Discharge by John, 2nd lord Madertie, to Sir James Drummond of Machanie, kt., his brother, of heirship, 3 November 1623, RH15/123/1 (National Records of Scotland).

uses too, including official black robes that marked out state officials. In August 1668 the advocate James Cumming bought a black velvet gown laced with gold lace and trimmed with gold embroidered buttons and loops for the marquis of Montrose.[22] Black was also used for clerical dress, as is revealed in a letter sent by James Strachauchin, parson of Fethercarne, to Thomas Strathauchin of Carmly, in the mid-sixteenth century (and so just prior to the Reformation in Scotland) asking for his black gown, vestments, and silver chalice.[23]

European ways of using black were on show in Scotland, as in September 1508 when the divine and historian, David Calderwood (1575–1650), recalled the arrival of Ulrich, duke of Württemberg (1487–1550). The duke was:

> a young man of comelie behaviour, accompanied with twenty-foure in traine, came to see the countrie. He was convoyed from place to place by noblemen, by the king's directioun, and weill interteaned. His traine were all clothed in blacke.[24]

As John McGavin has noted, this represents a sobriety in dress of which Calderwood would have approved. As such, it was a style more usually expected from clergy in Scotland, and unlikely to be adopted by the high-ranking Scots nobility unless they were in mourning.[25]

Scottish Alternatives to Fashionable Black

Some of the Scottish soldiers who fought for Gustavus Adolphus, king of Sweden (1594–1632), during the Thirty Years' War wore their national dress.[26] This style, including a plaid and bonnet, was captured in a woodcut of 1631.[27] While very distinctive, these soldiers were not representative of all Scots, and there were attempts to regulate this style. Many, especially those from the middling sort and

---

22 Sundry small accounts of the family of Montrose discharged, 4 August 1668, GD220/6/748, no. 16 (National Records of Scotland).

23 Letter to Thomas Strathauchin of Carmly from Mr. James Strachauchin parson of Fethercarne, 21 May, no year but mid-sixteenth century, GD45/14/779 (National Records of Scotland).

24 David Calderwood: *The History of the Kirk of Scotland*, ed. by Thomas Thomson, vol. 6. Edinburgh 1845, 783.

25 I am very grateful to Professor John McGavin for this reference and insight.

26 Henry McClintock: *Old Highland Dress and Tartans*, 2nd ed. Dundalk 1949 and id.: *Old Irish and Highland Dress*. Dundalk 1950.

27 Unknown artist: *Scottish Soldiers in the Service of Gustavus Adolphus*, 1631, woodcut, New York Public Library Digital Collections, PC ARMY-(M-Z).

elite, favored fashionable dress for everyday wear. While hunting, however, the elite often wore more traditional clothing and by the 1670s the plaid was worn with a short-waisted doublet of a style that had dropped out of fashion in the 1660s.[28]

By the early eighteenth century, the Jacobite supporters of the exiled Stuart kings, began to favor wearing the plaid as a sign of their support for the "king over the water". However, Vicci Coltman has noted that while much has been made of Bonnie Prince Charlie (1720–1780) actively wearing tartan to stress his ties to Scotland during his campaign to recover his throne in 1745–1746, he did not always wear it, citing his appearance on 29 July 1745. For his first meetings in Scotland, the prince was dressed in:

> a plain black coat with a plain shirt not very clean and a cambric stock fixed with a plain silver buckle, a fair round wig out of the buckle, a plain hatt [...] he had black stockings and brass buckles in his shoes.[29]

However, the context for this black suit was very significant because Charles Edward Stuart was travelling incognito in his bid to rally support in Scotland. As Alexander MacDonald of Glenaladale recalled, "we were immediately told [...] that this youth was also ane English clergyman who had long been possess'd with a desire to see and converse with Highlanders."[30] These simple black clothes made the prince look the part, but, as Jacqueline Riding has noted, his real identity was given away by how people who knew who he was behaved towards him.[31]

Reasons for Travel

Some Scots left their homeland because of economic opportunities or necessity, but this was not the motivation for the group under consideration here.

---

28 See, for example, John Michael Wright: *Lord Mungo Murray [Am Morair Mungo Moireach]*, 1683, oil on canvas, 88½ x 60¾ inches (224.8 x 154.3 cm), National Galleries of Scotland, PG 997.

29 George Lockhart Esq. of Carnwath: *The Lockhart Papers*, vol. 2. London 1817, 480; Viccy Coltman: Party-coloured Plaid? Portraits of Eighteenth-Century Scots in Tartan, in: *Textile History* 41 (2010), 213. Also see Robin Nicholson: The Tartan Portraits of Prince Charles Edward Stuart. Identity and Iconography, in: *British Journal for Eighteenth Century Studies* 21 (1998), 145–160.

30 Jacqueline Riding: *Jacobites. A New History of the '45 Rebellion*. London 2016, 85.

31 Ibid., 85.

Their reasons for heading to Europe included education and learning how to be a gentleman, as is indicated by the letter of advice sent by Sir Robert Gordon (1580–1656) to his nephew, the eleven-year-old John, fourteenth earl of Sutherland, c. 1620. Sir Robert was certain that "Ther can be no accomplished gentleman without travelling abrod in other kingdomes."[32] This idea held true into the second half of the century. In 1661 the marquis of Argyll noted that "he that hath lived lock'd up in one Kingdom" was "but a degree beyond a Country-man, who was never put out of the bounds of his parish."[33] With this thought in mind, William Moncreif wrote from Versailles to the laird of Blair Drummond, younger, on 3 July 1699, describing the proposed route for a grand tour that Lord Hay wished to join.[34] Alternatively men traveled for the sake of their health, as in the case of Robert, earl of Lothian, who was granted a license to travel to Spa in the Low Countries, or "to any other suitable place, [and] there to remain for a year for recovery of his health".[35] Others sought a military career, or a life in trade, or both, as in the case of James Spens who wrote to his parents who lived on the Canongate in Edinburgh on 12 November 1631 informing them that he had taken his discharge from Spens of Wormiston and left the king of Sweden's service. He had gone to Holland but now planned to travel for seven years in the East Indies with Bessie Cowan's son, George Borthwick.[36] In all of these examples, the men were often away for long periods of time, meaning that they might spend weeks or months in the same place so their appearance was important, making a lasting impression of those they met and stayed with.

Travel writing, whether in the form of journals, letters, or accounts, provides evidence of how individuals encountered and responded to national difference.[37] Clothing often played a key role in this. It might be when they encountered unfamiliar clothes, such as when the Presbyterian, William, earl of Lothian, visited the

32 Sir William Fraser (ed.): *The Sutherland Book, vol. 2: Correspondence.* Edinburgh 1892, 365.
33 Archibald Campbell: *Instructions to a Son.* London 1661, 72; Claire Jackson: *Restoration Scotland, 1660–1690. Royalist Politics, Religion and Ideas.* Woodbridge 2003, 31.
34 Letters (5) addressed to the laird of Blairdrummond and others, 1693–1699, GD24/1/471, fols. 3–4 (National Records of Scotland).
35 Licence to Robert, Earl of Lothian, to travel to Spa in the Low Countries or to any other suitable place, there to remain for a year for recovery of his health, 1609–1624, GD40/2/19/1/5 (National Records of Scotland).
36 James Spens, son of James Spens, Edinburgh. To his mother and father, addressed to his mother in Canongate beneath the cross above John Ramsay's land, 12 November 1631, RH9/2/241 (National Records of Scotland).
37 John McGavin: Thomas Ker of Reddon's Trip to the Low Countries, 1620, in: Sarah Carpenter and Sarah Dunnigan (eds.): *Joyous Sweit Imaginatioun. Essays on Scottish Literature in Honour of R. D. S. Jack.* Amsterdam 2007, 157–159.

sisters of the Catholic eighth marquis of Argyll. The three women had become nuns and lived in Antwerp, Brussels, and Lothian, and they carefully recorded the different colors of their habits.[38] For Scots going into exile in Europe, their clothes often indicated how they integrated themselves into their new lives. The travel account books of David Melville, third earl of Leven (1660–1728), which cover the period from 1684–1686 when he was in exile, reveal a man with money to spend adapting to life in a new country. Resident in the Low Countries because of his involvement in the Rye House plot to kill Charles II and his younger brother, James duke of York and Albany, Melville proved himself a loyal supporter of William of Orange. While he was a Presbyterian, he recorded very little detail about the color of his clothing purchases that were bought locally, with the exception of a pair of black fringed gloves and a pair of black silk stockings.[39] A similar theme runs through the accounts of Sir David Nairne (1655–1740), who accompanied James VII and II (1633–1701) into exile, and worked as clerk of the foreign office at St Germain. Nairne dressed carefully yet elegantly in the French style: on 6 November 1699 he bought himself a black coat and breeches, in October 1702 he spent £58 14s on a new sword and a new suit, and on 25 January 1697 and 6 January 1700 he bought new wigs costing 39 livres and 52 livres, respectively.[40] For both men, black remained an integral part of their new wardrobes as they adapted to life away from Scotland.

The Virtue of Black According to Andrew Fletcher

It is in the letters of the first case study, Andrew Fletcher of Saltoun, East Lothian (1655–1716) – a writer, politician, and opponent of the 1707 act of Union between Scotland and England – that the need for a black suit was seen to be so important.[41] He gave this advice to his nephew Andrew, who was studying in Leiden before he traveled to Paris to meet his uncle in 1716. Fletcher's advice focused on three key points. Firstly, that "black cloath [...] will always be of good use to you and save you the trouble of making a sutte

---

38 Travel journal of William, Earl of Lothian, no year, 30 March/9 April to 2 March/12 April, GD40/15/58, (National Records of Scotland).
39 Note-book containing personal accounts of the Earl of Leven while in the Low Countries, 1684–1686, un-paginated, GD26/6/139 (National Records of Scotland).
40 Edward Corp: *A Court in Exile. The Stuarts in France, 1689–1718*. Cambridge 2009, 148.
41 Irene J. Murray: Letters of Andrew Fletcher of Saltoun and His Family, 1715–1716, in: *Scottish History Society*, 4th series, vol. 2, Miscellany 10. Edinburgh 1965, 145–173. For the wider context see Paul H. Scott: *Andrew Fletcher and the Treaty of the Union*. Edinburgh 1992.

immediately upon your coming to town." Secondly, that black was a sound choice for travel clothes on this occasion because "There is no hazard of traveling with a black suttee since you go not a horseback."[42] However, "It were redicoulous for you to post from thence since it is but the gaining of 3 days and will spoyle your black suttee."[43] Thirdly, that black had the added virtue of being able to serve as mourning as well as fashionable dress so that those who do not dress in black "will be in good pickle and must at least wait 3 days in their chamber to cloathes". The clever compromise was to have the suit made in advance to his uncle's specifications:

> There is no alteration in the fashion of the coat but that the slive must not be as mine was made [diagram] but thus [diagram]. This is the outside of the flap [diagram] others cut it thus [diagram] but the best is to make it very large and then if there be any alteration it is easily mended.[44]

So, with careful planning, a black suit made in Leiden could be made in the style that fulfilled all of the subtle details of a Parisian suit, ensuring its wearer immediate access to French society. While Fletcher was evidently at home in Paris, he did admit that the city has its fashion failings, stating "Bring with you lickways a pair of black silk stockings in you can get them good and cheap for they are very dear here" and "there is no cloath lick the Dutch black."[45]

Not surprisingly, Andrew Fletcher of Saltoun wore black himself, and he informed his nephew that he had "travelled from Bruxelles in my black sutt and since it has never bin off my back."[46] He was far from unique: indeed, as Michel Pastoreau observed, black clothes were a regular occurrence in the clothing choices of the sixteenth century Augsburg accountant, Matthäus Schwarz (1497–1574).[47] However, Schwarz also tailored his wardrobe so that he could acknowledge and conform to local taste and fashions when he traveled to Milan and Venice in 1515 and 1516.[48] His son, Veit Konrad (1541–1587), followed suit when he went to Verona and Venice in 1556.[49] Both men dressed in black Italian styles in order to succeed in business, and their choices reveal the

42 Murray, Letters, 166.
43 Ibid.
44 Ibid.
45 Murray, Letters, 166.
46 Ibid.
47 Pastoreau, Black, 99.
48 Ulinka Rublack and Maria Hayward (eds.): *The First Book of Fashion. The Books of Clothes of Matthäus & Veit Konrad Schwarz of Augsburg.* London 2015, 75–80.
49 Ibid., 204–206.

value of local knowledge that they, like Fletcher's nephew, accessed by asking family, friends, or business associates.

However, if conforming to local fashions while travelling was accepted as polite and prudent, was there a danger of going too far? James Howell, who was Welsh yet thought of himself as English when he wrote his *Instructions for Forreine Travel* (1642), noted how his countrymen "strive to degenerate as much as they can from Englishmen", which they did in a variety of ways, including the blending of language especially the *Inglese Italiano*. When he left home he changed "out of his country fashion, and indeed out of himself", while on his return he ought to "come home to himselfe, fashioned to such a carriage in his apparell, gesture, and conversation, as in his owne country is most plausible."[50] While this was a valid point of view, foreign fashions worn home were not always well received as revealed by the recollection of a call made by Lady Faudonside to Mr. Davidson with her son, John Ker. John was:

> then ane young gentleman latelie come from France, pransing in his French garb, with his short scarlet cloake and his long caudie rapier, according to the mode of those tymes.[51]

As this example reveals, not everyone believed that fashion should cross borders: indeed, this was an example of a disapproving Scot who believed that French fashion should stay in France.

Traveling further afield potentially posed more challenges because, while European dress might be acceptable, in most quarters at least, William Feilding, first earl of Denbigh (1587–1643), might well have been regarded as "going native". Feilding traveled to Persia and India between 1631 and 1633, and on his return he was painted by Sir Anthony van Dyck.[52] He wore an Indian-style jacket that also incorporated elements of the fashionable doublet with loose "trousers" of the pyjamas type, while his native servant, called "Jacke", was dressed in a sherwani and turban.[53] However, how far these were clothes for his portrait, as opposed to everyday wear once back in England, is hard to tell; nevertheless, they reveal a lasting interest in the clothing styles that Feilding had encountered on his travels.

---

50 Larkin, Making of Englishmen, 50.
51 Quoted in David Mathew: *Scotland under Charles I*. London 1955, 52.
52 Anthony van Dyck: *William Feilding, 1st earl of Denbigh*, 1633–1634, oil on canvas, 247.5 x 148.5 cm, National Gallery, NG 5633.
53 Karen Hearn: *Van Dyck & Britan*. London 2009, 98–99.

Black: The Mind-Set and Alternatives

The second case study draws on the diary that Samuel Pepys kept during the 1660s because he provides invaluable insights into why and when he wore particular garments.[54] Pepys is of interest because he was from the middling sort and at the height of his career he was Chief Secretary to the Admiralty, an office that gave him access to the court of Charles II. In 1660 Pepys traveled to the Netherlands in order to accompany Charles II back to England. While there, he bought Dutch clothes in order to integrate into society at The Hague. As such, he appreciated how to take on the style of another country in order to facilitate his current role; however, in the context of this discussion, it is what his diary reveals about the relationship with black clothing that is most important. Pepys shows that wearing black reflected a particular mind-set, and it could be habitual. In 1665 Pepys was evidently very comfortable wearing black because on 11 June he noted in his diary:

> dressed myself in my late new black silk camelot suit; and when full ready, comes my new one of colour'd Farrinden, which my wife puts me out of love with; which vexes [me] but I think it is only my not being used to wear Colours which makes it look a little unusual upon me.[55]

He was not alone in noting problems with colored clothing. In 1716 Andrew Fletcher stated that:

> if the heats be great about the time of your arrival, and you buy a coloured suttee, it must be of stuff, which will do you no service; and about the end of August a cloath lined with silk will be in Season.[56]

Pepys's discomfort in wearing colored clothing partially explains why he invested money in keeping his black clothes presentable. So on 30 March 1662, which was Easter Sunday, he commented "having my old black suit new furbished I was pretty neat in clothes today".[57] Black had other benefits including allowing Pepys to dress down when required, as was the case on 15 November 1664: "that I might not be too fine for the business that I intend this day, I did leave off my fine cloth

---

54 For Pepys, see Claire Tomalin: *Samuel Pepys. The Unequalled Self*. London 2002. Also see Kay Staniland: Samuel Pepys and his Wardrobe, in: *Costume* 37 (2003), 41–50 and id.: Samuel Pepys and his Wardrobe, in: *Costume* 39 (2005), 53–63.
55 Latham and Matthews, Diary, vol. 6, 125.
56 Murray, Letters, 165.
57 Latham and Matthews, Diary, vol. 3, 54.

new suit lined with plush and put on my poor black suit."[58] On other occasions, black was combined with strong colors, as on 29 November 1663: "Lords Day – This morning I put on my best black cloth suit trimmed with Scarlet ribbon, very neat, with my cloak lined with velvett and a new beaver, which altogether is very noble, with my black silk knit canons I bought a month ago."[59] This combination of black and color was a common theme in men's wardrobe as two brief examples make clear. The first is a portrait of *James Hamilton, Earl of Arran, Later 3rd Marquis of Hamilton* painted in 1623 and his black suit contrasts strongly with his scarlet stockings.[60] The second is the account for items bought by the laird of Glenorchy from James Rae in Edinburgh, 1639, that included the finest black satin, silver plate breast buttons, purple ribbons, Holland cloth, purple Spanish taffeta, and a fine black English hat.[61]

Pepys's diary also reveals that new clothes, including new black clothes, were often worn for the first time on a Sunday, as on 8 May 1664: "Lords day – this day my new tailor, Mr Langford, brought me home a new black cloth suit and cloak lined with silk moyre."[62] While black was well suited to a day of prayer and spiritual reflection, other factors influenced Pepys's choices, including the opportunity to show off new clothes, as he did on 10 May 1663: "put on a black cloth suit with white lynings under all, as the fashion is to wear, to appear under the breeches."[63] He also often wore his best clothes as on 17 April 1664: "I put on my best cloth black suit and my velvet cloak."[64]

Fashionable black garments could be worn as mourning or worn with other items of mourning as on 11 February 1666: "Lords day – put on a new black cloth suit to an old coat that I make to be in mourning at court, where they are all for the king of Spain."[65] A few months later Pepys was in official, court mourning again, and he noted on 22 April 1666: "Lords day – put on my new black cloak-coat; long, down to my knees and with Sir W Batten to White-hall where all in deep mourning for the queen's mother."[66]

---

58 Ibid., vol. 5, 322.

59 Ibid., vol. 4, 400.

60 Daniel Mytens: *James Hamilton, 3rd Marquis and 1st Duke of Hamilton*, 1623, oil on canvas, 200.7 x 125.1 cm, Tate Britain, NO3474, Presented by Colin Agnew and Charles Romer Williams, 1919.

61 Miscellaneous receipts, account due by the laird of Glenorchy to James Rae, merchant, burgess of Edinburgh, 1639. Paid 23 January 1640, GD112/29/15, no. 36 (National Records of Scotland).

62 Latham and Matthews, Diary, vol. 5, 144.

63 Ibid., vol. 4, 130.

64 Ibid., vol. 5, 125.

65 Ibid., vol. 7, 39.

66 Ibid., vol. 7, 106.

As Pepys indicates, black was a frequent choice when getting dressed because it allowed him to present himself in so many different ways that were suited to the occasion. He was not alone in understanding the value of well chosen black garments. In 1703 Nicholas Blundell (1669–1737), who was a member of a recusant family, and who had been educated at the Jesuit College in St Omer, was considering marriage.[67] He arranged to visit Heythrop Park, Oxfordshire, the home of Sir John Webb, with hopes of marrying Frances, daughter of Marmaduke, third lord Langdale and granddaughter of Lady Webb. Before setting out, he went on 12 April "to Liverpool to have a black coat made by Edward Porter for my journey to Heythrop".[68] The sober coat must have worked because on 28 April Nicholas "presented my diamond ring" and in May he "presented my gilt coffee spoons".[69] On 3 June he bought a wedding ring in London, and on 11 June he "tried on my wedding suit there".[70] The implication is that his London-made wedding suit was not black and a similar pattern can be seen in the choices of William Hamilton, third duke of Hamilton (1634–1694). For instance, on 19 August 1690 James Marshall wrote to Mr. David Crawforde, reporting that he had shipped from London the duke of Hamilton's "black suit and vest, two plaine musline cravates and 2 p[ai]r of rufles and a p[ai]r of best black silk stockings".[71] While black suits served many purposes, when the duke wanted to demonstrate his loyalty to William III and Mary II he wore "a new sute with gold buttons and brocade wastcoat to complement his majestie with" while attending the king's birthday ball.[72]

Alternatives to black included grey, such as the fine grey Spanish cloth bought by the laird of Glenorchy from James Campbell in November 1657.[73] While subdued, "sad colour" was evidently desirable, as is indicated by the purchase of sad-colored silk for a pair of breeches, a large skin for pockets, and a pair of cloth-colored stockings for the young laird of Glenorchy from Alexander Rankene, merchant in Perth, in the early 1670s.[74] In the same period, the accounts by Pitfoddels

---

67 Ralph Houlbrooke (ed.): *English Family Life. An Anthology from Diaries.* Oxford 1988, 243.
68 Frank Tyrer and John J. Bagley (eds.): *The Great Diurnal of Nicholas Blundell of Little Crosby, Lancashire,* vol. 1. Chester 1968, 31–38.
69 Ibid., 41.
70 Ibid., 42. They were married on 17 June, ibid., 43.
71 James Marshall, London, to Mr. David Crawforde, 19 August 1690, GD406/1/3679 (National Records of Scotland).
72 Marshall, Conscience, 33.
73 Accounts of special interest, account for tailoring due by the laird of Glenorchy to James Campbell, 22 November 1657, GD112/35/10, no. 12 (National Records of Scotland).
74 Miscellaneous receipts, account due by the laird of Glenorchy to Alexander Rankene, merchant in Perth, 1671–1673, paid on precept, 6 January 1674, GD112/29/30, no. 1 (National Records of Scotland).

to Andrew Dempster included a sad cloth coat to the lord.[75] Sad-colored fabrics could also reflect fashionable change as in the 18 yards of new sad-colored and black-striped silk bought by the duchess of Hamilton from Thomas Aliborne, from the "Hen and Chickings" in Covent Garden.[76] As Pepys, Blundell, and Hamilton demonstrate, black was a safe yet sophisticated choice for men that held true across national and social boundaries.

The Sense of a Scots Community

Seventeenth-century Scots traveled widely in Europe for business, education and leisure, but there were some places where they congregated such as Veere, Leiden, and Saumur.[77] This resulted in a sense of community, as can be seen in the letter of Annabella Lothian, who was living in La Rochelle in March 1649. She wrote:

> It is hard to receaue lettres now since passages for the most pairte ar stopped from Paris so ye may wret with the ships that cumes ather to bourdeous or the Rochell derecting your lettres to bourdeous to Mr broun there and to the Rochell to Mr Masson, no scots cume to ather of those pairts that knows not those two men.[78]

While the Scots in these communities were bound together by ties of kinship and business, they also integrated with the local population by means of trade, marriage, and a shared religious outlook. At the Scottish staple at Veere, the former cloth merchant from Dundee, Sir William Davidson of Curriehill (1615–1689), became Conservator and agent of Charles II.[79] He married a local woman and

---

75 Accounts for tailoring due by Pitfoddels to Andrew Dempster, 1671–1672, GD237/11/96, no. 2–3 (National Records of Scotland).

76 Thomas Aliborne, from the hen and Chickings in Covent Garden, to the duchess of Hamilton, 15 May 1690, GD406/1/3683 (National Records of Scotland).

77 See Douglas Catterall: *Community without Borders. Scots, Migrants and the Changing Face of Power in the Dutch Republic, c. 1600–1700*. Boston 2002; Alexia Grosjean and Steve Murdoch: *Scottish Communities Abroad in the Early Modern Period*. Leiden 2005 and Steve Murdoch: *Network North: Scottish Kin, Commercial and Covert Associations in Northern Europe, 1603–1746*. Leiden 2006.

78 Annabella, countess dowager of Lothian, to the countess of Lothian, 16/6 March 1649, GD40/2/3, no. 1 (National Records of Scotland).

79 For Davidson's predecessor, see Victor Enthoven: Thomas Cunningham (1604–1669). Conservator of the Scottish Court at Veere, in: David Dickson et al (eds.): *Irish and Scottish Mercantile Networks in Europe and Overseas in the Seventeenth and Eighteenth Centuries*. Gent 2007, 39–66.

dressed in the Netherlandish style, with his white linen contrasting against the black of his clothes.[80]

Gravitating towards local Scottish communities in Europe was not always an advantage for the Scottish traveler. In December 1678 Lord William Hamilton wrote to the duke of Hamilton, explaining that although "your Grace desired that I might not be known at Poitiers", this was impossible, "by reason of there being severall Scotts and Inglish students here who at my verie first appearing knew me."[81] However, these communities were always shifting in composition and dressing the part could only make a person fit in so far. This is evident from the letter sent by James Fall to the duke of Hamilton, explaining that he and his fellow countrymen will leave Paris soon and Lord William wants William Hamilton sent over to look after him, for "it very much weights his spirit to be left among strangers."[82]

The Verbal Virtues of Black

An English royalist, John Bargrave, who traveled extensively, advised fellow travelers that "If his apparel be fashionably, it matters not how plain it be, it being a ridiculous vanity to go gaudy amongst strangers."[83] The language that Bargrave used to justify a particular style is reminiscent of that used by Castiglione, and it can be found running throughout sixteenth- and seventeenth-century correspondence. In March 1676, William, third duke of Hamilton, informed his son James, earl of Arran, that he was:

> to be governed and follow his advice [Mr. Forbes] as absolutely as if it wer mine, and if in the least you faill in it [...] I intend imediatly on the knowledge therof to call you home.[84]

---

80 Abraham Lambertsz van den Tempel: *Sir William Davidson of Curriehill with his Son Charles*, c. 1664, oil on canvas, 140 x 108 cm, National Galleries of Scotland, acc. no. 2462.
81 Lord William Hamilton, Poitiers, to the duke of Hamilton, 13 December 1678, GD406/1/6125 (National Records of Scotland).
82 James Fall, Paris, to the duke of Hamilton, 6 September 1681, GD406/1/6197, (National Records of Scotland).
83 Travel journal of John Bargrave, un-foliated, Lit MS/E/39, Canterbury Cathedral Archives and Library.
84 The duke of Hamilton, London, to James, earl of Arran, 29 March 1676, GD406/1/5878 (National Records of Scotland).

Later in the year the duke objected to James engaging "in things unfit for you, as balls, masquerades, unnecessary clothes and tennis".[85] As a result Mr. Forbes tried to reassure the duke that once in Paris James's clothes would be "neither rich nor gaudy, but plain and fashionable".[86]

A very similar use of language runs through the third case study, which considers the letters sent by Michael Young, tutor and companion to the two eldest sons of William, third earl of Lothian: Robert, lord Kerr of Newbattle, aged 15, and William, aged 12.[87] When confronted with more flamboyance than they were used to, dressing in that style was justified in several ways. The first option was to blame the locals. In December 1651 Michael Young wrote from Leiden stating that "the students here are very gallant in apparel. Beyond what they used to be in any part of France", but all was well because "it is more difficult to restrain Lord Kerr from buying books than clothes."[88] The second possibility was to cite court etiquette. This worked when the boys visited the Stuarts resident at The Hague where:

> The fashion of the country did requyre that the Gentlemen should be clothed after that maner which though [it] may appear a little beyond what is ordinary in our Countrey yet it was very sober in respect of what is usual in Holland.[89]

Here, a combination of honoring local fashionable styles while showing their loyalty to the exiled Stuarts justified additional expense on suitable clothes. Young was not the only Scot writing home and he had to defend how his charges were dressed when their father announced that his sons "have been reported very fyn in their Clothes". Young refuted this claim by recourse to the language of Castiglione, stating that "Their fynnesse was never any other than a decent neatnesse [...] their Clothes being always very sober." This was backed up with a reminder that his Lordship had kept them so short of money that "wee could very scarcely doe of prodigality or gaudienesse in apparell".[90]

---

85 Rosalind Marshall: *The Days of Duchess Anne. Life in the Household of the Duchess of Hamilton, 1656–1716.* London 1973, 136.

86 Marshall, Days of Duchess Anne, 138.

87 Margaret F. Moore: The Education of a Scottish Nobleman's Sons in the Seventeenth Century, in: *Scottish Historical Review* 31 (1952), 1–15.

88 Michael Young to the countess of Lothian, 30/20 December 1651, GD40/2/3, no. 7 (National Records of Scotland).

89 Note of accounts from March 25/15 1651 until March 25/15 1652, GD40/2/3/61B (National Records of Scotland).

90 Michael Young to Lothian, 8/18 February 1654, GD40/2/3, no. 27 (National Records of Scotland).

A third option was to invoke a language of thrift, as in December 1651, when Michael Young assured Lord Lothian that:

> it is fit each of them have ane spare suit handsomely mounted besides their sommer and winder suits as the seasons come about and ye fashion of the place requyreth. We shall indeavour that wee be prodigul in nothing.[91]

He used the same phrase, "sordid nor prodigall", earlier in the year, indicating that this was an effective phrase.[92] Three years later Young informed the countess of Lothian that her sons "will be as frugal as honesty permits, but their suits, though plain, must be in the fashion with ribbons and other things."[93]

While the color of their clothes was usually not mentioned, some black items were specified including a black suit and black stockings.[94] At Paris "wee bought only a Black broydered Belt and a Hat for my L Kerr, both were very necessair and though wee know that men doe not goo naked at Saumur, yet wee finde that many of them doe send for such things as those from Paris."[95] However, other evidence suggests that black was not the norm because when their grandmother died in 1652 and their grandfather died in 1656 they did not have suitable clothing. That this was so is clear from a letter that Lord Kerr wrote to his mother in 1652: "If you think fit Madam that wee put our selves in murning, you will command us with the first and inable us to doe soe for as present it is not in our power."[96]

Mourning clothes were to be found across Europe, and the underlying ideas cut across national boundaries. Here, too, the style of language that Castiglione used permeated discussions of how mourning clothes should look. Emphasis was placed on the depth of shade, the blackness of the black, in tandem with a lack of decoration and shine, as a physical demonstration of their sense of loss. While resident in Utrecht, Colin Campbell received news of his mother's death in January 1700, and he was anxious to reassure his father that he

91 Michael Young to Lothian, 12/2 December 1651, GD40/2/3, no. 6 (National Records of Scotland).
92 Michael Young to Lothian, 27/17 May 1651, GD40/2/3, no. 13 (National Records of Scotland).
93 Michael Young to the countess of Lothian, 26 October/5 November 1654, GD40/2/3, no. 40 (National Records of Scotland).
94 Detailed notes of expenses during absence abroad, GD40/2/3/61G (National Records of Scotland).
95 Michael Young to the countess of Lothian, end of January 1654, GD40/2/3, no. 25 (National Records of Scotland).
96 Lord Kerr to the countess of Lothian, 24 October/4 September 1652, GD40/2/3, no. 57 (National Records of Scotland).

had "put John and my self in as deep mourning as if I had been on the place" [i.e. in Scotland].[97] The word "deep" recurred in a letter sent by David Monro, in December 1708, when he described a black mourning suit that was "deep enough for any accept a wife, father or mother".[98] The Laird of Glenorchy's response to the death of his daughter-in-law, Frances, who died on 4 February 1691, indicates that while he mourned her, dressed in the black clothing ordered specially for the occasion, life went on, and by mid February he sent for gray clothes for "death coms in at on dore & hearshipe at the other."[99]

Conclusions

As this brief discussion suggests, a black suit was acceptable anywhere in sixteenth- and seventeenth-century northern Europe, but to really fit in, it needed to reflect local fashions in terms of cut and decoration. As such, the black suit was a staple item in a wealthy man's wardrobe, regardless of where he lived. However, it would be rare that all his suits were black; if there was a preponderance of black, it was often offset by colored trimmings, white lace, and metal buttons. The value and virtue of the black suit was linked to the language used to describe it. While words such as "sobriety" and "not gaudy" conjured up a language of the subdued, this was tempered by a desire for fashionability and elegance. The challenge here was that all of these qualities were in the eye of the beholder, with one man's "sobriety" being another's flamboyance. Ultimately, the value of travel was reflected in this wish to embrace local styles in order to know how to dress when they returned home. Lord Ancram summed this up well when he wrote to the marquis of Lothian in the 1650s:

> rather than to loyter at home or sculk in the Highlands especially in these winter warres' that the boys should go to Paris 'to perfyte their fencing and other manly qualityes, whereof they may yet have use when all these storms are over. But by any means do not forbid, but allow them to follow their dauncing with best masters at Paris, where they must spend tyme. They cum [from] home to get the right garb of the world.[100]

---

97 Colin Campbell of Ardmaddy, Utrecht, to Breadalbane, his father, 22 January 1700, GD112/39/181/3 (National Records of Scotland).

98 David Monro, Edinburgh, not addressed, 29 December 1708, GD157/2790 (National Records of Scotland).

99 Breadalbane to Carwhin, February 13 or 15 February, n.y. GD112/39/151/17 (National Records of Scotland).

100 Quoted in Moore, Education, 15.

Thomas Weller

"He knows them by their dress": Dress and Otherness in Early Modern Spain

Abstract: *In the sixteenth and seventeenth centuries people perceived themselves as members of particular ethnic groups and considered dress to be an important marker of, alternatively, similarity or otherness. Whereas the construction of self and other in literary texts and costume books has been widely discussed, relatively little is known about the relevance of "national" dress in social practice. Against this backdrop, this article discusses the extent to which people in early modern Spain and Spanish America were able to recognize foreigners and ethnoreligious others by the way they dressed. Focusing on two groups, moriscos (Muslims converted to Christianity) within the Spanish realms and foreign Protestants, it demonstrates how a person's outward appearance could reveal, but also conceal, his or her origin. Dress served as an important marker of ethnic and religious difference, but it always remained an ambiguous signifier.*

In the sixteenth century, Western Europe saw an unprecedented interest in dress and fashion. Not by coincidence, this process went hand in hand with a new perception of the self and the individual's place in society. Renaissance men and women showed who they were or who they aspired to be not least by the way they dressed.[1] The growing number of sumptuary laws issued by political authorities across Europe since the Late Middle Ages highlights the role of dress as an important marker of difference.[2] By regulating the outward appearance of their subjects, early modern rulers not only aimed at preventing people from wasting their money in luxury, but also tried to guarantee the legibility of the social universe. In the eyes of contemporaries, a person's outward appearance

---

1 Ulinka Rublack: *Dressing Up. Cultural Identity in Renaissance Europe.* Oxford 2010; Anne Hollander: *Seeing Through Clothes.* Los Angeles 1993; Stephen Greenblatt: *Renaissance Self-Fashioning. From More to Shakespeare.* Chicago 1980; Neithard Bulst and Robert Jütte (eds.): *Zwischen Sein und Schein. Kleidung und Identität in der ständischen Gesellschaft.* Freiburg 1993.
2 Giorgio Riello and Ulinka Rublack (eds.): *The Right to Dress. Sumptuary Laws in a Global Perspective, c. 1200–1800.* Cambridge 2019; Alan Hunt: *Governance of the Consuming Passions. A History of Sumptuary Law.* New York 1996; Catherine Kovesi Killerby: *Sumptuary Law in Italy 1200–1500.* Oxford 2002; Neithard Bulst: Zum Problem städtischer und territorialer Kleider-, Aufwands- und Luxusgesetzgebung in Deutschland (13. bis Mitte 16. Jahrhundert), in: André Gouron and Albert Rigaudière (eds.): *Renaissance du pouvoir législatif et genèse de l'Etat.* Montpellier 1988, 29–57.

reflected his or her place within the social order. Therefore, members of the lower estates were strictly forbidden to wear garments reserved for the higher ranks.[3] However, even in a society as obsessed by rank and hierarchy as that of pre-revolutionary Europe, social status was but one feature among others.[4] Accordingly, many sumptuary laws contained special regulations for religious or ethnic minorities.[5]

Costume books, a new literary genre that became extremely popular at this time, also showed a world divided into perfectly distinguishable groups of people who dressed differently according to their social rank, occupational status, gender, religious affiliation, and – last but not least – ethnic origin and place of residence.[6] In this manner, authors like Christoph Weiditz, Hans Weigel, Cesare Vecellio, and François Desprez presented to their readers a broad range of regional costumes from all over the world.[7] However, the seemingly naturalistic depictions of men and women wearing their respective "national" dress could also deceive. Due to

---

3 Martin Dinges: Von der "Lesbarkeit der Welt" zum universalierten Wandel durch individu-elle Strategien. Die Soziale Funktion der Kleidung in der höfischen Gesellschaft, in: Bulst and Jütte, Sein und Schein, 90–112; Thomas Weller: "Von ihrer schändlichen und teuffelischen Hoffart sich nicht abwenden lassen wollen … ". Kleider- und Aufwandsordnungen als Spiegel "guter Ordnung", in: Irene Dingel and Armin Kohnle (eds.): *Gute Ordnung. Ordnungsmodelle und Ordnungsvorstellungen im Zeitalter der Reformation.* Leipzig 2014, 203–219.

4 For the importance of rank see: Barbara Stollberg-Rilinger: Rang vor Gericht. Zur Verrechtlichung sozialer Rangkonflikte in der frühen Neuzeit, in: *Zeitschrift für Historische Forschung* 28 (2001), 385–418; Marian Füssel and Thomas Weller (eds.): *Ordnung und Distinktion. Praktiken sozialer Repräsentation in der ständischen Gesellschaft.* Münster 2005; Marian Füssel: Die relationale Gesellschaft. Zur Konstitution ständischer Ordnung in der Frühen Neuzeit aus praxeologischer Perspektive, in: Dagmar Freist (ed.): *Diskurse – Körper – Artefakte. Historische Praxeologie in der Frühneuzeitforschung.* Bielefeld 2015, 115–137.

5 For the intersection of these differences, see Dror Wahrmann: *The Making of the Modern Self. Identity and Culture in Eighteenth-Century England.* New Haven 2004.

6 Rublack, Dressing Up, 146–163; Ulrike Ilg: The Cultural Significance of Costume Books in Sixteenth-Century Europe, in: Catherine Richardson (ed.): *Clothing Culture 1350–1650.* Aldershot 2004, 29–48; Leslie Schick: The place of dress in pre-modern costumes albums, in: Suraiya Faroqhi and Christopher K. Neumann (eds.): *Ottoman Costumes from Textile to Identity.* Istanbul 2004, 93–102; Odile Blanc: Ethnologie et merveille dans quelques livres de costumes français, in: Marie Viallon (ed.): *Paraître et se vêtir au XVIe siècle.* Saint-Étienne 2008, 79–94.

7 Theodor Hampe (ed.): *Das Trachtenbuch des Christoph Weiditz von seinen Reisen nach Spanien (1529) und den Niederlanden (1531/32).* Berlin 1927; Hans Weigel: *Habitus praecipuo-rum populorum [. . .]. Trachtenbuch, darin fast allerley und der fürnembsten Nationen [. . .] klei-dungen [. . .] mit allem vleiß abgerissen.* Nürnberg 1577; Margaret F. Rosentahl and Ann Rosalind Jones (eds.): *Cesare Vecellio's Habiti Antichi et Moderni. The Clothing of the Renaissance World.* London 2008; François Desprez: *Receuil de la diversité des habits, qui sont de present en usage, tant en pays d'Europe, Asie, Affrique et Isles sauvages.* Paris 1562.

genre conventions, costume books were "more likely to affirm local, national, gender and rank-specific identities than cosmopolitanism and universal values".[8] In many cases the authors themselves pursued a "nationalistic" agenda and thus presented a biased or distorted view of other cultures.[9] By doing so, they deliberately ignored an important aspect of contemporary fashion. At the same time as costume books were becoming popular, fashionable clothing items and materials started to circulate ever faster across cultural and political borders. The adoption of foreign styles and their mixture with autochthonous elements was quite frequent among European elites.[10] Nevertheless, the popularity of this genre shows that sixteenth and seventeenth-century contemporaries perceived themselves as members of different ethnic groups and considered dress as an important marker of "national" differences.[11] Whereas the construction of self and other in humanist discourse in general and costume books in particular has been widely discussed, relatively little is known about the relevance of dress as a marker of "national" difference and belonging in social practice.

Against this backdrop, this article discusses the extent to which people in early modern Spain and Spanish America were able to recognize foreigners and ethnoreligious others by the way they dressed. The Spanish monarchy is of particular interest for this question for various reasons. In the sixteenth and seventeenth centuries the so-called Spanish dress served as a model for aristocratic and bourgeois elites across Europe.[12] However, early modern Spain was by no means a monolithic cultural entity. As a paradigmatic case of a composite monarchy, it encompassed different territories and ethnic groups under one dynasty.[13] Among the Iberian subjects of the Catholic Kings were also large religious and ethnic minorities, who had been forced to convert to Christianity and to assimilate

8 Rublack, Dressing Up, 162.
9 Ibid., 146–163.
10 The contributions to this issue provide many cases in point.
11 For pre-modern concepts of nation and the rise of early modern nationalism, see Caspar Hirschi: *The Origins of Nationalism. An Alternative History from Ancient Rome to Early Modern Germany*. Cambridge 2012.
12 José Luis Colomer and Amalia Descalzo (eds): *Spanish Fashion at the Courts of Early Modern Europe*, vol. 1. Madrid 2014; Milena Hajná: Moda al servicio del poder. La vestimenta en la sociedad noble de la Europa Central en la Edad Moderna y las influencias de España, in: Miguel Cabañas Bravo, Amelia López-Yarto Elizalde, and Wilfredo Rincón García (eds.): *Arte, poder y sociedad en la España de los siglos XV a XX*. Madrid 2008, 71–82.
13 Pedro Cardim et.al. (eds.): *Polycentric Monarchies. How did Early Modern Spain and Portugal Achieve and Maintain a Global Hegemony*. Brighton 2012; Antonio Álvarez-Ossorio Alvariño et al. (eds.): *La monarquía de las naciones. Patria, nación y naturaleza en la Monarquía de España*. Madrid 2004.

to the dominant Christian culture at the beginning of the early modern period.[14] As I will show, dress regulations accompanied and fostered this process in a significant way. Apart from Jews and Muslims, who were perceived by many Spaniards as "foreigners" within – although they had been living on the Iberian Peninsula for centuries – early modern Spain was also confronted with increasing migration from other European territories.[15] Commercial hubs like Seville, one of the most important centers of world trade in the sixteenth century, attracted thousands of foreigners. Many of these were Protestants or came from territories that were continuously at war with the Spanish Monarchy. By focusing on these two groups, ethnoreligious minorities within the Spanish realms and foreign migrants, I will analyze the extent to which dress served as a marker of otherness. As I will show, in sixteenth- and seventeenth-century Spain and Spanish America a person's outward appearance could reveal, but also conceal, his or her origin. Dress served as an important marker of ethnic and religious difference, but it was always an ambiguous signifier.

Foreigners Within: Dress Regulations and Ethnoreligious Minorities in Medieval and Early Modern Spain

As in other parts of Europe, Jews and Muslims living under Christian rule in the medieval Iberian kingdoms were subject to special dress regulations. The authorities not only obliged them to wear distinctive marks on their clothing to

---

14 Mark D. Meyerson and Edward D. English (eds.): *Christians, Muslims, and Jews in Medieval and Early Modern Spain. Interaction and Cultural Change*. Notre Dame, IN 2000; Christian Windler: Religiöse Minderheiten im christlichen Spanien, in: Peer Schmidt (ed.): *Kleine Geschichte Spaniens*. Stuttgart 2002, 105–121; Patrick Leonard Harvey: *Muslims in Spain, 1500–1614*. Chicago, IL 2006; Mary Elizabeth Perry: *The Handless Maiden. Moriscos and the Politics of Religion in Early Modern Spain*. Princeton 2007; Antonio Domínguez Ortiz and Bernard Vincent: *Historia de los moriscos. Vida y tragedia de una minoría*. Madrid 1978; Jane S. Gerber: *The Jews of Spain. A History of the Sephardic Experience*. New York 1992; Elie Kedourie (ed.): *Spain and the Jews. The Sephardi Experience 1492 and After*. London 1992; Dolores J. Sloan: *The Sephardic Jews of Spain and Portugal. Survival of an Imperiled Culture in the Fifteenth and Sixteenth centuries*. Jefferson, NC 2009; Julio Caro Baroja: *Los Judíos en la España Moderna y Contemporánea*. Madrid 1978.
15 For the perception of Muslims, Jews, and their descendants as "others within", see Antonio Feros: *Speaking of Spain. The Evolution of Race and Nation in the Hispanic World*. Cambridge, MS 2017, 76–108.

make them easily recognizable, but also prohibited them from wearing specific garments or materials that were considered signs of social distinction, such as gold, silver, and silk. Regardless of their economic situation, non-Christians were not allowed to dress better than Christian commoners did; thus, religious discrimination went hand in hand with social stigmatization.[16] However, it seems that these regulations were scarcely obeyed, despite being constantly repeated and confirmed, and that cross-cultural influences between Christians, Muslims, and Jews were quite frequent during the Middle Ages. The famous historian Ibn Khaldun, whose family had abandoned Andalusia after the fall of Seville in 1248, criticized Andalusian Muslims for subjecting themselves to Christians by adopting their dress.[17] In Nasrid Granada, Muslim authorities worried about the blurring of religious lines, since many Christians dressed like Muslims.[18] In spite of the limited obedience to their dress regulations, it appears that medieval rulers, both Christian and Muslim, aimed at making religious difference visible through dress. These regulations took a different direction only after 1492, when the coexistence of the three monotheistic religions on the Iberian Peninsula came to a definite end.

Whereas in the medieval Iberian kingdoms the separation of religious minorities had been enforced, in early modern Spain rulers aimed at homogenizing their subjects in both religious and cultural aspects. In 1492 and 1502 respectively, the Catholic Kings obliged all remaining Jews and Muslims either to convert to Christianity or to leave the Spanish kingdoms. Both royal edicts were soon followed by ordinances on Jewish and Muslim customs and dress.[19] It is a characteristic feature of sumptuary legislation in early modern Spain that

---

16 José Damián González Arce: *Apariencia y poder. La legislación suntuaria castellana en los siglos XIII y XIV*. Jaén 1998, 170–177; Maria Filomena Lopes de Barros: Body, Baths, and Cloth. Muslim and Christian Perceptions in Medieval Portugal, in: *Portuguese Studies* 21 (2005), 1–12; Ana Isabel Carrasco Manchado: *De la convivencia a la exclusión. Imágenes legislativas de mudéjares y moriscos. Siglos XIII–XVII*. Madrid 2012. For Jewish dress in other parts of early modern Europe, see the contributions by Flora Cassen and Cornelia Aust to this issue.
17 Ibn Khaldun: *The Muqaddimah. An Introduction to History*, trans. Franz Rosenthal, ed. N.J. Daewood, Princeton 1967, 322.
18 Manuela Marín: Signos visuales de la identidad andalusi, in: ead. (ed.): *Tejer y vestir. De la antigüedad al islam*. Madrid 2001, 137–180, here 143–152.
19 Raymond B. Waddington and Arthur H. Williamson (eds.): *The Expulsion of the Jews. 1492 and After*. New York 1994; Carrasco Manchado, De la convivencia, 223–240; Antonio Gallego y Burín and Alfonso Gamir Sandoval: *Los moriscos del reino de Granada segun el sínodo de Guadix de 1554*. Granada 1968; Rafael Benítez Sánchez-Blanco: Carlos V y los moriscos granadinos, in: Joaquín Pérez Villanueva and Bartolomé Escandell Bonet (eds.): *Historia de la Inquisición en Espana y America*, vol 1. Madrid 1984, 474–487; David Coleman: *Creating Christian Granada. Society and Religious Culture in an Old-World Frontier City, 1492–1600*. Ithaca, NY 2003.

it was never limited to the restriction of luxurious garments according to rank and status but always intersected with laws regulating the sartorial practices of ethnoreligious minorities.[20] In order to guarantee the most complete assimilation, *conversos* (converted Jews) and *moriscos* (converted Muslims) were obliged not only to believe but also to live and dress like Christians. From the very beginning, however, this measure had a paradoxical effect: the increasing disappearance of visible differences fostered mistrust of New Christians, who were suspected of clandestinely clinging to their old faith and customs.[21] Especially in case of the *moriscos*, who proved to be more resilient to forced assimilation, the prohibition of religious practice and cultural habits "reinforced each other and supported the equation of social deviance (Morisco customs) with religious deviance (heresy)".[22] However, although there still were significant differences in eating habits, ritual practice, religious holidays, and the like, as a result of continuous cross-cultural influence the difference between Muslim and Christian dressing styles was not as clear-cut as one might think, especially in those regions with large Muslim populations.[23] In the Kingdom of Granada, a territory that had been under Muslim rule for more than seven centuries and that was conquered by the Christians only in 1492, people seemed to dress in a very similar way regardless of their religion. Thus, when the new Christian rulers of Granada started to prohibit "Moorish dress", it was not quite clear what that actually meant. In 1511, reconfirming previous legislation, Juana of

---

20 For Spanish sumptuary legislation in the early modern period see Amanda Wunder: Spanish Fashion and Sumptuary Legislation from the Thirteenth to the Eighteenth Century, in: Riello and Rublack, Right to Dress, 243–272; Ruth de la Puerta Escribano: Las leyes suntuarias y la restricción de lujo en el vestir, in: José Luis Colomer and Amalia Descalzo (eds): *Spanish Fahsion at the Courts of Early Modern Europe*, vol. 1. Madrid 2014, 209–231; ead.: Reyes, moda y legislación jurídica en la España moderna, in: *Ars Longa* 9/10 (2000), 65–72; Saúl Martínez Bermejo: Beyond Luxury. Sumptuary Legislation in 17th-Century Castile, in: Gunther Lottes et. al. (eds.): *Making, Using and Resisting the Law in European History*. Pisa 2008, 93–108; Antonio Álvarez-Ossorio Alvariño: Rango y apariencia. El decoro y la quiebra de la distinción en Castilla (ss. XVI–XVIII), in: *Revista de Historia Moderna* 17 (1998/99), 263–278; Antonio Pérez Martin: El derecho y el vestido en el antiguo regimen, in: *Anales de Derecho* 16 (1998), 261–289.
21 Philip Hersch, Angus MacKay, and Geraldine MacKendrick: The Semiology of Dress in Late Medieval and Early Modern Spain, in: *Razo* 7 (1987), 95–110, esp. 106–110; David M. Gitlitz: *Secrecy and Deceit. The Religion of the Crypto-Jews.* Philadelphia 1996, 523–530.
22 Deborah Root: Speaking Christian. Orthodoxy and Difference in Sixteenth Century Spain, in: *Representations* 23 (1988), 119–132, quote on 126. Leonard Patrick Harvey: The Political, Social, and Cultural History of the Moriscos, in: Salma Khadra Jayyusi and Manuela Marín (eds.): *The Legacy of Muslim Spain.* Leiden 1992, 201–234.
23 See Javier Irigoyen-García: *Moors Dresses as Moors. Clothing, Social Distinction, and Ethnicity in Early Modern Iberia.* Toronto 2017.

Castile forbade the production of "Morisco clothing" (*ropa morisca*).[24] Since the Morisco tailors of Granada did not know precisely what kind of clothes they were forbidden to produce, they asked the city council for further instructions. The answer of the local authority is very telling: it was not able or willing to give a precise definition. The city council permitted the "aforementioned tailors" to produce "hoods for slashed tunics and four spans long for men, and doublets in the Castilian style and hose for men, and *ropones*, which they call *cotas*." Furthermore they were allowed to fashion "all kind of men's clothing except for *marlotas*" (Moorish tunics), but they were forbidden "to cut or make any kind of female clothing *a la morisca*."[25] Even when the authorities prohibited specific garments like the *almalafa*, a large veil used by women to cover the head and the upper body, the prohibiting laws often addressed Morisco and Old Christian women alike.[26] [Figure 1]

In 1567 Philipp II issued a new decree on Moorish dress, in which he mandated

> that none of the said newly converted in the aforementioned Kingdom of Granada nor their descendants can make or tailor veiled gowns (*almalafas*), Moorish tunics (*marlotas*), hose, or any other sort of clothing such as they used to wear during the time of the Moors, and that new dresses be made like those that the Old Christian women wear, that is, cloaks and tunics.[27]

Although the monarch explicitly confirmed the regulations issued by his predecessors, the decree widely ignored the "complex cultural reality of Granada that had been acknowledged in the previous legislation".[28] The alleged difference between Christian and Moorish clothing had never been that obvious,

---

24 Gallego y Burin and Gamir Sandoval, Los moriscos, 174.

25 Ibid., 175; Irigoyen-García, Moors, 103–104. The Spanish original reads: "Que los dichos sastres pueden hacer y cortar capuces de sayas de jirones de cuatro cuartas para hombres, y jubones a la castellana y calzas para hombres, y ropones, que ellos dicen cotas, y toda ropa de hombres, excepto marlotas; e que no corten ni hagan ropa alguna para mujeres a la morisca."

26 Gallego y Burin and Gamir Sandoval, Los moriscos, 179; Irigoyen-García, Moors, 105; Coleman, Creating Christian Granada, 63; Harvey, Muslims in Spain, 72, 212.

27 *Pregmaticas y provisiones de S. M. el Rey don Philippe nuestro señor, sobre la lengua y vestidos, y otras cosas que an de hazer los naturales deste Reyno de Granada.* Granada 1567, fol. 2r–v. Quoted in: Irigoyen-García, Moors, 110, 226. The Spanish original reads: "ningunos de los dichos nueuamente conuertidos del dicho reyno de Granada, ni descendientes dellos, no puedan hazer ni cortar de nueuo almalafas ni marlotas, ni otras calças ni vestidos, de las que usauan y trayan en tiempo de moros, y que los vestidos que de nuevo hizieren sean conforme a los que traen las christianas viejas, conuiene a saber, mantos y sayas."

28 Irigoyen-García, Moors, 110.

Figure 1: Morisco Woman wearing an *amalafa*, in: Christoph Weiditz: *Trachtenbuch*, c. 1530–1540. Courtesy ©Germanisches Nationalmuseum Nürnberg, Hs 22474, fol. 97.

neither "during the time of the Moors" nor after 1492. Although dressing styles changed after the fall of Granada, these changes affected not only the former Muslim community but also Old Christians. According to Francisco Núñez Muley, a Morisco nobleman from Granada, by the middle of the sixteenth century the outward appearance of Moriscos was almost indistinguishable from that of Old Christians. In a memorandum addressed to the Royal Audiencia of Granada, in which he protested against the new dress regulations, he claimed that the Morisco men (and to some extent women) of Granada had been dressing in the "Castilian manner" since the 1520s.[29]

Even though this might have been an exaggeration, and probably was not true for the rural regions of Granada, Núñez Muley's memorandum demonstrates that the authorities' efforts to regulate the sartorial practices of the Moriscos followed a paradoxical logic: the more similar the latter became to

---

29 Francisco Núñez Muley: *A Memorandum for the President of the Royal Audiencia and Chancery Court of the City and Kingdom of Granada.* Transl. by Vincent Barletta. Chicago 2007; Irigoyen-García, Moors, 115; Harvey, Muslims of Spain, 213; Louis Cardaillac: Le vêtement des morisques, in: Haïm Vidal Sephiha (ed.): *Signes et marques du convers. Espagne, XVe–XVIe siècles.* Aix-en-Provence 1993, 15–30.

Old Christians, the more legislation perceived and treated them as an essentially distinct group. In practice, however, "the Moorishness of the Moriscos" often "existed only in the eye of the beholder", independent of the clothes they were actually wearing.[30] Thus it was not the textile object itself, but its wearer and the specific context in which he or she wore a specific garment that made the latter a marker of religious or ethnic difference. For the same reason, supposedly Moorish clothing could generate different meanings if it was worn by non-Moriscos. While authorities obliged the Moriscos to dress in a "Castilian manner" and prohibited the production of "Moorish" clothing by Morisco tailors, garments *a la morisca* remained fashionable among the Old Christian nobility in many parts of the Iberian Peninsula. Although these garments were no longer part of Castilian noblemen's everyday clothing, as they had been in the Middle Ages, aristocrats still wore them on certain occasions. In the so-called game of canes (*juego de cañas*), a popular equestrian game that was performed at urban and courtly feasts in all parts of the Iberian Peninsula, the participants used to dress as Moors. Their attire consisted of leather boots (*borceguíes*), the Moorish tunic (*marlota*), a hooded cape (*capellar*) and a turban.[31] [Figure 2] Regardless of the royal decree of 1567 that prohibited the production of any

Figure 2: Participant in the Game of Canes, in: Anonymous, *Códice de trajes*, between 1500 and 1599. Courtesy Biblioteca Nacional de España, RES/ 285, fol. 1r.

---

30 Irigoyen-García, Moors, 19, 101.
31 Ibid., 8–11, 27–56.

kind of Moorish clothing in the Kingdom of Granada, even the king himself continued dressing *a la morisca* when he participated in the game of canes together with other noblemen.[32] On these occasions, the same textile objects that were perceived as markers of ethnicity and condemned as signs of religious and social deviance, when used by Moriscos, served as status symbols for the Old Christian nobility, since only noblemen were allowed to participate in the game of canes. As the example of Moorish clothing shows, "dress as a marker of ethnic identity can also deceive", since it "generates social meanings [...] that go beyond its mere materiality".[33] In the following, I will discuss whether this also holds true for other ethnic and religious groups and their specific dressing habits.

Suspicious Strangers: Foreign Heretics and Enemies of the Crown

Many strangers who came from outside the Spanish Monarchy were regarded with the same suspicion as Moriscos, who were increasingly treated as foreigners on their own soil and who were finally expelled from the territories of the Spanish Monarchy in 1609.[34] In the sixteenth century, the influx of gold, silver, and other colonial products from Spain's American possessions attracted traders from many European countries.[35] However, not all of these traders were welcome

---

32 Teófilo Ruiz: *A King Travels. Festive Traditions in Late Medieval and Early Modern Spain.* Princeton 2012, 215.

33 Irigoyen-García, Moors, 16.

34 Mercedes García-Arenal and Gerard Wiegers (eds.): *The Expulsion of the Moriscos from Spain. A Mediteranean Diaspora.* Leiden 2014. For the presence of foreigners on the Iberian Peninsula and their perception, see the still ground-breaking study by Antonio Domínguez Ortiz: Los extranjeros en la vida espanola, in: *Estudios de historia social de España* 4:2 (1960), 293–426, more recently Bernardo José García García and Óscar Recio Morales (eds): *Las corporaciones de nación en la monarquía hispánica. Identidad, patronazgo y redes de sociabilidad.* Madrid 2014; Óscar Recio Morales and Thomas Glesener (eds.): *Los extranjeros y la nación en España y la América española.* Madrid 2012; David González Cruz (ed.): *Extranjeros y enemigos en Iberoamérica. La visión del otro.* Madrid 2011; id.: *Pueblos indígenas y extranjeros en la Monarquía Hispánica. La imagen del otro en tiempos de guerra.* Madrid 2010; María Begoña Villar García and Pilar Pezzi Cristóbal (eds.): *Los extranjeros en la España moderna.* Málaga 2003; Tamar Herzog: *Defining Nations. Immigrants and Citizens in Early Modern Spain and Spanish America.* New Haven 2003.

35 See among others Juan José Iglesias Rodríguez and José Jaime García Bernal (eds.): *Andalucía en el mundo atlántico moderno. Agentes y escenarios.* Madrid 2016; Ana Crespo

on the Iberian Peninsula. Since many of the foreigners were Protestants, the Catholic clergy and the notorious Spanish Inquisition soon became alarmed. In the 1560s, the Spanish Inquisition started to visit all incoming ships in search of heretical books and writings. On some occasions, whole crews were arrested and burned at the stake. By the end of the sixteenth century, however, tempers had cooled down and Spanish authorities started tacitly to tolerate the presence of foreign Protestants in Seville, Cádiz, and other trading port cities, and to some extent even in America.[36]

Religious denomination, however, was just one side of the coin. The other was the question of ethnic origin and "national" belonging. While the Spanish Monarchy was at war with England, France, and the Northern Provinces of the Netherlands, traders from these countries were officially banned from Spanish territories and not allowed to enter Spanish ports. One might wonder, though, how Spanish authorities were able to distinguish enemies from friends, that is, English, French, and Dutchmen from Irishmen, Germans, or the inhabitants of the Southern Netherlands, who also spoke French and Dutch but remained loyal to the Spanish Crown after the outbreak of the Dutch rebellion. Personal documents and passports hardly existed or were still at an embryonic stage and thus easy to falsify or manipulate.[37] Linguistic differences played an important part in making distinctions, but they were anything but clear-cut.[38] Apart from language,

---

Solana (ed.): *Comunidades transnacionales. Colonias de mercaderes extranjeros en el Mundo Atlántico (1500–1830)*. Madrid 2010; Eberhard Crailsheim: *The Spanish Connection. French and Flemish Merchcant Networks in Seville (1570–1650)*. Cologne 2016; Hermann Kellenbenz (ed.): *Fremde Kaufleute auf der Iberischen Halbinsel*. Cologne 1970.

36 Thomas Weller: Trading Goods – Trading Faith? Religious Conflict and Commercial Interests in Early Modern Spain, in: Isabel Karreman, Inga Mai Groote, and Cornel Zwierlein (eds.): *Forgetting Faith? Negotiating Confessional Conflict in Early Modern Europe*. Berlin 2012, 221–239; Pauline Croft: Englishmen and the Spanish Inquisition, 1558–1625, in: *The English Historical Review* 87 (1972), 249–268; Werner Thomas: *La represión del protestantismo en España, 1517–1648*. Leuven 2001; id.: *Los protestantes y la Inquisición en España en tiempos de Reforma y Contrarreforma*. Leuven 2001; Joël Graf: *Die Inquisition und ausländische Protestanten in Spanisch-Amerika (1560–1770). Rechtspraktiken und Rechtsräume*. Köln 2017.

37 .Valentin Groebner: *Who are you? Identification, deception, and surveillance in early modern Europe*. Brooklyn, NY 2007; id.: Describing the Person, Reading the Signs in Late Medieval and Renaissance Europe. Identity Papers, Vested Figures, and the Limits of Identification 1400–1600, in: Jane Caplan and John Torpey (eds.): *Documenting Individual Identity. The Development of State Practices in the Modern World*. Princeton, NJ 2001, 15–27.

38 Iñaki López Martín: Embargo and Protectionist Policies in Late Sixteenth and Early Seventeenth-Century Hispano-Dutch Relations in the Western Mediterranean, in: *Mediterranean Studies* 7 (1998), S. 191–219; id.: Los unos y los otros: comercio, guerra e identidad. Flamencos y holandeses en la Monarquía Hispánica (ca. 1560–1609), in: Carmen Sanz Ayán and Bernardo

however, there was a second important marker of difference that is frequently mentioned in contemporary sources and often in combination with language.

At the beginning of the year 1587, the Duke of Medina Sidonia, future commander-in-chief of the Great Armada that would set course for England one year later, arrested dozens of vessels presumed to be Dutch in the port of Sanlúcar de Barrameda, Seville's outer harbor where the duke had his residence.[39] In order to find out where the ships' crews came from, the ducal authorities first spoke to members of the local Flemish and German community, the so-called *nación flamenca y alemana* of Sanlúcar de Barrameda. Most of the members of this community were also merchants who had lived in Sanlúcar for many years. These witnesses denounced the vast majority of the foreign ships and crews as "rebels". 38-year-old Cornieles Adrián was sure that most of the foreign ships and crews were Dutch. According to the interrogation records, he recognized them by their "language and dress" (*traje y habla*), since he had seen the crewmembers and spoke to them on several occasions in town.[40] In the same fashion Lorenzo Aponte, Juan Hanze, Bernardo Lorenzo, and Andres Juanes explicitly mentioned "language and dress" (*el vestido y lenguaje de las gentes, sus lenguas y trajes, su lengua y vestidos*) as unmistakable markers that revealed the Dutch origin of the foreign sailors and merchants.[41]

Unfortunately, none of these witnesses mentioned specific garments or details of the clothing that made them sure that the crews came from the rebellious parts of the Netherlands.[42] Nevertheless, there is evidence of some specific pieces of clothing or accessories which were regarded as markers of "foreignness" in Spain and Spanish America. In 1590 the shipmaster and surgeon Nicolás Alés from the city of Lille (now French but at the time part of the Spanish Netherlands) was captured as a pirate on the coast of Yucatán (Mexico). Apart from accusing him of piracy, the Spanish authorities assumed that Alés was Protestant. Sebastían

---

José García García (eds.): *Banca, crédito y capital. La monarquía hispánica y los antiguos Países Bajos (1505–1700)*. Madrid 2006, 425–457.

39 Thomas Weller: Fronteras fluidas. Los Países Bajos, la Hansa y el embargo general de 1586–1587, in: *e-Spania* 24 (2016). URL: *http://journals.openedition.org/e-spania/25760* (30 Jan. 2019); Luis Salas Almela: Poder señorial, comercio y guerra. Sanlúcar de Barrameda y la política de embargos de la Monarquía Hispánica, 1585–1641, in: *Cuadernos de Historia Moderna* 33 (2008), 35–59.

40 Archivo General de la Fundación Casa de Medina Sidonia [AGFCMS], leg. 979, Declaration by Cornieles Adrián, Sanlúcar, 15, January 1587.

41 Ibid., Declarations by Lorenço Aponte and Iuan Hance, Sanlúcar, 14, January 1587, Declarations by Andres Iuanes and Bernardo Lorenço, Sanlúcar, 15, January 1587.

42 For Spanish sailors' dress see Pablo E. Pérez-Mallaína: *Spain's Men of the Sea. Daily Life on the Indies Fleets in the Sixteenth Century*. Baltimore 1998, 145–152.

Herrera, a resident of the city of Mérida, declared that he had seen Alés in his town "wearing earrings and having his ears perforated and that this was clearly a sign of Protestantism (*señal de luteranos*)". Herrera knew this because he had seen Protestants in England wearing the same kind of earrings. Being confronted with this testimony, Alés replied that he wore only one earring, as Catholic and Protestant soldiers in France did, regardless of their denomination, and that there was "no religious symbolism" in it (*no había señal ni cosa de religion*).[43] In the same fashion, Leonardo Salina, a cleric from Cozumel in Yucatán, suspected the crew of a French vessel to be Protestant because some of the sailors wore earrings in the same manner as some pirates whose detention the cleric had witnessed some years earlier in Puerto Rico. In 1590, a monk named Francisco Zapata, resident of the city of Trinidad de Guatemala, on the Pacific coast, told Inquisitors about a journey through the Netherlands he had undertaken 15 years earlier. On this voyage, he had noticed a special fashion in hats that Dutch Protestants "used as a symbol". According to Zapata the Dutch Protestants "used to cut the brims of their hats and fix together the hats' ends with buckles and buttons" (*tomaron por seña cortar las alas de los sombreros y las puntas prenderlas con hebillas y botones*). When he became aware that the same fashion had spread to the General Captaincy of Guatemala, the worried monk alerted the Inquisition to the menace of a Protestant infiltration of this province.[44]

As these examples show, the sixteenth-century inhabitants of Spanish America obviously associated specific styles of dress with foreign origin and Protestant belief. As to the earrings, these suspicions were not far-fetched. Men's earrings were indeed popular among English pirates and sailors but also among aristocrats and courtiers. Sir Walter Raleigh had himself portrayed wearing a pair of pearls in his left ear in 1588. Robert Carr, first Earl of Somerset, also shows off with a precious earring on a seventeenth-century painting. The famous Chandos Portrait of 1610 shows a male person, presumably William Shakespeare, wearing a golden earring. [Figures 3, 4, and 5] Although one of the captured pirates argued that French soldiers also used earrings, among Spaniards, apparently, they were rather uncommon. In Renaissance Italy, earrings served as a distinguishing sign for Jewish women. Contemporary paintings also show male "heathens" and religious

---

43 Archivo General de la Nación [AGN], México, Inquisición, Proceedings against Nicolás de Alés, 1590, quoted in: Eleonora Poggio: *Foráneos y arraigados. Migración, inclusión y exclusión social de néerlandeses y alemanes en Nueva España, 1560–1650*, PhD thesis, *Universidad Pablo de Olavide*. Sevilla 2015, 93.
44 AGN, Inquisición, Denunciation by Francisco Zapata concerning Protestant dress, quoted in Poggio, Foráneos y arraigados, 94.

Figure 3: Unknown English artist: *Sir Walter Ralegh (Raleigh)*, oil on panel, 1588. Courtesy ©National Portrait Gallery, London.

Figure 4: *Robert Carr, Earl of Somerset*, after John Hoskins, oil on panel, after 1630, based on a work of c. 1625–1630. Courtesy ©National Portrait Gallery, London.

Figure 5: *William Shakespeare*, associated with John Taylor, oil on canvas, feigned oval, c. 1600–1610, Courtesy ©National Portrait Gallery, London.

others wearing earrings.[45] However, even in the sixteenth century fashions changed rapidly, and often spread from one country to another. This seems to be the case with the "Protestant" headgear, which Francisco Zapata had first observed in the Netherlands and later in New Spain. It is hard to believe that the people who wore these hats in a remote city on New Spain's Pacific coast really were Dutch Protestants.

From Foreigners to Spaniards: Dress and Cultural Assimilation

So far, I have discussed the case of foreigners who visited Spain only for a short time, mostly merchants and sailors who came for business and returned to their

---

45 Diane Owen Hughes: Distinguishing Signs. Ear-Rings, Jews, and Franciscan Regulation in the Italian Renaissance City, in: *Past & Present* 112 (1986), 3–59, 20; Penny Howell Jolly: Marked Difference. Earrings and 'The Other' in Fifteenth-Century Flemish Art, in: Désirée G. Koslin and Janet E. Snyder (eds.): *Encountering Medieval Textiles and Dress. Objects, Texts, Images.* New York 2002, 195–207.

home countries after reloading their ships with new merchandise. What happened with those foreigners who decided to stay longer or to settle permanently in Spanish territories? Did they adapt their way of living – and clothing – to Spanish habits? Historians have answered this question in quite different ways. Hipólito Sancho de Sopranis, one of the first Spanish historians to study the presence of foreigners in the bay of Cádiz, came to the conclusion that the Flemings who settled there never became integrated into local society but rather formed a separate community. Their "isolation and lack of intermingling with the Spanish element" was a result of their supposed "ostentatious character" that did not work well with the "natural dignity of the Spaniards". According to Sancho de Sopranis, sumptuousness in private life and clothing was a "characteristic of the Flemish race".[46] Sancho de Sopranis wrote his article in 1960, during the Franco regime, which might explain some of his ideas on the supposed cultural differences between Spaniards and Flemings. In the very same year, however, Antonio Domínguez Ortiz drew a completely different picture of the foreign merchants in Spain and their relation to Spanish society. According to Domínguez Ortiz, most of them assimilated quite rapidly to Spanish culture, including its flaws:

> From their social environment, infused with aristocratic values, they [the foreign merchants] adopted forms of ostentation and luxury in clothing and household which formed the counterpart to the mercantile spirit that predominated at that time in other latitudes of the European continent, as Max Weber's penetrating analyses have shown.[47]

As evidence to prove his thesis, Domínguez Ortiz quotes an inventory dating from the year 1684. The owner of the goods, Enrique Lepín from Hamburg, had lived for many years in Seville and married a "Spanish" woman. Although his wife, Susana Antonia de León, was born and raised in Seville, she was the daughter of another immigrant from Hamburg.[48] Among Lepín's possessions

---

46 "Y aún podría agregarse otro factor que explique el aislamiento de los germánicos [sic!] y su falta de compenetración con el elemento español: su carácter ostentoso que les hacía poco soportables a la natural dignidad española [. . .]. La fastuosidad en la vida privada es una de las características de la raza flamenca.", Hipólito Sancho de Sopranis: Las naciones extranjeras en Cádiz durante el siglo XVII, in: *Estudios de Historia Social de España* 4:2 (1960), 753–877, here 764.

47 "Podemos decir que se españolizaron también en los defectos, tomando de aquel medio ambiente saturado de caballeresco espíritu de ostentación los hábitos de lujo en vestidos, casa y menaje que eran el polo opuesto de aquel otro espíritu mercantil parsimonioso y utilitario que por las mismas fechas triunfaba en otras latitudes de Europa, según han puesto de manifiesto los penetrantes análisis de Max Weber.", Domínguez Ortiz, Los extranjeros, 323.

48 For Lepín's family relations see José Manuel Díaz Blanco: Un mercader alemán en Andaluccía. Enrique Lepín entre Sevilla y Cádiz (siglos XVII–XVIII), in: Juan José Iglesias

were two coaches valued at 2,000 ducats. As measured by the amount of trade goods, which was projected at 30,000 ducats, Domínguez Ortiz sees in the two carriages clear evidence of a genuinely Spanish aspiration to demonstrate one's status. Nonetheless, one may rightfully wonder whether the sometimes ruinous investment in such forms of symbolic capital was confined to Spanish society alone. If we consider the extensive number of sumptuary laws in the Holy Roman Empire, for example, the interpretation of Domínguez Ortiz does not seem very convincing. Instead, it seems that the need for ostentatious luxury and social distinction was a general characteristic of *Ancien Régime* society, regardless of the region in which one lived.[49] Unfortunately, the inventory of 1684 does not list Lepín's garments. However, Lepín drew up a second one in 1706, three years before he died, which is much more detailed and also contains information about the merchant's wardrobe.[50] Already in 1684, Lepín was a well-respected member of Seville's commercial elite; towards the end of his life, he was among the wealthiest merchants of the city. As his inventory shows, he was very well integrated into Spanish society, also in religious terms. Although Lepín's family was Protestant, he lived as a Catholic and was member of various religious brotherhoods. His inventory lists hundreds of Catholic devotional objects, such as rosaries, depictions and statues of various saints and the Virgin Mary, as well as altar cloths and even chasubles, which was nothing exceptional for Seville's upper-class households.[51] Against this backdrop, it is not surprising that Lepín's wardrobe did not differ much from that of other wealthy merchants.[52] Among his clothes we find cassocks, doublets and trousers made of black silk and taffeta, as well as several black capes, which form part of the typical Spanish dress.[53]

Rodríguez, Manuel F. Fernández Chaves, and Rafel M. Pérez Rodríguez (eds.): *Comercio y cultura en la Edad Moderna. Comunicaciones de la XIII reunión científica de la Fundación Española de Historia Moderna*. Sevilla 2015, 283–298.

49 Thomas Weller: Madre de todos los vicios? Müßiggang und ostentativer Konsum im Spanien des Siglo de Oro und im Heiligen Römischen Reich Deutscher Nation, in: Martin Baxmeyer, Michaela Peters, and Ursel Schaub (eds): *El sabio y el ocio. Zu Gelehrsamkeit und Muße in der spanischen Literatur und Kultur des Siglo de Oro. Festschrift für Christoph Strosetzki zum 60. Geburtstag*. Tübingen 2009, 203–216.

50 Archivo Histórico Provincial de Sevilla [AHPS], Protocolos notariales [PNS], leg. 3778, fol. 1000ff. [folio numbers illegible on the following sheets].

51 Francisco Núñez Roldán: *La vida cotidiana en la Sevilla del Siglo de Oro*. Madrid 2004, 217–220.

52 Ibid., 51–70.

53 Carmen Bernis: La moda en la Espana de Felipe II a traves del retrato de corte, in: Santiago Saavedra (ed.): *Alonso Sánchez Coello y eI retrato en la corte de Felipe II*. Madrid 1990, 65–111; Amalia Descalzo: Spanish Male Costume in the Habsburg Period, in: Colomer and Descalzo,

However, it appears that Lepín did not always dress entirely in black, since he also owned a "red woollen coat with plush lining" (*un sobretodo de carro de oro con foro de felpa, encarnado*), a white waistcoat with golden flowers, silver-colored doublets and two "light brown capes" (*capas de color de canela*).[54] In the second half of the seventeenth century, however, due to French influences, colorful garments had increasingly replaced the traditional black dress *a la española*, even at the royal court in Madrid.[55] Thus, in this aspect, Enrique Lepín's wardrobe reflected only a general tendency that definitely had nothing to do with his foreign origin or cultural background.

The question remains, however, whether Lepín and his German and Flemish compatriots changed their style of dress after moving to Spain. According to a royal decree of 1563, foreigners were allowed to use their foreign clothes up to six months after their arrival to Spain, even if their garments contravened Spanish sumptuary laws. Only after that period were they obliged to keep to the royal decree, with the exception of those foreigners who wanted to visit the royal court, who had to obey to Spanish dress regulations from the moment of their arrival.[56] In fact, before foreign diplomats had their audience at the royal court, the envoys and their entourage usually had to be fitted out with new clothes *a la española*.[57] For that purpose, each member of a Hanseatic embassy to Madrid in 1607 charged 1,600 Reichstaler to the Hanseatic Diet (a sum four times as high as the annual salary of the Hanseatic Syndic Johannes Domann, who headed the legation to Madrid).[58] Nevertheless, not only courtiers but also merchants who settled at the big trading places soon took over Spanish dressing habits. According to the Belgian historian Eddy Stols,

> the Flemings who lived in Seville rapidly adapted to the habits of Spanish society and to the city's general atmosphere. Being so different because of their physiognomy, with red

Spanish Fashion, vol.1, 15–31; José Luis Colomer: Black and the Royal Image, in: ibid., 77–112; Rafael García Serrano (ed.): *La moda española en el Siglo de Oro*. Toledo 2015.

54 AHPS, PNS, leg. 3778, fol. 1000ff.

55 Carmen Bernis: El "vestido francés" en la corte de Felipe IV, in: *Archivo Español de Arte* 55 (1982), 201–208. See also the contribution by Gabriel Guarino to this issue.

56 *Premática de los vestidos y trajes, la qual mandó el rey nuestro señor se publicasse el año de mill y quinientos y sesenta y tres*. Madrid 1590, fol. 5. See Puerta, Sumptuary Legislation, 213–214.

57 Milena Hajna: El final del viaje. Audiencias de los embajadores delante del rey de España en los siglos XVI y XVII, in: Josef Opatrný (ed.): *Las relacciones checo-españolas. Viajeros y testimonios*. Prague 2009, 15–25, here 21.

58 Wilhelm Pauli: Aus den Aufzeichnungen des Lübecker Bürgermeisters Henrich Brokes, in: *Zeitschrift des Vereins für Lübeckische Geschichte und Altertumskunde* 1 (1860), 79–92, 173–183, 281–347, here 308.

cheeks and blond beards and rather tall in stature, they soon changed their colored dress for the sober black *a la española.*[59]

However, the Spanish fashion with its predilection for black soon spread to other parts of Europe. In 1529, the Augsburg patrician Matthäus Schwarz had himself portrayed dressed entirely in black and wearing a Spanish cape.[60] [Figure 6] In the Low Countries black clothing also became extremely popular in the sixteenth century. Apparently not even the Dutch rebellion provoked any change in dressing habits, although some authors argue that "black in the United Provinces" was "different in character from the power-black of the Spanish Empire".[61] Bearing this in mind, Stols's assertion that Flemish merchants changed their colored clothing for the sober Spanish black is rather surprising. It is hard to believe that they really started to wear black clothes only after coming to Spain. Anyway, what might have changed was how these clothes were perceived. When a Dutch or a Flemish merchant dressed in black in his home country, this usually was not a political statement. It did not say anything about his feelings towards the Spanish Monarchy. Whether he was loyal to the Spanish crown or sympathizing with the Dutch rebels, the "Spanish" black remained first and foremost a marker of social prestige.[62] When the same merchant travelled to Spain, however, the very same clothes could generate different meanings.[63]

Conclusion

In sixteenth- and seventeenth-century Spain dress was a multi-layered and always ambiguous marker of difference. Many Spaniards judged foreigners and supposed ethnoreligious minorities by their dress, and sometimes denounced

59 "Rápidamente se adaptaban los flamencos sevillanos a las costumbres de la sociedad española y el ambiente general de la ciudad. Tan diferentes por su fisionomía de mejillas rojas y barbas rubias y por su estatura alta, pronto dejaban sus trajes coloridos para adoptar el sobrio vestido negro a la española." Eddy Stols: La colonia flamenca de Sevilla y el comercio de los Países Bajos Españoles en la primera mitad del siglo XVII, in: *Anuario de historia económica y social* 2 (1969), 363–361, here 367.
60 Ulinka Rublack and Maria Hayward (eds.): *The First Book of Fashion. The Book of Clothes of Matthäus and Veit Konrad Schwarz of Augsburg.* London 2015, 299.
61 John Harvey: *Men in Black.* London 1995, 89.
62 Colomer, Black, 95.
63 For the symbology of black in general and its manifold meanings see: Michel Pastoureau: *Black. The History of a Color.* Princeton, NJ 2009, and the contribution by Maria Hayward to this issue.

Figure 6: Matthäus Schwarz wearing a Spanish cape, in: Matthäus Schwarz of Augsburg:
Trachtenbuch, 1520–1560 [18th century copy]. Courtesy Gottfried Wilhelm Leibniz
Bibliothek – Niedersächsische Landesbibliothek, Hannover, Ms XVII, 988, fol. 94.

them to the authorities, thinking them to be enemies of the Crown or suspicious elements that threatened public order or the purity of Catholic faith. However, vestimentary signifiers were often ambiguous. For that reason, it is hard to believe that the Flemish merchants of Sanlúcar de Barrameda were able to tell whether a foreigner was from the Northern or Southern part of the Netherlands, only by looking at his garments. More likely, as in the case of the Moriscos, their otherness existed only in the eye of the beholder. As the examples discussed in this article show, it was never the textile object alone but its wearer and the social context in which he or she wore a specific garment that made the latter a marker of ethnic or religious difference.

However, we should not forget that dress was only one factor among others by which to identify and classify strangers. Even though the Flemish merchants of Seville dressed like Spaniards, as Eddy Stols asserts, their red cheeks, blond beards and tall stature – in Stols's words – still revealed their foreign origin. In contrast to those physical characteristics, which were difficult to change, it was easy to change one's dress, even though this could prove very costly. If migrants adopted the dressing style of their new environment, they probably did so for good reasons. We should bear in mind that during the Dutch rebellion anybody who spoke Dutch was liable to be suspected of making common cause with the rebellious provinces. Most of the German merchants came from Protestant cities and lived as Catholics in Spain. Thus, in times of war and religious persecution, neither Flemish nor Dutch nor German immigrants were very eager to attract public attention. They tried rather to show themselves as loyal subjects of the Spanish Crown and as true Catholics. The same holds true for the Moriscos, who also had to face suspicion and hatred. In this regard also, "the act of dressing became a much more important 'signifying practice' for many in this period."[64] Dress was not only a mirror of individual taste and a medium of Renaissance self-fashioning; for certain individuals and under certain circumstances it could turn into something even more important – a question of survival.

---

64 Rublack, Dressing Up, 25.

Flora Cassen

Jewish Travelers in Early Modern Italy: Visible and Invisible Resistance to the Jewish Badge

Abstract: *Sartorial discrimination was one of the ways that pre-modern European rulers sought to define and demean Europe's Jews. The Jewish badge was an external mark placed on the Jews' bodies to identify them; however, it was a removable or "mobile" mark. As a result, whatever the badge did to or communicated about the Jews was usually not permanent and often was subject to negotiations among Jews, their neighbors, and the authorities. Using examples from the Duchy of Milan in the second half of the sixteenth century, a time of increasingly strict enforcement of anti-Jewish sign regulations, this essay focuses on how traveling Jews in particular were harassed for not wearing the yellow badge or hat. It explores how sartorial discrimination threatened these Jews' freedom of movement as well as their ability to choose how to represent their own identity. And it shows that the Jews resisted the authorities' attempts to stigmatize them in a variety of ways, including, counter-intuitively, by being recognizably Jewish.*

Honoré de Balzac (1799–1850) understood a long time ago that "dress is the most immense modification experienced by man in society, it weighs on his entire existence [...] it dominates opinions, it determines them, it reigns."[1] In addition to experiencing the power of dress, men and women also used clothing to gain agency in their lives and to influence their positions in society. Indeed, historians have shown that in medieval and early modern times, people used dress to fashion their selves and produce identity in a variety of social settings, ranging from the courts to the streets.[2] This essay deals with a specific type of dress code, the

---

1 Cited by Philip Mansel: *Dressed to Rule. Royal and Court Costume from Louis XIV to Elizabeth II.* New Haven 2005, xiii.

2 Susan Crane: *The Performance of Self. Ritual, Clothing, and Identity during the Hundred Years War.* Philadelphia 2002; Carole Collier Frick: *Dressing Renaissance Florence. Families,*

Note: I am grateful to Cornelia Aust, Denise Klein, and Thomas Weller for inviting me to the conference "Dress and Cultural Difference in Early Modern Europe" at the Leibniz Institute. I thank them and all the participants for their helpful comments.

so-called "Jewish badge", which is a generic term to denote the variety of sarto-rial signs that Jews were forced to wear in Europe after 1215.[3] In contrast to volun-tary dress codes, which were freely chosen and worn with pride, the Jewish badge was a mark imposed from above in order to differentiate Jews from the rest of society. But it, too, whether it was a hat, a badge, or other marker of difference, functioned and acquired meaning in the context of the specific society in which it was applied. For a Jewish badge or hat to be effective, two conditions needed to be met. First, it needed to be understood as a marker of Jewishness both by Jews and the surrounding society. Second, it needed to be enforced by local authori-ties. Using examples from my research in the Duchy of Milan in the second half of the sixteenth century, a time of increasingly strict enforcement of anti-Jewish sign regulations, this essay focuses on how traveling Jews in particular were har-assed for not wearing the yellow badge or hat. It explores how sartorial discrimi-nation threatened these Jews' freedom of movement as well as their ability to choose how to represent their own identity. And it will show that the Jews re-sisted the authorities' attempts to stigmatize them in a variety of ways, including, counter-intuitively, by being recognizably Jewish. For, as the cases examined in the article will suggest, their goal was not so much to be invisible, as it was to remain in control of their image.

Brief Background

In 1215 at the Fourth Lateran Council, Pope Innocent III argued that Jews and Muslims needed to be distinguishable from Christians through their clothing. The purpose of such distinction, as stated in the conciliar canon, was to prevent acci-dental sexual intercourse between Christians and Muslims or Jews, although the extent to which miscegenation actually occurred is debated. Both Jewish and Christian religious authorities prohibited relations with members of the other group, and there were virtually no Muslims in Europe, except in diverse border-lands such as the Southern Iberian Peninsula or Sicily.[4] Because the pope did not

---

Fortunes, and Fine Clothing. Baltimore 2002; Ulinka Rublack: *Dressing Up. Cultural Identity in Renaissance Europe*. Oxford 2010; Javier Irigoyen-García: *Moors Dressed as Moors. Clothing, Social Distinction and Ethnicity in Early Modern Iberia*. Toronto 2017.

3 Scholars have traditionally referred to these signs as "the Jewish badge", because it often was a brightly colored badge, though as this essay will show, it could also be a hat, a veil, or a cloak.

4 Solomon Grayzel: *The Church and the Jews in the XIIIth Century, 1198–1254*. 2nd ed. New York 1966, 308–309. For the full text of the Canon in Latin with English translation, see Norman P. Tanner: *Decrees of the Ecumenical Councils*. London 1990, 266. On the frequency of sexual

specify what this distinction should look like, local rulers came up with a wide variety of different signs: blue stripes in Sicily, a red cape in Rome, the Tablets of the Law in England, a yellow wheel in France, a pointed hat in Germany, a red badge in Hungary.[5] In the Duchy of Milan, it was not until the end of the fourteenth century, that distinctive sign laws were first issued. Early on, the Jews had to wear a yellow round badge and, starting from the sixteenth century, a yellow hat. The rationale most often given for imposing a badge or hat was to ensure the Jews' recognition. As Bernardino da Siena, a popular preaching friar, said: "there could be Jews here in the audience, but we don't know because we can't recognize them [...]".[6] But, as I've argued elsewhere, the circumstances surrounding its introduction or imposition often suggest other motives as well. For example, authorities sometimes issued Jewish badge laws only to have Jewish individuals or communities pay for the permission not to wear it, revealing the financial motivations behind such laws. At other times, power struggles between religious and secular – and local, regional, and central – authorities were played out by taking aim at Jewish populations in rival territories.[7] Moreover, as the following examples involving Jewish travelers who were punished for non-compliance will suggest, Jews were often recognizable even without the mark.

Traveling as a Jew

When the badge was first introduced in Northern Italy in the late fourteenth century, the penalties for not complying ranged from fines to physical punishments to

---

intercourse between Jews and Christians, see David Nirenberg: *Communities of Violence. Persecution of Minorities in the Middle Ages.* Princeton 1996, 138–156; but Elliott Horowitz: Families and Their Fortunes. The Jews of Early Modern Italy, in: David Biale (ed.): *Cultures of the Jews. A New History.* 5 vols. New York 2002, vol. 2, 278–279, makes the point that in the fifteenth century "sexual relations across religious lines [...] continued to plague many Italian Jewish communities", though Robert Bonfil: *Jewish Life in Renaissance Italy.* Berkeley 1996, 111–116, disagrees and thinks it was a rather infrequent problem. Bonfil also challenges the idea that court cases involving sexual intercourse between Jews and Christians reflect typical patterns of intermingling between Jews and Christians during the Renaissance. Bonfil: Jews, Christians and Sex in Renaissance Italy. A Historiographical Problem, in: *Jewish History* 26 (2012), 101–111.

5 Guido Kisch: The Yellow Badge in History, in: *Historia Judaica* 4, no. 2 (1942), 105–109.

6 Cited by Nirit Ben-Aryeh Debby: Jews and Judaism in the Rhetoric of Popular Preachers. The Florentine Sermons of Giovanni Dominici (1356–1419) and Bernardino da Siena (1380–1444), in: *Jewish History* 14 (2000), 175–200, here 185.

7 Flora Cassen: *Marking the Jews in Renaissance Italy. Politics, Religion, and the Power of Symbols.* Cambridge 2017, 189–192.

prison sentences. Yet, prior to 1555, enforcement was lax – there is no record of a Jew being fined or chastised for failure to wear the distinctive mark and only one instance of a Jew being arrested for such an offense. That one incident is a telling case involving an attempt by an official to extort money from Vitale Sacerdoti, the wealthiest Jew of Alessandria, a small town in the vicinity of Milan.[8] In July 1531, Vitale wrote to the podestà (or mayor) of Alessandria claiming that the fiscal advocate, Stephano Carabello, had found a "new way to rob money from the hands of the Jews": he looked to see if Jewish women wore the distinctive sign.[9] Carabello had arrested Vitale's wife and niece at a public celebration, even though they were wearing the sign and everybody knew that they were Jewish. To free them, Vitale had been forced to pay two hundred scudi; the women were now waiting to stand trial. Vitale pleaded for an annulment of the trial and a reimbursement of the bail. The podestà transmitted his letter to the Senate, which answered that the podestà could proceed as he saw fit.[10]

Up to 1560, Vitale's case was a unique incident in which imprisonment for failure to heed distinctive sign laws was used in a thinly veiled attack on a wealthy Jewish businessman. By contrast, between 1560 and 1570, and especially after 1566, the archival record shows that dozens of Jews were arrested for not wearing the yellow hat. This increased enforcement coincided with strengthening Spanish rule in the northwestern region of the peninsula. Lombardy had been one of the major battlefields of the Italian Wars that wrecked the peninsula during the first half of the sixteenth century. After defeating the French in 1522, Holy Roman Emperor Charles V returned Milan to the Sforza family. When Francesco II Sforza died without an heir, however, the duchy devolved to Habsburg rule and, in 1544, Charles V gave Milan to his son, the future Philip II

---

8 Renata Segre: *Gli ebrei lombardi nell'età spagnola*. Turin 1973, 77–78, 24–25, 53, 66, 91–93, 100. Vitale Sacerdoti's parents had moved to Italy after being expelled from Spain in 1492. He was born in Alessandria around 1510 and quickly became a moneylender whose business brought him in contact with both Italian and Spanish officials. As a result of his prominent position, he also served as one of the leaders of the Jews of Milan. His son, Simone Sacerdoti, took over the family business and served King Philip II as a spy. See also Cassen: Philip II of Spain and His Italian Jewish Spy, in: *Journal of Early Modern History* 21 (2017), 318–342.
9 Archivio di Stato di Milano (thereafter ASM), Fondo Culto 2159, 150: "Nuova inventione et nuova via per ricoperare danari o per dire meglio rapargli dale mani delli hebrei ha trovato il signor Stephano Carabello advocato fiscale in Alesandria laquale è che va cercando se le done delli hebrei portano li segni."
10 ASM, Fondo Culto 2159, 150. Record of the podestà's subsequent actions could not be located. Perhaps he dropped the case.

of Spain.[11] Early on, Philip strove to maintain the status quo between the different groups and communities of the Duchy, but over time the Jews' position grew increasingly precarious, ending with their expulsion from the Duchy in 1597.[12]

One indication that the Jewish badge was being enforced more strictly was that more Jews were getting arrested for failing to wear it. Remarkably, nearly all of the arrested and imprisoned Jews in the period between 1560 and 1570 were foreigners traveling in the Duchy for business or because of family matters. For example, a Jewish man identified as Jacob and two other Jews were detained in Cremona city for not wearing the yellow hat while traveling.[13] On their way from Alessandria to Vigevano, Benedetto and Graziado of Mestre were arrested by the podestà of Mortara, even though, as they wrote the governor, they showed the podestà an "authentic copy" of the decree that exempted the Jews from wearing the yellow hat while traveling.[14] Lazarino Pugieto and

---

11 For more on the history and structure of Spanish rule in Milan, see Giuseppe De Luca: Struttura e dinamiche della ativita finanziarie milanesi tra cinquecento e seicento, in: Elena Brambilla and Giovanni Muto (eds.): *La Lombardia spagnola. Nuovi indirizzi di ricerca*. Milan 1997, 31–76; Giuseppe Galasso: Il sistema imperiale spagnolo da Filippo II a Filippo IV, in: Paolo Pissavino and Gianvittorio Signorotto (eds.): *Lombardia borromaica, Lombardia spagnola, 1554–1659*. Rome 1995; Gianvittorio Signorotto: Equilibri politici, istituzioni e rapporti di potere in età spagnola, in: Livio Antonielli and Giorgio Chittolini (eds.): *Storia della Lombardia, dal 1350 al 1650*. Rome 2001, 101–126; and id.: Milano e la monarchia cattolica. Spagnoli e lombardi al governo dello Stato, in: Maria Canella and Antonella Grandellini (eds.), *Grandezza e splendori della Lombardia spagnola, 1535–1701*. Milan 2002, 37–45; and also Romano Canosa: *Milano nel seicento. Grandezza e miseria nell'Italia spagnola*. Milan 1993; and id.: *La vita quotidiana a Milano in età spagnola*. Milan 1996; and Benedetto Croce: *La Spagna nella vita italiana durante la rinascenza*. 2nd ed. Bari 1922.

12 Cassen: The Last Spanish Expulsion in Europe: Milan 1565–1597, in: *Association for Jewish Studies Review* 38 (2014), 55–98; Segre, Gli ebrei Lombardi, 80–127; Geoffrey Parker: *Philip II*. Boston 1978, 193; Shlomo Simonsohn: *The Jews in the Duchy of Milan. A Documentry History of the Jews of Italy*. Jerusalem 1982, xxxiii–xxxvii.

13 ASM, Fondo Culto 2160, 33: "Detenuti in Cremona, li fid^{mi} serv^i di V.E. Jacob di Scalini et doi altri hebrei fuori di essa città per haver per camino portato li capelli negri." The letter is undated, but filed with documents from the second half of the 1560s.

14 ASM, Cancelleria Spagnola, Carteggio Generale, cart. 271: "Perché portavano di viaggio li capelli negri in testa furono tra Mortara et Vigev° pure in campagna presi dalli sbirri del podestà di Mortara, et conduti in prigione, al quale podestà ancor che si sia mostrata une copia autentica del decreto fatto in Cons° Secreto per lo quale v.ecc^a dechiara non esser tenuti li hebrei portare capelli giali di camino." The Jews' letter is not dated, but it is archived with documentation related to Milan's Spanish administration from the second half of the sixteenth century. The same file also contained an order issued by the king of France in 1520 ordering that all Jews, including those traveling, wear a yellow hat. It is telling, perhaps, that the podestà had to go back all the way to the French administration to justify his actions. The two Jews were released on bail. For more, see Cassen, Marking the Jews, 90.

Moyses Fereves, bankers from Genoa with business in the Duchy of Milan, requested an exemption because they feared their identification as Jews might lead bandits to rob them.[15] They needed the governor's intervention because they were in a serious quandary: wear the yellow hat and suffer violence or take it off and risk being arrested and fined. Another Jew from Milan, the physician Zacharia, explained to the governor that he was a respected physician who knew many secrets, but he could not practice medicine with the yellow hat and had therefore been forced to move to Genoa where medical doctors are allowed to wear a black *bereta*.[16] In Como in 1566, so many traveling Jews were harassed that local Jews took their case to the governor:

> The sir podestà of Como has tormented several Jews who did not wear the yellow hat when they were traveling, against several declarations your Excellency has made in similar cases by which it is permitted to said Jews not to wear such yellow hat or badge. [...] We therefore implore your Excellency to command the sir podestà of Como to stop harassing the said Jews for the indicated reason, cancelling all the trials and securities paid. Doing this is important for any Jew who will transit through your dominions in the future.[17]

As a consequence, the podestà of Como and Lodi, where similar incidents had been taking place, received letters from the governor prohibiting them from maltreating Jews who did not wear the yellow hat when traveling.[18]

---

15 ASM, Fondo Culto 2159, 173: "Ma perché in quella parti vi si trovano molti banditi et [disauiali] che conoscendo i supplicanti hebrei come loro nemici ma piu presto desiderosi del loro denaro li potrebbono a mazzore e farli altro danno et ingiuria conosendoli essere hebrei." Not dated, but filed with documents from the 1560s. The Jews were expelled from Genoa in 1567, which thus constitutes a potential *terminus ad quem*.

16 Ibid., 140: "Sacharia ebreo dottore de medecina fid. ser. di V. ecc^a si trova dio gratia in sua professione di medicar dotato de varii secreti pro salvate de infermi come ha demostrato in molte occasioni si qua nel stato di Milano dove habitava per essergli nato, et perché non poteva senza grande opprobrio della professione sua exercire detta sua arte qua nel stato per l'ordine fatto in esso di portar tutti li ebrei la bereta gialla fu forzato rebitarsi fuori de esso stato e stantiasi in Genova dove gli è permesso il portar la bereta nera come alli altri medici." Not dated, but filed with documents from the 1560s.

17 Ibid., fasc. 1: "Il s^r Podesta di Como travaglia alchuni Hebrei quali non havevano per viaggio portato il capello o sia baretta gialda contra diverse declaratione fatte per Vra ecc^a in simile casi per le quale è licito a detti Hebrei il non portar tal capello sive baretta gialda [...] Supp^no Vra Ecc^a sia servita ordinare al s^r Podesta di Como che non molesta detti hebrei per la recitate causa, annulando ogni processo fatto et sigurta datta, la qual cosa, anco servi, in l'avenire per qualonche altro Hebreo occorrera fare transito nella sua giurisdittione ilche."

18 Ibid.

The focus on foreign Jews is intriguing and needs to be explained, as does the question of how these Jews were recognized. If they were arrested for failing to wear the yellow hat, they must have been distinguishable by other means. But if Jews were identifiable, what was the purpose of the distinctive sign? At a minimum, the arrests suggest that Jews were recognizable even without the badge, and that the claim that it made Jews recognizable (thereby protecting Christians) was only part of the story. To probe these questions further, let us examine the case of Leone Segele.[19] While most Jews were released after paying a fine, Segele's case was the subject of a full and thorough investigation. It is a curious episode, not least because the color of the hat – the matter under dispute – seems to keep changing.

In 1560, Leone Segele, a Jew from Piedmont, was arrested in Lodi for wearing a black hat instead of the yellow one. The podestà who arrested him described the hat as a black felt hat of the kind that is worn in Mondevi and Piedmont. He [Leone] gave it to a Jewish youngster asking him to cover it according to the custom of the Jews. The youngster covered it in the way that it looks now with a black veil and a black braid at the extremity of the hat.[20]

In his defense Leone presented three arguments. First, he was a foreigner. Second, upon arriving in the Duchy, he went to a hatter and asked: "Maestro [. . .]. please make me a hat according to the decree recently issued concerning the hats and caps of the Jews." That was the hat he wore at the time of his arrest. Third, he had been in Lodi only one day before being arrested.[21] The podestà then heard the testimonies of two other Jews who had traveled with Leone. Sara of Verona declared that she knew from her son Marco that Leone was from Piedmont and confirmed his story: he had bought a new hat in Alessandria, was arrested with it in Lodi after just one day, and, contrary to the arresting officer's

---

19 Cassen, Marking the Jews, 54–55.

20 ASM, Fondo Culto 2159, 203: "capello di feltro negro come si usava nel de Mondevi et piemonte lo diede ad un giovine Hebreo dicendoli che lo copresse a la usanzza de gli hebrei il qual lo coperse come hora sta con un vello a torno nero et un passamano negro per l'estremio dil capello."

21 This was a reference to the three-day grace period that the Jews often, though by no means always, received when traveling. Ibid.: "Il primo che esso Leone gia quatro anni et oltra habita nel Mondevi in Piamonte nella giurisdictione del Illmo et Ecc^mo Sr Ducca di Savoia. Il secundo che gia giorni sei passati gionto egli in Alessandria ando da un capellaro et gli disse maestro io voglio andare sin a Lodi et piu oltri anchora pero fattime un capello secondo l'ordine delle cride novamente fatte circa il portar de berette et capelli per li hebrei et cossi il detto maestro li ordino il detto capello con il qual è stato preso et li disse che era secondo l'ordine. Il terzo che esso Leone era solamente gionto lunedi la sera in Lodi che fu alli quatro dil presente et il giorno sequente a la matina fu preso."

statement, wore an orange and golden colored hat.[22] The next witness, Moses Sacerdote, testified that in Alessandria a Jewish teenager warned them to wear the yellow stripe or face certain arrest.[23] Moses was able to borrow a stripe from the boy, but not Leone. That is why he commissioned a new hat from a local hatter. Contradicting Leone's statement, Moses then said that on the day of the arrest, Leone was not wearing his hat and gave two reasons for this failure: first, it was raining; second, Vitale Sacerdoti had told Leone that the governor had granted him the right to wear a golden and silver hat. Seeing that his hat was the same color as Vitale's, Leone thought he was in good standing.[24] Confused, the podestà sent the governor a letter about "the hat that Leone wore and with which he was found [to inquire] whether it appears to you [the governor] that with a hat of such color [Leone] ought to be excused [...] and what should be done either in absolving him, or in condemning him".[25] Penned in the margin, the governor's decision ordered the podestà to release Leone but not without reminding him that he must wear the yellow hat.

Did Leone wear a black hat, an orange stripe, or a yellow hat? Or did he, like Vitale Sacerdoti, wear a silver and golden hat? Color codes are full of shades and nuance; they vary with time, place, and individual perspectives. Although silver and gold could be described as shades of yellow, they did not indubitably conform to the type of yellow that Jews had to wear, or Sacerdoti would not have needed the governor's approval to wear his hat. Naturally, Jews resisted being defined negatively and unilaterally from above. A silver-golden color was preferable to the "true Jewish yellow". It was less stigmatizing than the correct yellow for Jews, though it did not relieve them from the constant threat of being arrested. That Vitale Sacerdoti, one of the most powerful Jews in the duchy, felt the need to receive assurances from the governor reveals how much the Jews – including local, wealthy, and well-connected ones – feared arrest. A few years after Segele's trial, in 1569, Vitale wrote the governor that,

---

22 Ibid., 203–204: "ha visto portare le brette et capelli ranzi et di color d'oro." *Ranzi* probably is *rancio*, an old word for orange. Dante used it in *Inferno* XXIII, 100–101: "Le cappe rance / son di piombo sì grosse."

23 He does not seem to have been related to Vitale Sacerdoti. The name Sacerdote/i is the Italian equivalent of Cohen and was common.

24 ASM, Fondo Culto 2159, 205: "et anchora perché piovea, et che Vidale de Sacerdoti in Alessandria li disse che un li portavano li capelli di quelo medema colore dil suo con l'oro et argento et che havendoli visti v.ecc[za] disse che stafevano bene." This Vitale Sacerdoti is the same man who was blackmailed in 1531. For more, see above note 8.

25 Ibid., 206: "Ho volutto il tutto referire a v.ecc[za] et insieme mandarli il cappello qual portave et con quale è stato trovato accio se a lei parera che con haverlo portato de simil color sia excusato et [...] che haver da fare o in absolverlo o in condenarlo."

now old and frail, he needed a servant to help him walk and would like that person to be relieved of the obligation to wear a yellow hat.[26] The sense of anguish felt by all the Jews was indeed palpable in the letter written by the Jews of Como in which they begged the governor to order the podestà to stop arresting traveling Jews.[27]

The Jewish community was small – on the eve of the expulsion in 1592 there were fewer than nine hundred Jews in the duchy – and decentralized, with hubs in Cremona and Pavia.[28] This made their close relations with Jewish centers outside of the Duchy essential, particularly as the Jews of Milan were exceptionally mobile and often on the road for business, family, or religious reasons. Now these social ties, so important to their survival as a community, were under assault and local Jews realized that, while they were relatively protected at home, they too could be targeted if traveling.

The archives preserved only one case concerning the arrest of a local Jew. Interestingly, this was also the sole case involving a woman: Laura Volterra of Castelnovo, an old, deaf lady in her seventies.[29] On May 30, 1567, Bernardo Vistarino and four other men claimed they saw her walking around town dressed like a Christian woman and lacking the yellow collar.[30] At her interrogation, Laura denied the allegation and showed her badge to the officers, who described it as: "[a] strip of yellow or orange fabric sown around the neck of her black collar".[31] After giving her statement, Laura was released on bail and the podestà recorded the testimonies of a series of witnesses. In addition to Vistarino and his four companions, who testified against Laura, seven more witnesses, all Christians, defended her, emphasizing that she was a good, honorable, and honest person.[32]

---

26 Ibid., fasc. 4, 198: "Et ritrovandosi vechio infermo et che piu no puo andare senz'un servitore che portando la beretta o capelli gialdo vien mispresato il padrone et ser^re pero ricorre da v.ecca con ogni humilta."

27 Cassen, Marking the Jews, 114 and note 285.

28 Simonsohn, Jews in the Duchy of Milan, vol. 3, 1817–1818; Cassen, The Last Spanish Expulsion in Europe.

29 Excluding, of course, Vitale Sacerdoti's niece and daughters, mentioned above in note 8. But that was in the 1530s. In the 1560s, Laura Volterra seems to have been the only woman.

30 ASM, Fondo Culto 2159, 243: "Primo il di 30 di maggio dell anno presente fu accusata [...] Laura Ebrea da Bernardo Vistarino come detta Laura non portana il colleto gialdo, ne alcuno segno da Ebrea, anzi che andana per la detta terra di Castelnovo in habito da Christiana."

31 Ibid., 245: "Laura [...] dice che non è vero che lei sia andata senza segnale, anzi che sempre l'ha portato, come mostro al'hora haverlo, qual segno era una lista di sorgia gialda, o sia ranciata cocita intorno al collo, al colleto negro."

32 Ibid.: "Che essa Laura è persona di bona voce, conditione et fama."

Dante Torto and his wife told the podestà that Bernardino Vistarino and the four other accusers went up to Laura saying that she was not dressed in a Jewess' habit. Laura responded by showing them her sign, which Dante Torto's wife described as "[a] strip of orange fabric around her neck sown to a black thing underneath her sheepskin jacket". She added that she could clearly see it, though she did not know whether Laura's accusers had seen it too.[33] Bruno Grasso testified that she was hard of hearing, approximately seventy years old, and wore "a sign of a faded color sown around her neck and hanging in the middle of her chest".[34] Marco Antonio Lazaro and Marchino Berro confirmed that she was old and deaf. Hieronimo da Borgo and Bernardo dalla Torre had not seen Laura on that day but had heard that she was wearing her sign. They questioned the credibility of the accusers by noting that two of the four prosecution witnesses were related to Vistarino.[35] The governor read the report and decided to pardon Laura but demanded that she be firmly told to wear the sign as prescribed.[36]

Laura's case confirms that the arrests burdened and intimidated all Jews, locals and foreigners alike. Her arrest seems particularly cruel, though, as she was deaf and elderly and well-regarded by many in Castelnovo. Moreover, the yellow collar was not necessary to identify her or her Jewishness, since she was well known in town and none of the witnesses report her having to introduce herself to them.

By then, much of the northwestern region of the Italian Peninsula, including the Duchy of Milan, was under Spanish control. From Milan, Spanish officials regularly wrote letters to officials elsewhere complaining about their difficulties identifying travelers and securing the borders. But, as the governor of Milan wrote to King Philip II in 1572, Jews posed a particular problem:

> One of the things that the Duke [of Savoy] concedes to them [Jews] but that to me seems very unreasonable is the permission that they go without a sign. Among many other problems that this will provoke, there is the fact that there will be many Jews from Spain and

---

33 Ibid., 246: "Che detta Laura risposte vedete qua il mio segno et mostro il petto dove haveva una lista di sargia ranciata intorno al collo cucita a una cossa negra che haveva di sotto dalla giamarra qual lista appareva chiaramente che si poteva vederre, ma se li testimonii sopranominati la vedessero lei non lo sa."
34 Ibid., 246–247: "Che difficilmente ode et è vechia al suo aspetto di anni settanta et rare volve escie di casa [...] subito gli mostro un segno di collor smarrito largo dua dita cucito intorno al collo che pendena a meggio el petto dicendogli questo e il segnale."
35 Ibid., 248.
36 Ibid., 250: "Chel podestà per questa volta non molesti la detta [Laura], advertandola che da qui inanzi porti il segno come si ha ordinato."

other nations in Piedmont, but that it will not be possible henceforth to prove that they are Jewish when they transit through Spanish provinces for they will say that they are Christian merchants.[37]

Indeed, Jewish travelers were twice suspect: first, for being Jewish – or secretly Jewish, if they were of Iberian origin – and, second, for being mobile, for traveling, for being part of a group of people with connections across the Mediterranean and beyond. Yet, as the examples cited above reveal, the Jews, even when they were traveling foreigners, were often recognizable without a sign.

How Were the Jews Recognized?

Frequently, traveling Jews were recognized and arrested because they were seen with local Jews. Joseph and Jacob, for example, were arrested in Felizano after stopping at the house of a Jew.[38] It may be, in fact, that traveling Jews wanted to be recognizable in order to facilitate their associations with local Jews. In strange cities and towns, coreligionists probably provided a sense of familiarity that inspired confidence to travelers.[39] Other cases, though, are more intriguing. After spotting Adam and three other Jews from Mantua on the road, an officer from Cremona followed them for ten miles before arresting them.[40] The officer seems to have doubted his first impression, so he watched them closely for ten miles before concluding that they were indeed Jewish and proceeding to imprison them. It is not clear what in their appearance, dress, or actions revealed them to be Jewish, but there must have been subtle clues.

Was it that they spoke Hebrew or a form of Judeo-Italian? Bonfil argues that the Jews' cultural language was Hebrew and that their Italian "was often a somewhat ridiculous fashion of speaking [. . .], with transpositions of gender

---

37 Archivo General Simancas, Estado, leg. 1234, 56; Haim Beinart: Settlement of the Jews in the Duchy of Savoie in the Wake of the Privilege of 1572, in: Attilio Milano, Alexander Rofe, and Daniel Carpi (eds.): *Scritti in Memoria di Leone Carpi*. Jerusalem 1967, 96.

38 ASM, Cancelleria Spagnola, Carteggio Generale, 39.

39 Kerry Wallach: *Passing Illusions. Jewish Visibility in Weimar Germany*. Ann Arbor 2017, 1, makes a similar point about Jews in Weimar Germany: "[T]he acts of choosing to remain hidden and to be seen were not mutually exclusive, and they operated both in tension and intersection with one another. Many Jews cultivated a complex identity in order to pass for non-Jewish in some contexts (such as with non-Jews or in unknown company) and yet still perceivably Jewish in others (for example, when around other Jews)."

40 ASM, Fondo Culto 2160, 198.

from masculine and feminine and vice versa, in accordance with Hebrew usage, and phrases that were nothing more than literal translations of the original Hebrew idiomatic expressions."[41]

Yet other scholars argue that, notwithstanding their cultural and religious distinctiveness, the Jews were generally well integrated and spoke good Italian.[42] Alternatively, were these Jews arrested because aspects of their behavior set them apart from Christians? In the cities of Counter-Reformation Italy, sacred objects were placed almost everywhere, partly as a means of crowd control or violence prevention. In that context, simply failing to acknowledge a sacred object identified a person as foreign or Jewish.[43] For instance, Theodori, a banker from Alessandria, who was arrested in November 1566 upon arriving in Valenza, may have neglected to react appropriately to a sacred statue placed at the entrance of the city.[44]

Or is it possible that the Jews were easily identified because they already dressed differently? We have little information on how Jewish men dressed, but Jewish women readily admitted to wearing highly distinctive accessories. In 1566, the Jews of Milan wrote to the governor to complain about the increasingly harsh distinctive-sign rules. They asked that an orange ribbon replace the yellow hat and that women be totally exempt because they were already recognizable "by their clothing and by the ornaments on their heads".[45] Likewise in Genoa in 1587, the doge and the *governatori* issued a proclamation forcing all male Jews to wear a yellow badge, called a *fresetto*, on their hats and another one on their coat, collar, or jacket. Jewish women, however, were exempt because "their headwear is already so different from ours that they are undoubtedly recognizable".[46] Apparently Jewish women

---

41 Bonfil, Jewish Life in Renaissance Italy, 48, 239–240. For more on Judeo-Italian, see Umberto Fortis: *La parlate degli ebrei di Venezia e le parlate giudeo-Italiane.* Florence 2006; Umberto Cassuto: Parlata ebraica, in: *Vessillo Israelitico* 57 (1909), 254–260.

42 Ariel Toaff: *Love, Work and Death. Jewish Life in Medieval Umbria.* London 1996, 166–194; Elizabeth Borgolotto: Al mio carisimo fratello Salomone hebreo in Fiorenza in casa de Laudadio hebreo. La lettre du Juif Simone (1470?), in: *Materia Giudaica. Rivista dell'associazione italiana per lo studio del giudaismo* 8, no. 1 (2003) 199–208.

43 Edward Muir: The Virgin on the Street Corner. The Place of the Sacred in Italian Cities, in: Steven Ozment (ed.): *Religion and Culture in the Renaissance and Reformation.* Kirksville, MO 1989, 25–42.

44 ASM, Fondo Culto 2159, 78: "Havevano in testa un capello negro nel entrar nel detto loco di Valenta a cavallo."

45 Ibid., 240.

46 Archivio di Stato di Genoa, Archivio Segreto, n. 833, c. 156, M. D. S; and Cassen, Marking the Jews, 155–187.

readily distinguished themselves from Christians through fashion.[47] What distinguished men was less clear, though the experiences of Jewish foreigners in the Duchy of Milan suggest a variety of possibilities, including the possibility that these Jews were recognizable despite their efforts to blend in. However, I contend that Jews may actually have preferred to be distinguishable because it helped them meet local Jews and contributed to asserting more beneficial interpretations of Judaism.

The Many Ways of Jewish Resistance

As we saw, Jews took a variety of actions in response to being forcibly marked, ranging from negotiations, to payments for individual or collective exemptions, to non-compliance at the risk of fines or imprisonment, to placing the badge on a location on their clothing where it could be shown or not (for example in a fold or under a collar) and to playing with its size or color. But their boldest and perhaps most surprising form of resistance may have been their recognizability. In a recent article, Maria Diemling and Larry Ray argued that early modern Jews resisted the dominant Christian powers of Europe in a variety of ways. Using concepts from postcolonial studies, Diemling and Ray call the early modern Jew a "subaltern figure", and understand resistance along a spectrum going from active fighting to "multiple forms of everyday social practices that are embedded in alternative cultural identities, even if they do not manifest as overt heroic opposition". Many of the Jews' acts of resistance that Diemling and Ray record were small and some of them were hidden, but even seemingly trivial everyday acts – such as avoidance of Christian prayer spaces, the usage of Hebrew, mockery of Christians inside the home, Jewish dietary laws and so on – can be interpreted as acts of resistance for they "asserted a sense of Jewish agency despite Christian domination".[48] Building on Ray and Diemling's

---

47 For more on Jewish women's dress, Maria Giuseppina Muzzarelli: Il Vestito Degli Ebrei, in: *Zakhor* 4 (2000), 161–168; Diane Owen Hughes: Regulating Women's Fashion, in: Christiane Klapisch-Zuber (ed.): *A History of Women in the West, vol. 2: Silences of the Middle Ages.* Cambridge 1994, vol. 2, 136–158; Id., Distinguishing Signs: Ear-Rings, Jews and Franciscan Rhetoric in the Italian Renaissance City, in: *Past and Present* 112 (1986), 22–24; Rosita Levi Pisetzky: *Storia Del Costume in Italia.* 5 vols. Milan 1964, vol. 3, 45–125. Pisetzky argues that extravagant headdress was a mark of nobility for women.
48 Maria Diemling and Larry Ray: Arendt's "Conscious Pariah" and the Ambiguous Figure of the Subaltern, in: *European Journal of Social Theory* 19 (2016), 503–520. Whereas Diemling and Ray have found Jewish resistance in Hannah Arendt's notion that the Jews' pariahness could

findings, I would argue that being visibly Jewish, too, afforded Jews a sense of agency. For early modern Italian Jews, to remain in control of their image and to choose what their appearance meant to the world was more important (and perhaps also safer) than blending in.

One of the difficulties in trying to understand the Jewish badge is that the meaning of symbols is inherently fluid and changing. Yellow can be a color of opprobrium, but also of royalty; a circle can represent the perfect celestial spheres or be a mark of shame. Interestingly, fluidity was both the primary tool and the goal of the Jews' resistance. They lived in a world that had long espoused a conception of them as the enemies of Christians – responsible for the death of Christ and guilty ever after. Some scholars have called this image the "hermeneutical" Jew: a character that existed only on paper but the fear of which frequently determined Jewish-Christian relations.[49] The Jewish badge represented a kind of "hermeneutical Jew" as the badge contained layers upon layers of anti-Jewish stereotypes. The Italian poet, Battista Guarini, had summarized them in a short poem published in 1516, entitled "Why the Jews wear the letter O?" In response, he wrote:

> Condemned to eternal torment, the Hebrew bears it as a sign of his grief;
> Or perhaps this vowel is used as a Zero, indicating his nonentity among men;
> Or since the Jews get rich through usury, it indicates how they get much out of nothing.[50]

The first is a theological explanation referring to the Jews' rejection of Jesus and their subsequent exile and servitude. Just like Cain, who was exiled and marked on his forehead for murdering his brother, the Jews must be exiled and branded for their guilt in Jesus' death.[51] In the second and third lines, he tells us that it also stood for both the low status of

---

be willed, others have more explicitly conceptualized it in terms of power and opposition to power, see for example Biale: *Power and Powerlessness in Jewish History*. New York 1986, 58–86; and Yaacov Deutsch: Jewish Anti-Christian Invectives and Christian Awareness. An Unstudied Form of Interaction in the Early Modern Period, in: *Leo Baeck Institute Yearbook* 55 (2010), 41–61.

49 Jeremy Cohen: *Living Letters of the Law. Ideas of the Jew in Medieval Christianity*. Berkeley 1999, 155–156, 359–363, 391–400.

50 David Werner Amram: *The Makers of Hebrew Books in Italy*. 2nd ed. London 1963, 83.

51 Cassen, Marking the Jews, 20–49. In 1208, just seven years before the Fourth Lateran Council, Innocent III wrote a letter to the count of Nevers, in which he associated Cain and his sign to the Jews and their guilt. Simonsohn: *Apostolic See and the Jews. Documents*. Toronto 1988, vol. 1, 92–93; Cohen, *Living Letters of the Law*, 28–29, 55, 249 (n90), 361 (n118); Mellinkoff: *The Mark of Cain*. Berkeley 1981, 14–21; Gilbert Dahan: L'exégèse de Cain et Abel du XIIe au XIVe siècle en Occident, in: *Recherches en Théologie ancienne et médiévales* 49–50

Jews and their practice of usury.[52] This association between the badge and moneylending is particularly important in the Italian context, for both issues often were proclaimed at the same time.[53] And here, too, Guarini refers to traditional Church teachings. The Jews' inferior condition, or "nonentity" as he calls it, followed from their continued disbelief, and the charging of interest, the Church argued, was tantamount to selling time or sinfully creating wealth "out of nothing". In addition, Guarini was probably drawing on a long history of negative stereotypes involving the Jews' relation with money. Already in 1154, Bernard of Clairvaux had used the verb "to judaize" to refer to the lending of money at interest.[54] In artwork, illuminated Bibles or other manuscripts, and even in scribal doodles, one could see depictions of the Jews' exclusive devotion to money (which functioned also, by extension, as illustrations of their excessive materiality).[55] There was even a French poem, *Mystère du Jour et du Jugement*, composed in the fourteenth century, that linked the round badge to money and to the Jews' allegiance to the antichrist.[56] And in Italy in the fifteenth

---

(1982), 21–89; Irven Resnick: *Marks of Distinction. Christian Perceptions of Jews in the High Middle Ages*. Washington, DC 2012, 206–212.

52 For more on Jews and moneylending in Italy, see Luciano Allegra: *La città vertical. Usurai, mercanti e tessitori nella Chieri del cinquecento*. Milan 1987, 71–82; Benjamin Ravid: 'Contra Judaeos' in Seventeenth-Century Italy. Two Responses to the 'Discorso' of Simone Luzzatto by Melchiore Palontrotti and Giulio Morosini, in: *AJS Review* 7 (1982), 301–351; F. R. Salter: The Jews in Fifteenth-Century Florence and Savonarola's Establishment of a Montis Pietatis, in: *Cambridge Historical Journal* 5 (1936), 193–211; Kenneth R. Stow: Papal and Royal Attitudes toward Jewish Lending in the Thirteenth Century, in: *AJS Review* 6 (1981), 161–184; Ariel Toaff: Il commercio del denaro e le comunità ebraiche 'di confine' (Pittigliano, Sorano, Monte San Savino, Lipiano) tra cinquecento e seicento, in: Vittore Colorni et al. (eds.): *Italia Judaica*. Rome 1986, 99–117. For general background, see Joseph Shatzmiller: *Shylock Reconsidered. Jews, Moneylending, and Medieval Society*. Berkeley 1990.

53 Cassen, Marking the Jews, 50–82.

54 Jeremy Cohen, Living Letters of the Law, 236.

55 For French, Spanish, and English visual sources, see Sara Lipton: *Images of Intolerance. The Representation of Jews and Judaism in the Bible Moralisée*. New Haven 1999, 30–53; Pamela Patton: *Art of Estrangement. Redefining Jews in Reconquest Spain*. University Park 2012, 54–62; Cecil Roth: Portraits and Caricatures of Medieval English Jews, in: Jewish Publication Society (ed.): *Essays and Portraits in Anglo-Jewish History*. Philadelphia 1962, 22–25; Frank Felsenstein: *Anti-Semitic Stereotypes. A Paradigm of Otherness in English Popular Culture, 1660–1830*. Baltimore 1995, 27–29; Sara Lipton: Isaac and Antichrist in the Archives, in: *Past and Present* 232 (2016), 3–44.

56 Danièle Sansy: Marquer la difference. L'imposition de la rouelle aux XIIIe et XIVe siècles, in: *Médiévales* 41 (2001), 15–36, here 29. In this poem the Jews mint coins with an effigy of the antichrist to wear as a sign that they are faithful to the antichrist. The text is illustrated with

century, Franciscan Friars were waging a vehement campaign against Jewish moneylending.[57] Their sermons – perhaps not coincidentally, given the parallels just laid out – also included calls for the Jews to wear the badge.

The Jews' resistance to the Jewish badge (including by not hiding their identity) thus needs to be seen against the backdrop of this symbolic realm where they were forced to play the villain. Their goal was less to blend in than to preserve the fluidity of their identities: the possibility that they might be viewed negatively on one day but more positively on another. In other words, they fought for the prospect of defining themselves on their own terms. In identity theory, as understood by sociologists, societies are complex organizations made of people who possess multiple identities because they occupy multiple roles, are members of multiple groups, and claim multiple personal characteristics. For instance, a Jewish man could be a father, a respected religious leader, a merchant, and a moneylender. These roles coexisted and were sometimes expressed concurrently, but at other times they were not. Each of these identities corresponded to a context and a set of expected behaviors. By behaving as any honest moneylender or scrupulous merchant would, the Jewish man was confirming his identity and earning the trust and the business of his clients, who in the Duchy of Milan were majority Christian.[58] The discriminatory marks disrupted that system. Forced to wear a sign, the O-badge or other sign that symbolized one's egregious religious errors, dishonest lending practices, and inherent threat, how could a Jewish moneylender still engage in his business? Could a Jewish merchant still travel safely? Could a Christian still trust his longstanding Jewish neighbor? Above all, the badge deprived the Jews of the possibility of holding multiple roles in society; instead they were reduced to the sign and its negative connotations.[59] The Jewish badge thus acted as a negative status symbol – one that diminished the condition of the Jews, curtailed their rights and rendered them more vulnerable to both physical violence and financial

---

images of Jews wearing badges of different colors. For more on representations of Jews and the antichrist, see Debra Higgs Strickland: Antichrist and the Jews in Medieval Art and Protestant Propaganda, in: *Studies in Iconography 32* (2011), 1–50.

57 Bonfil, Jewish Life in Renaissance Italy, 22–37.

58 Peter J. Burke and Jan E. Stets: *Identity Theory*. Oxford 2009, 112–129.

59 Scholars have identified this reductionism as a key element in phenomena such as stereotyping and racism. See David T. Goldberg: Racial Europeanization, in: *Ethnic and Racial Studies* 29 (2006), 331–364; and Alana Lentin: *Racism. A Beginner's Guide*. Oxford 2008, 32–55.

insecurity. This explains the Jews' willingness to engage in a variety of resistance behaviors to avoid being marked. Paradoxically, it also explains their reluctance to make their Judaism invisible. If they could determine how Jewishness was symbolized, they had greater latitude to control how it was seen and understood by others; if they were not seen, all that was left were the harmful representations of them.

Cornelia Aust

From Noble Dress to Jewish Attire: Jewish Appearances in the Polish-Lithuanian Commonwealth and the Holy Roman Empire

Abstract: *This article examines the different styles of attire that had emerged by the eighteenth century among Jews in Poland and German-speaking lands. It argues that Jews in both regions developed their attire from older styles of dress that had fallen out of fashion among German burghers and Polish noblemen, respectively. Nevertheless, the distinguishability of Jews and Christians and distinctions among Jews according to social status, gender, and geographic origin were never clear-cut issues.*

Picturing a Hasidic Jew in Jerusalem or New York today, with a long black coat, a silk or satin caftan on Sabbath, and a black (fur) hat, many believe that this or similar attire has been the typical dress of (East European) Jews throughout time.[1] However, dress and appearance have always undergone continual change and are a rather fluid marker of identity and belonging. Though Jewish law traditionally prescribes that Jews be distinguishable from their non-Jewish neighbors, and Christian and Jewish authorities have since the thirteenth century explicitly stipulated distinctive dress, such normative prescriptions do not allow for the conclusion that Jewish men and women have always been recognizable by their dress. Likewise, the fact that Jews were sometimes forced to wear distinctive signs does not mean that they were otherwise invisible as Jews or could pass as Christians when not wearing a discriminatory sign.[2] Nevertheless, by the end of the eighteenth century there seems to have been a clear sense of a "Jewish attire".

---

1 On today's Hasidic dress see: Eric Silverman: *A Cultural History of Jewish Dress*. London 2013, 112–131.

2 On discriminatory signs in late medieval Italy see: Flora Cassen: *Marking the Jews in Renaissance Italy. Politics, Religion, and the Power of Symbols*. Cambridge 2017. For passing as a non-Jew see for a modern example: Kerry Wallach: *Passing Illusions. Jewish Visibility in Weimar Germany*. Ann Arbor 2017.

In this article, I trace some developments concerning the dress and appearance of Jews, mostly men, of the early modern period in German-speaking lands, with a particular emphasis on Fürth (near Nuremberg) in Middle Franconia and Frankfurt am Main, and compare them with similar developments in early modern Poland.[3] I ask how and when such a general term like "Jewish attire" emerged and what it meant for those who wore so-called "Jewish attire" or "Jewish dress". Did they even conceive it as "Jewish dress"? Where and when did visual difference play a particular role? Looking at such different sources as sumptuary laws, inventories, "ethnographic" descriptions, and costume books, I sketch out a highly complex picture in which perceived differences intersected, not only between Jews and Christians, but also among Jews themselves, concerning, for example, socioeconomic status, gender, and geography.

The External Perception of Jewish Dress

The insistence of Christian and Jewish authorities that Jews and Christians should be easily distinguishable in their outward appearance points to the possibility that, by the thirteenth century, Jews and Christians could often not be easily told apart.[4] Both the Fourth Lateran Council of 1215 and the thirteenth-century *takkanot Shum* – the ordinances of the three Jewish communities of Speyer, Worms, and Mainz in the Rhineland – insisted that Jews had to be visually distinguishable from their Christian neighbors. Regulations of religious, royal, and urban authorities following the Fourth Lateran Council usually insisted on distinctive signs, including different forms of yellow (or red) patch, or specific hats, while rabbinical and communal Jewish ordinances insisted more generally that Jewish men not cut their hair and beard like Christians, that Jews observe the biblical prohibition of *sha'atnets* (the mixing of wool and linen), and that they generally not dress like Christians.[5] As Flora Cassen has shown, this

---

3 On the dress of Jewish women in the early modern period see: Cornelia Aust: Covering the Female Jewish Body. Dress and Dress Regulations in Early Modern Ashkenaz, in: *Central Europe* 17 (2019) [forthcoming].

4 In antiquity, however, Cohen argues that Jews were not visibly distinctive from their environment: Shaye J. D. Cohen: *The Beginnings of Jewishness. Boundaries, Varieties, Uncertainties.* Berkeley 1999, 27–28, 31–33.

5 Alfred Rubens: *A History of Jewish Costume*, 2nd ed. London 1973, 80–97. On the medieval Jewish hat see: Sara Lipton: *Dark Mirror. The Medieval Origins of Anti-Jewish Iconography.* New York 2014, 21–54; Naomi Lubrich: The Wandering Hat. Iterations of the Medieval Jewish

insistence does not necessarily mean that Jews, whether local or foreign, were not recognizable. Locally, Jews were usually known to their neighbors and may have been recognizable by the language they spoke to each other. When traveling they may have behaved differently from Christians in specific situations, for example by not making the sign of the cross when passing statues of the Virgin Mary or other sacred objects.[6]

Turning eastward, we know relatively little about the kind of dress worn by Jews in sixteenth-century Poland. As in other regions, religious and political authorities tried to enforce the stigmatization of Jews through specific markers, as for example with the Breslau synod of 1267, which prescribed that Jews wear a specific hat. Although such hats are depicted in church windows and elsewhere, these images provide little information regarding what Jews actually did or did not wear. In 1538, the Polish Sejm in Piotrków took up the issue. The political authorities decreed:

> As the Jews abolished an old custom, namely the sign, which allowed to distinguish them from the Christians, and as they began to wear exactly the same clothes as the Christians, so that they became unrecognizable among Christians: therefore We command that all Jews and each of them should further wear a beret, or a hat or another headgear in a bright, meaning yellow, color, everywhere in Our Kingdom.

The order further stated that travelers were exempted from this regulation and that it was permitted to remove or conceal all signs of this kind while traveling.[7] This decree provides some hint that Polish Jews indeed dressed in similar clothes as their non-Jewish neighbors. Nevertheless, we can assume that Jews and non-Jews

Pointed Cap, in: *Jewish History* 29 (2015), 203–244. On the "yellow batch", its reach and some of the implications of wearing it see Flora Cassen's article in this volume. On the *takkanot Shum*: Rainer Josef Barzen: Die Schum-Gemeinden und ihre Rechtssatzungen. Geschichte und Wirkungsgeschichte, in: Pia Heberer and Ursula Reuter (eds.): *Die SchUM-Gemeinden Speyer – Worms – Mainz*. Regensburg 2013, 23–35.

6 Cassen, Marking the Jews in Renaissance Italy, 99–102. On stigma signs see also: Robert Jütte: Stigma-Symbole. Kleidung als identitätsstiftendes Merkmal bei spätmittelalterlichen und frühneuzeitlichen Randgruppen (Juden, Dirnen, Aussätzige, Bettler), in: *Saeculum (Zwischen Sein und Schein. Kleidung und Identität in der ständischen Gesellschaft)* 44 (1993), 65–89.

7 De judaeis, Petrikov 1538, in: Jozafat Ohryzko (ed.): *Volumina Legum: przedruk zbioru praw staraniem XX. pijarów w Warszawie, od roku 1732 do roku 1782 wydanego*, vol. 1: *Ab anno 1347 ad annum 1547*, Warsaw 1980 [reprint of Petersburg 1859], no. 525, 258–259. On regulations in Poland more generally see: Magda Teter: "There should be no love between us and them." Social Life and the Bounds of Jewish and Canon Law in Early Modern Poland, in: Adam Teller, Magda Teter, and Antony Polonsky (eds.): *Social and Cultural Boundaries in Pre-Modern Poland*. Oxford 2010, 249–270, esp. 264.

were well aware of the boundaries of each community. We can assume that here, like in Italy and elsewhere in Europe, the wearing of a special sign had a largely symbolic function. Traveling without such a sign afforded travelers protection on their already dangerous travels. In daily life, when most inhabitants already knew who belonged to the local Jewish community, specific signs served not only to keep up communal borders but also to refer to these borders symbolically.

Christian and Jewish insistence on strict sartorial boundaries or stigmatizing markers of difference shows that distinguishability was important to authorities of both religions. However, this does not mean that contemporaries were always able to tell Jews apart, as a polemical letter from the early sixteenth century suggests. At the beginning of the sixteenth century a dispute began between Johannes Pfefferkorn, a converted Jew from Cologne, and the famous humanist Johannes Reuchlin. Following Pfefferkorn's attempts to convince the Emperor Maximilian I to confiscate all Jewish books with allegedly anti-Christian content, including the Talmud, a set of anonymous satirical letters was published in 1515, followed by a second extended edition in 1517. These *Letters of Obscure Men* (*Epistolae Obscurorum Virorum*) were mostly a humanist defense of Reuchlin, who had turned against Pfefferkorn, as well as an attack on scholastic theology and on Pfefferkorn as a Jewish convert.[8] In the second letter of the collection, a certain master Johannes Pellifex writes to the master Ortivinus Gratius and relates an episode that he had recently experienced in Frankfurt. He had gone to the Frankfurt fair, where he had walked together with a local student toward the market square. They came across two men, whose outward appearance was rather respectable. Both men wore black robes and large pointed hoods. The author, Pellifex, thus believed them to be two *magistri nostri* – theologians – and honored them by lifting his hat. The student was shocked and told Pellifex that these two men were clearly Jews, who obviously should not be greeted this way. Pellifex immediately regretted his action but defended himself by excusing his *faux pas* by his ignorance, as he had indeed taken them for two scholars. The remainder of the letter discusses the issue, remarking that Jews were actually always to wear a yellow ring on their gowns, and complaining about the fact that

---

8 On the debate and the *Letters of Obscure Men* see: Thomas Bartoldus: Humanismus und Talmudstreit. Pfefferkorn, Reuchlin und die "Dunkelmännerbriefe" (1515/17), in: Arne Domrös, Thomas Bartoldus, and Julian Voloj (eds.): *Judentum und Antijudaismus in der deutschen Literatur im Mittelalter und an der Wende zur Neuzeit*. Berlin 2002, 179–228. On the anti-Jewish tone of the *Letters of Obscure Men* see: Winfried Frey: Die "Epistolae obscurorum virorum" – ein antijüdisches Pamphlet?, in: Renate Heuer (ed.): *Probleme deutsch-jüdischer Identität*. Bad Soden 1986, 147–172.

the burghers of Frankfurt allowed the local Jews to walk around like scholars.[9] Although this imaginary letter emerged from a polemic, it offers hints that in sixteenth-century Frankfurt Jews did not necessarily wear clothes that made them immediately recognizable on the street. Nevertheless, the local student was well aware that they were Jews, though he claims that he saw the yellow ring attached to their clothes.

About 200 years later, Johann Jacob Schudt (1664–1772), the well-known "ethnographer" of the Jews of Frankfurt, took up this story from the *Letters of Obscure Men* in his *Jewish Curiosities (Jüdische Merkwürdigkeiten)*, published in 1714.[10] Schudt, who showed considerable interest in Jewish daily life – though not without serious discontent with his Jewish neighbors – recounts the encounter from the *Epistolae Obscurorum Virorum* but notes that actually it was no longer necessary for Jews to wear yellow signs on their dress.[11] He informs his readers, rather, that "the Jews wear black coats, black hats, generally clothes of dark color and around the neck a collar made from linen; the older and most distinguished ones also a round white linen ruff with many pleads and tucks, which, in addition to the beret, have their origin in the former Spanish costume".[12] Thus, Schudt describes here the adoption of a specific costume that was probably most common in sixteenth- and seventeenth-century Spain. The linen ruff, especially when it came "with many pleads and tucks", was its most characteristic part. According to Schudt, Jews had adopted this costume and retained it when it became otherwise unfashionable. Despite Schudt's repeatedly anti-Jewish tone, one may assume that the changes he describes in Jewish dress are nevertheless reliable. Thus, by the early eighteenth century, Jews were most likely recognizable by their dress, at least in Frankfurt.

A similar phenomenon can be observed in the attire of Polish Jews, though we have few sources that can confirm what Jews wore before the second half of the eighteenth century. It seems that they mostly followed the style of the lower

---

9 Karl Riha (ed.): *Dunkelmännerbriefe. Epistolae obscurorum virorum an Magister Ortuin Gratius aus Deventer.* Frankfurt am Main 1991, 13–15.

10 On Schudt and his work see: Yaacov Deutsch: Jüdische Merckwürdigkeiten. Ethnography in Early Modern Frankfurt, in: Fritz Backhaus et al. (eds.): *The Frankfurt Judengasse. Jewish Life in an Early Modern German City.* Frankfurt am Main 2010, 73–84.

11 Officially, stigmatory signs were often abolished in the eighteenth century; in Frankfurt am Main in 1728, in the Habsburg Empire only in 1765. This, however, does not mean that Jews indeed wore those discriminatory signs until their annulment.

12 Johann Jakob Schudt: *Jüdische Merckwürdigkeiten vorstelende was sich Curieuses und denckwürdiges in den neuen Zeiten bey einigen Jahrhunderten mit denen in alle IV Teile der Welt, sonderlich durch Teutschland, zerstreuten Juden zugetragen, Sammt einer vollständigen Franckfurter Juden-Chronik.* Frankfurt am Main 1717, part 2, book VI, chapter 14, 247–248.

nobility, including such typical items as the *żupan*, a long coat worn visibly under the outer garment, the *delja*, a long overcoat with long arms, and a wide belt.[13] Nevertheless, Jewish communal authorities had sought to maintain a sartorial difference between Jews and non-Jews, especially the *szlachta*, the Polish nobility.

Practices of Difference among Early Modern Ashkenazim

The desire for sartorial distinction between Jews and Christians might not be surprising; however, early modern Jews assigned meaning to dress as a marker of *internal* difference as well. In general, Ashkenazi Jews (at least north of the Alps) are considered a unit; if inner-Jewish differences are taken into account, Ashkenazim are usually distinguished primarily from Sephardim. The latter had become an important part of Western and, to some extent, Central European Jewish life during the seventeenth century, when they settled increasingly in commercial centers like Amsterdam, Hamburg, and, later, London.[14] In all three cities they encountered Ashkenazi Jews, locals as well as refugees, who arrived during the war-ridden seventeenth century from various German territories and from Poland-Lithuania, having fled from the repercussions of either the Thirty Years' War or the Khmelnytsky Uprisings of 1648/49.

The relation between Ashkenazim and Sephardim often proved complicated. In both Amsterdam and Hamburg Sephardic Jews financially supported Ashkenazi refugees, though they mostly attempted to remove the Jewish poor from the city and to send them elsewhere. Though Ashkenazim and Sephardim did business together, they maintained separate communities and did not intermarry. Often Sephardic Jews were not only wealthier than their Ashkenazi brethren but also thought of themselves as superior in a vague cultural sense.

---

13 Tamar Somogyi: *Die Schejnen und die Prosten. Untersuchungen zum Schönheitsideal der Ostjuden in Bezug auf Körper und Kleidung unter besonderer Berücksichtigung des Chassidismus.* Berlin 1982, 159–163. For a discussion of early modern noble dress in Poland see the contribution by Beata Biedrońska-Słota and Maria Molanda in this volume.
14 On Amsterdam see: Yosef Kaplan: Amsterdam and Ashkenazic Migration in the Seventeenth Century, in: *Studia Rosenthaliana* 23:2 (1989), 22–44; Daniel Swetschinski: *Reluctant Cosmopolitans. The Portuguese Jews of Seventeenth-Century Amsterdam.* London 2000. On Hamburg see: Jutta Braden: *Hamburger Judenpolitik im Zeitalter lutherischer Orthodoxie: 1590–1710.* Hamburg 2001.

This included the Jews' outward appearance, as Menasseh ben Israel from Amsterdam noted in his famous address to Oliver Cromwell for the readmission of the Jews to England in 1655. While he argued for the Jews' economic usefulness and political harmlessness,[15] he also blatantly displayed a condescending attitude toward northern European Ashkenazim. Concerning their appearance he remarks that "especially at Prague, Vienna and Franckfurt [sic] [they are] very much favoured by the most mild and most gracious Emperours, but despised of the people, being a Nation not very finely garnished by reasons of their vile clothing".[16] Despite being esthetically unpleasant, these Ashkenazim had close ties to imperial power, and thus, Menasseh ben Israel argued, why should the much more pleasant and civilized Sephardim not be allowed to resettle in England.

Though the term Ashkenazim referred to Jews who descended from medieval Jewish inhabitants of the Rhineland and came to include Jews from northern France, England, northern Italy, Bohemia, Moravia, and eventually the Polish-Lithuanian Commonwealth, noticeable differences existed between different groups of Ashkenazim since the seventeenth century at the latest. Jews from early modern Poland and German-speaking lands could be distinguished for example by liturgy and customs (*minhag*).[17] These differences were not only expressed on an intellectual level and in rabbinical writings, but also in folk literature, in which we find mention of apparent differences between Polish and German Jews in matters of everyday life such as food and dress.

Around 1675, a satirical Yiddish poem by an anonymous author was printed in Prague. Entitled "Di beshraybung fun ashkenaz un polak" (A description of Ashkenaz and Polak), the title already set a clear distinction between two Jewish entities: those Jews from the German-speaking lands and those from Poland. Eventually, the poem complicates things further as it introduces Jews from Prague as distinct from the other two groups. It probably is "the most famous

---

15 Lucien Wolf (ed.): *Menasseh ben Israel's Mission to Oliver Cromwell. Being a Reprint of the Pamphlets Published by Mensasseh ben Israel to Promote the Re-admission of the Jews to England, 1649–1656.* London 1901. See also: Jonathan Karp: *The Politics of Jewish Commerce. Economic Thought and Emancipation in Europe, 1638–1848.* Cambridge 2008, 32–37.
16 Wolf, Menasseh ben Israel's Mission, 86.
17 See for example: Adam Teller: Jewish Literary Responses to the Events of 1648–1649 and the Creation of a Polish-Jewish Consciousness, in: Benjamin Nathans and Gabriella Safran (eds.): *Culture Front. Representing Jews in Eastern Europe.* Philadelphia 2008, 17–45; Joseph Davis: The Reception of the "Shulḥan 'Arukh" and the Formation of Ashkenazic Jewish Identity, in: *AJS Review* 26 (2002), 251–276; Elkhanan Reiner: The Rise of an Urban Community. Some Insights on the Transition from the Medieval Ashkenazi to the 16th Century Jewish Community in Poland, in: *Kwartalnik Historii Żydów* 207 (2003), 363–372.

and elaborate literary example for the expression of a pre-Haskalah [Jewish en-lightenment] inner Ashkenazic bias".[18] The poem describes a Polish Jew wander-ing through German lands, probably one of the refugees of 1648/49 or from the later Northern War (1655–1660) between Sweden and the Polish-Lithuanian Commonwealth. The anonymous author[19] mentions several shortcomings of Polish Jews, including infidelity in marriage, superficial religiosity, fraudulence, and theft, but also complains about the lack of hospitality in Jewish communities in German lands. He mentions explicitly Frankfurt, Worms, Fürth, Hamburg, Halberstadt, Friedberg and many others. According to the author, Jews in these communities mistrusted Polish Jews and took them for thieves; they hardly let them into their houses and tried to send them away with little food and as quickly as possible. The author also mocks Jews of the German lands for their outward appearance, for wearing only one coat and one hat on weekdays and Shabbat and for wearing shoes that were studded with nails. Moreover, their beard was trimmed short, leaving only a *kamats*, which refers either to some kind of goatee or to a mustache with a small goatee in the form of the Hebrew vowel point *kamats*, which also was called a *kamats-berdele* in Yiddish.[20] In con-trast, the author describes the dress of the Polak, consisting of a *shupits* (a long winter coat with fur; Polish *żupan* or *żupica*) and a *shoibn* (a long overcoat with fur; Polish *szuba*)[21] with its wide sleeves, as making for a more dignified appear-ance, even though the Ashkenaz pokes fun at him.

---

18 Diana Matut: What Happened in Hamburg ... A Yiddish Document about Polish Jews in Germany during the Early Modern Period, in: Marion Aptroot et al. (eds.): *Leket. Jiddistik heute/ Yiddisch Studies Today*. Düsseldorf 2012, 321–355, quotation 331. The poem has been published by Max Weinreich: Tsvei yidishe shpotlider oif yidn, in: *Filologishe shriftn* 3 (1929), c. 537–554. On the satirical poem in general see: Ewa Geller: Aschkenas und Polak. Ein Jahrhunderte während der Antagonismus, exemplarisch dargestellt an einem jiddischen Streitlied aus dem 17. Jahrhundert, in: Nathanael Riemer (ed.): *Jewish Lifeworlds and Jewish Thought. Festschrift Presented to Karl E. Grözinger on the Occasion of his 70th Birthday*. Wiesbaden 2012, 357–368.

19 Max Weinreich and Maks Erik assumed that the author was probably a Polish Jew, who had traveled through German lands, while Ewa Geller argues that the language has the charac-ter of Western Yiddish and thus, the author might instead be a Jew from German lands. Geller, Aschkenas und Polak, 359, note 313.

20 Weinreich, Tsvei yidishe shpotlider oif yidn, c. 543.

21 The German term *Schaube* for an overcoat probably refers to a similar garment, used in six-teenth-century German lands, though it is difficult to say to what extent it differed from a *szuba*. See: Jutta Zander-Seidel: *Textiler Hausrat. Kleidung und Haustextilien in Nürnberg von 1500–1650*. Berlin 1990, 55. See also: Schaube, in: J.G. Krünitz (ed.): *Oekonomische Encyklopädie*, vol. 140. Berlin 1825, 545. URL: *http://www.kruenitz1.uni-trier.de/background/en tries_vol140b.htm* (22 Dec. 2018).

Though the differences in dress and outward appearance played only a minor role in this satirical poem and were not the most significant distinction the author described, the wording shows clear differences in dress that were fully developed by the second half of the seventeenth century. Thus, we see that geographic origin and the corresponding sartorial practices played a central role as a marker of inner-Jewish difference already in the seventeenth century. The image of the pre-Enlightenment Jew in "oriental" garb, including caftan and beard, versus the modern and enlightened Jew dressed in West-European fashion seems to be an invention of the Haskalah that sought to level out the differences among early modern Jews.[22]

Internal Restrictions: Jewish Sumptuary Laws

Jewish communities throughout Central and East Central Europe were concerned with their members' outward appearance throughout the early modern period. New ordinances (*takkanot*) that were more detailed than those of the thirteenth century emerged from the late sixteenth century onward. They were based on the older principles of a general distinguishability of Jews from non-Jews, the prohibition against mixing wool and linen, and the prohibition against wearing one's hair like non-Jews or to shaving one's beard completely, as well as a warning against excessive luxury and indecent female dress. These warnings and prohibitions were repeated in the early modern halakhic literature (Jewish legal texts), most prominently the *Shulchan Aruch* (The Set Table), first printed in 1565. In addition, the genre of communal ordinances began to develop. While earlier ordinances existed in fifteenth-century Spain and Italy,[23] the earliest known sumptuary laws in Central and East Central Europe are those of the Jewish community of Cracow from 1595.[24] These first sumptuary laws of a Jewish community in Poland are mostly concerned with the usage of luxury

---

22 For this phenomenon of the Haskalah period see: Kathrin Wittler: Orientalist Body Politics. Intermedia Encounters between German and Polish Jews around 1800, in: *Central Europe* 17 (2019), [forthcoming].

23 Rubens, A History of Jewish Costume, 184–185. In general see: Louis Finkelstein: *Jewish Self-Government in the Middle Ages*. New York 1924. On Italy: Diana Owen Hughes: Distinguishing Signs. Ear-Rings, Jews and Franciscan Rhetoric in the Italian Renaissance City, in: *Past & Present* 112:1 (1986), 3–59.

24 The communal ordinances are printed in: Majer Bałaban: Die Krakauer Judengemeinde-Ordnung von 1595 und ihre Nachträge, in: *Jahrbuch der Jüdisch-Literarischen Gesellschaft* 10 (1912), 296–360, 11 (1916) 88–114. On the ordinances see: Edward Fram: Hagbalat motarot

items, certain furs, stones, and gold and silver threads. The ordinances do not mention any garments in particular, but rather a variety of embellishments that Jews were to refrain from, at least if they did not belong to the small group of wealthy community members paying the highest taxes. Additional distinctions were made between items allowed within the Jewish quarter but prohibited outside of it, and items that were only acceptable on certain holidays and feasts.

The high degree of internal autonomy of the Jewish communities in the Polish-Lithuanian Commonwealth led to the emergence of transregional Jewish governing bodies. On the most central level these were the Council of the Four Lands (*Va'ad arba aratsot*), representing Jews from Great Poland, Little Poland, Ruthenia, and Volhynia, which adapted more organized forms in the 1580s; and the Lithuanian Council (*Va'ad medinat lita*), which emerged in the first half of the seventeenth century.[25] Already in 1607, the Council of the Four Lands explicitly prohibited the wearing of "clothes of non-Jews and prostitutes", even for the wealthiest. The ordinance does not specify what is meant by non-Jewish dress or by the dress of prostitutes, though one might assume that the latter refers to the dress of non-Jewish women in general, ridiculing them a "prostitutes", a rather common means of countering Christian dominance.[26] The same prohibition was repeated in 1637 in the ordinances of the Lithuanian Council, including an explicit warning to tailors and other artisans to observe these regulations when producing or (much more likely) altering used clothing. At this point a concrete garment is mentioned. The regulations prohibit men from wearing a *żupan* made of atlas and damask, with the exception of the very wealthy who paid over 4,000 ducats in community taxes annually.[27] This regulation, however, confirms that Jews indeed wore the *żupan*, which was usually tied together with a wide belt. Thus, Jews participated sartorially in early modern Polish society and adapted themselves toward the fashion of the Polish nobility in particular. Though the

---

be-kehilah ha-yehudit be-Krakov be-shalhe ha-me'ah ha-16 uve-re'shit ha-me'ah ha-17, in: *Gal-Ed* 18 (2002), 11–23.

25 The *takkanot* of the Council of the Four Lands did not survive, but have been reconstructed from other sources and published first in 1952 by Israel Halperin. Israel Halperin and Israel Bartal (eds.): *Pinkas va'ad arba' aratsot: likute takkanot, ketavim u-reshumot*, 2nd ed. Jerusalem 1989. The *takkanot* of the Lithuanian Council were published by Simon Dubnov (ed.): *Pinkas medinah o pinkas va'ad ha-kehilot ha-rashiyot bi-medinat Lita*. Berlin 1928. On Jewish autonomy in Poland see: Adam Teller: Telling the Difference. Some Comparative Perspectives on the Jews' Legal Status in the Polish-Lithuanian Commonwealth and the Holy Roman Empire, in: *Polin* 22 (2009), 109–141.

26 Maria Diemling: Navigating Christian Space. Jews and Christian Images in Early Modern German Lands, in: *Jewish Culture and History* 12 (2012), 397–410.

27 Halperin and Bartal, Pinkas va'ad arba' aratsot, 17–18; Dubnov, Pinkas medinah, 68, no. 313.

żupan was worn by nobility, it was also worn by Jews and some burghers as well; the finer distinctions were made through fabrics and embellishments. Poorer noblemen mostly wore a white linen or woolen *żupan,* whereas wealthier members of the nobility used brocade, silk, or velvet, embellished with gilt buttons and tied with expensive silk sashes (instead of simple woolen ones). In the sixteenth and seventeenth centuries even some better-off peasants owned a *żupan* and patterned belts, though these were probably not worn daily but as festive garments.[28] Thus, one might argue that the different estates or status groups (in the case of the Jews) competed against each other less in the specific garments worn and more in the richness and value of the fabrics and accessories (Figure 1).

As members of the Polish nobility increasingly adapted to a more Western European style of clothing, incorporating and adapting new fashionable cuts and accessories, it seems that Jews in Poland rather retained traditional garments, not unlike the developments in German lands to which we will return later. The last sumptuary laws regarding dress appeared in the minute book (*pinkas*) of the Lithuanian Council in 1761, three years before this central Jewish governing body was abolished, along with its Polish counterpart, the Council of the Four Lands, by the last Polish king, Stanisław August Poniatowski. The ordinances of 1761 did not prohibit the wearing of non-Jewish dress in particular, although they did state that it was forbidden to make new dresses from used Christian ones. On the other hand, the ordinances permitted Jews to buy used clothes even when made from silk or embroidered with gold and silver.[29] The ordinances, however, explicitly mentioned the caftan as a permitted garment, along with vests (*vestin*) and stomachers (*zalishkes*) to be worn during the week and Shabbat and at any place, including markets and streets, that is, spaces that were conceived as non-Jewish. It was likewise permitted to make these garments anew or to repair them. The caftan, a long buttoned coat-like garment, is thus mentioned as a garment of everyday use.[30]

28 Maria Bogucka: *The Lost World of the "Sarmatians". Custom as the Regulator of Polish Social Life in Early Modern Times.* Warsaw 1996, 103, 105–106, 108–109.
29 Dubnov, Pinkas medinah, 272, no. 1024–1026. The prohibition might be related to the traditional fears of reworking stolen goods. On Jews as fences see: Shaul Stampfer: Jews as Fences in Early Modern Poland and Beyond. Function, Ideology, Almost Philanthropy and Almost Diplomacy in a Complex Society, in: *Jewish Culture and History (Transformations and Intersections of Shtadlanut and Tzedakah in the Early Modern Period)* 19 (2018), 23–38.
30 Dubnov, Pinkas medinah, 272, no. 1025. See also: Somogyi, Die Schejnen und die Prosten, 166, 191–192.

Figure 1: Juif Polonois (Jewish Pole), 1765, Etching, in: Jean Baptiste Le Prince: *Habillements de diverses nations*, The British Museum Online Collection, Creative Commons: CC BY-NC-SA 4.0.

Communal sumptuary laws from the towns of Dubno, Tiktin (Tykocin), and Nieśwież from the same time period likewise did not stipulate any concrete prohibition against wearing non-Jewish dress. Evidently it was clear that Jewish attire differed in style and cut. The ordinances from Nieśwież, an important Jewish community in eighteenth-century Poland-Lithuania, focused rather on the embellishment of garments. Visible outer garments for women like the *tshuhai*, an overcoat, the *fartuch*, an apron, and bonnets were not to be interwoven or embroidered with silver and gold. The same embellishment, however, was permissible on the standard pieces of dress – caftan, vest, and stomachers (*zalishkes*) – worn as layers under an outer gown. Here, gold and silver embroideries were allowed as long as they were displayed only at home, but worn in reverse on the street and on the way to synagogue.[31] The embroidery was to remain invisible to the Christian eye. Thus the prohibition was concerned with the display of luxury and not with the distinguishability of Jewish men and women.

Dressed in "Jewish Attire"

A rare series of inventories from the small town of Biała Podlaska, near Warsaw, seems to confirm this impression.[32] Inventories are not simply "snapshots of reality"; they are created by individuals with specific intentions in mind. However, as "representations of the domestic" they can provide some glimpse into the ownership of particular garments.[33] Following the devastation of the noble town in 1764, which belonged to the Radziwiłł family, about 300 Jewish and 42 Christian burghers of the town submitted lists with damages to the Radziwiłłs. From the overall sum of nearly half a million zloty only about 10,000 zloty were claimed by the few Christian inhabitants, most of them

---

31 Anna Michałowska: *Gminy żydowskie w dawnej rzeczypospolitej. Wybór tekstów źródołwych.* Warsaw 2003, 127–128. On the garments see also: Somogyi, Die Schejnen und die Prosten, 199–204.

32 The inventories are found in: Akta tyczące się szkóć przez Karola Stanisława Kcia Radziwiłła i Jego poddanych przez rabunek r. 1764 poniefionych, Archiwum Warszawskie Radziwiłłów, XXIII [further AR XXIII], t. 7, pl. 2; t. 8, pl. 1 (AGAD Warsaw). On Biała Podlaska see: Andrzej W. Rachuba: Biała pod rządami Radziwiłłów w latach 1568–1813, in: Tadeusz Wasilewski and Tadeusz Krawczak (eds.): *Z nieznanej przeszłości Białej i Podlasia.* Biała Podlaska 1990, 37–65.

33 On the critical evaluation of inventories as a source see: Giorgio Riello: "Things Seen and Unseen." The Material Culture of Early Modern Inventories and Their Representation of Domestic Interiors, in: Paula Findlen (ed.): *Early Modern Things. Objects and Their Histories, 1500–1800.* London 2013, 125–150, esp. 127.

illiterate. Garments were not always mentioned in detail and, especially in the case of Jewish merchants, one must carefully distinguish between private pieces of dress and merchandise; none of the Christians, however, owned a *żupan* or a caftan. Most often the inventories mention a shirt (*koszula*), a shawl (*chusteczka*), and a bonnet (*czapka*), sometimes an apron, a hat, a scarf, and a pair of pants.[34] Most of the Jewish inventories, however, do mention a single *żupan*, and more rarely a *kontusz* and/or a caftan. If these are single items and not mentioned in conjunction with other textiles that might have been part of merchandise, one may assume that they were garments owned in addition to the ones worn when the damage to the town occurred.

Moreover, a cursory look at wanted notices in the Polish newspaper *Gazeta Warszawska* from the last quarter of the eighteenth century confirms that the inhabitants of the city, Jewish and Christian, must have had a very concrete idea of different types of dress. Between 1776 and 1788, and again between 1796 and 1806, 27 Jews were described in wanted notices, often after having fled from a first arrest or prison. When, for example, the authorities searched for a certain Faibus Jossiewicz, who had escaped after his arrest, he was described as follows:

> He is about 24 years old, of small stature, has red hair, a suchlike beard, a haggard and pale face, and speaks only Jewish-German [i.e. Yiddish] and Polish. At the time of his escape he wore Polish Jewish clothing and there was nothing exceptional beyond that, except that he was fast in his movements and spoke rather quickly.[35]

Most of the Jews' dress was similarly designated as Jewish in some way. A caftan is only mentioned once, the *żupan* eight times without any further definition and twice as a Jewish garment (*żupan żydowskie*). Nine times we find the attire described as Jewish; apparently the reader knew what was meant when he/she read "in a Jewish garment" (*w suknią żydowską*), "Polish-Jewish dress" (*polska-żydowska suknia/ w stroiu polski-żydowski*), or simply "in Jewish manner" (*po żydowsku*). In addition to the aforementioned *żupan*, the following garments were also described as Jewish: a black coat (*płaszcz czarny żydowskie*), a vest (*żydowska kamizielka*), and two different headcovers (*żydowska czapka, kapturek żydowski*). Only in seven cases is there no typical garment or additional descriptor "Jewish" to be found, while two Jews were dressed in different

---

34 AR XXIII, t. 7, pl. 2, 1–2, 226–310 (AGAD Warsaw).
35 *Gazeta Warszawska*, October 20, 1797, no. 84, supplement. This wanted-ad was published in German as Warsaw was under Prussian rule at the time.

styles: one in a long Polish garment (*suknia długa Polska*) and a certain Marek Moyźesz in French manner (*ubrany po Francusku*).[36]

Thus, those who described these Jews on the run, and presumably also those who read the wanted notices in the *Gazeta Warszawska*, had a relatively clear understanding of what was meant by Jewish dress or attire; what a Jewish hat or a Jewish vest looked like; and that a *żupan*, for example, was a piece of clothing often worn by Jews. In contrast, in German Jewish police lists with wanted notices from the first half of the eighteenth century onward, we do not find such general ascriptions, if we find descriptions of dress at all.[37] Detailing clothes made little sense, according to the authors of these lists, because many of the alleged criminals and vagabonds changed their clothing regularly. But even when dress was mentioned and described, generic terms like Jewish or German-Jewish dress are absent. This, however, does not mean that a specific Jewish attire did not develop in German-speaking lands, at least in parts of Jewish society.

From Spanish Dress to Honorary Garments

The attitudes toward Jewish dress and, certainly, the varieties of garments worn by early modern Jews, were even more diverse in German-speaking lands. Though depicted as a rather homogeneous group in the above-mentioned polemical poem mocking their habits of dress, Jewish communities were diverse in size, location, and social composition, and thus also in access to clothes, fabrics, and luxury items. The expulsions of the late medieval period had fundamentally changed the composition of Jewish communities in the German lands. The urban communities in the Rhineland and elsewhere had mostly vanished. Jews in Frankfurt am Main and Worms lived in separate parts of their respective cities;

---

36 *Gazeta Warszawska*, December 4, 1776, no. 97, supplement; May 9, 1781, no. 37, supplement; July 20, 1785, no. 85, supplement; August 3, 1785, no. 62, supplement; February 16, 1788, no. 14, supplement; April 19, 1796, no. 32, supplement; July 14, 1797, no. 56, supplement; October 20, 1797, no. 83, supplement; August, 31, 1798, no. 70, supplement; Ocotber 25, 1799, no. 86, supplement; December 30, 1800, no. 104, supplement; September 22, 1801, no. 76, supplement; December 15, 1801, no. 100, supplement; June 8, 1802, no. 46, supplement; November 8, 1803, no. 89, supplement; May 10, 1805, no. 38, supplement; November 4, 1806, no. 88, supplement.

37 See for example: *Acten-mäßige Designation derr von einer diebischen Juden-Bande verübten Kirchen-Raubereyen und gewaltsamen mörderischen Einbrüche, samt Angefügter Beschreibung derer meisten Jüdischen Erz-Diebe [. . .]*, 2nd ed. Coburg 1735; Acta betr. die in Hessen Schaumburgschen entdeckte Räuber und Diebesbande (1802–1804), HA I, Rep. 21, no. 206c 1, Fasz. 37 (Geheimes Preußisches Staatsarchiv Berlin); Criminalia 6.643, Steckbrief des Hochstifts Münster (Institut für Stadtgeschichte, Frankfurt am Main).

the Jews expelled from Nuremberg in 1499 resettled in Fürth, just outside of Nuremberg. Many small communities spread across villages and small towns, especially in Franconia. Other communities, like Halberstadt, were reestablished after the settlement of individual families of Court Jews, who built communities around family members and servants. Brandenburg-Prussia, marked by the devastations of the Thirty Years' War, readmitted Jews to its territories only in the late seventeenth century.[38]

No strong trans-regional representation of the Jewish communities developed in the German-speaking lands comparable to the Council of the Four Lands or the Lithuanian Council. Sumptuary laws were thus stipulated by local communities only, with the exception of the more general ordinances (*takkanot*) from seventeenth- and early eighteenth-century Moravia. Throughout the seventeenth and eighteenth centuries, relatively short regulations can be found in the Habsburg lands (Kremsier, Nikolsburg, and Prague) and in Friedberg and Halberstadt; more extensive laws are found in the three communities of Hamburg, Altona, Wandsbek, and in Frankfurt am Main, Fürth, and French Metz; while in Prussia, for example, no such ordinances are known from any relatively large Jewish community.[39] The shorter of these sumptuary laws usually prohibited various expensive fabrics, gold and silver threads, and similar luxury goods in general, often pertaining in particular to women. Some distinguished between Jewish and Christian space and prohibited some garments or

---

38 On the development of Jewish communities in Germany in general see: Jonathan Israel: *European Jewry in the Age of Mercantilism, 1550–1750*, 3rd ed. London 1998; Mordechai Breuer and Michael Graetz: *Tradition and Enlightenment 1600–1780*. New York 1996; Michael A. Meyer (ed.): *German-Jewish History in Modern Times*, vol. 1. New York 1996, 70–78, 82–121.

39 Israel Halperin: *Takkanot medinat Mehrin (5410–5508)*. Jerusalem 1952, 99–100, 160, 183–184, 198–200; Adolf Frankl-Grün: Die Gemeindeverfassung von Kremsier, in: *Monatsschrift für die Geschichte und Wissenschaft des Judentums* 40:4–6 (1896), 180–184, 209–219, 255–261; Abraham Naftali Zvi Roth (ed.): *Sefer takkanot Nikolsburg*. Jerusalem 1961; Yikutiel Kamelhar: *Sefer mofat ha-dor. Toldot rabbenu Yicheskiel Halevi Landau z"l*. Piotrków 1934; Stefan Litt: *Protokollbuch und Statuten der Jüdischen Gemeinde Friedberg (16.–18. Jahrhundert)*. Friedberg 2003. For Halberstadt, Fürth (1770) and Metz see: Stefan Litt (ed.): *Jüdische Gemeindestatuten aus dem aschkenasischen Kulturraum 1650–1850*. Göttingen 2014, 107–131, 132–273, 353–395; Andreas Würfel: *Historische Nachricht von der Judengemeinde in dem Hofmarkt Fürth Unterhalb Nürnberg 1. Die Beschreibung v. d. Juden Ansitz in d. Hofmark Fürth … ; 2. Das Tekunnos Büchlein d. Fürther Juden*. Frankfurt am Main 1754; Johann Jakob Schudt: *Neue Franckfurter Jüdische Kleider-Ordnung [. . .]*. Frankfurt am Main 1716; Heinz Mosche Graupe (ed.): *Die Statuten der drei Gemeinden Altona, Hamburg und Wandsbek. Quellen zur jüdischen Gemeindeorganisation im 17. und 18. Jahrhundert*. Hamburg 1973; Max Grunwald: Luxusverbot der Dreigemeinden (Hamburg – Altona – Wandsbek) aus dem Jahre 1715, in: *Jahrbuch für jüdische Volkskunde* 25 (1923), 227–234.

embellishments only outside of the Jewish home, street, or synagogue. The more extensive sumptuary laws likewise drew a number of social distinctions, according to status within the community (e.g. servants) or the amount of taxes a community member paid. Unsurprisingly, the most extensive sumptuary laws were from Hamburg/Altona/Wansbek and Metz, wealthy and well-connected Jewish communities.

For my purpose here, however, the sumptuary laws from Frankfurt am Main and from Fürth are the most interesting, as they seem to support the emergence of a particular Jewish attire, specific to at least some German Jews, in the eighteenth century at the latest. In both cases, one might argue that certain garments held honorary value and constituted part of a local Jewish identity. This feeling of belonging was based on membership in larger urban Jewish communities and on the holding of residential rights. This attitude was reflected in the sumptuary laws of both communities from the first decades of the eighteenth century. In both Frankfurt and Fürth the Shabbes cloak was of symbolic importance, as only full members of the community who received the so-called *Stättigkeit* (the right to settle permanently in the city) were allowed to wear it. The Frankfurt ordinances, which were promulgated after a devastating fire in the Jewish ghetto in 1711, were handed down only in an edition, including a translation into German, by Johann Jacob Schudt, the "ethnographer" of the Frankfurt Jewish community.[40] In the wake of the destruction of many houses in the Frankfurt Jewish street, the sumptuary laws stipulated that the Shabbes cloak should not be made from silk and that only young men who already owned such a cloak were allowed to wear it. Schudt commented that the Jews had a specific cloak for synagogue with a hole for the arms, i.e. without sleeves, which foreign Jews were not allowed to wear. Local Jews likewise were not allowed to wear it immediately after their wedding, but only once they officially received their *Stättigkeit*.[41] As mentioned earlier, Schudt also described the dress of Frankfurt Jewry as a typically Jewish dress with the black Shabbes cloak and a rather elaborate ruff.

Even though these were garments worn especially on Shabbat and on holidays, both remained the object of repeated dispute throughout the eighteenth century within the Jewish community in Frankfurt and between the elders and the magistrate. Both garments, cloak and ruff, had honorary meaning, and in

---

40 On Schudt, whose writings contain numerous anti-Jewish statements, see: Maria Diemling: The Ethnographer and the Jewish Body. Johann Jacob Schudt on the Civilisation Process of the Jews of Frankfurt, in: *Jewish Culture and History* 10 (2008), 95–110; Deutsch, Jüdische Merckwürdigkeiten. Ethnography in Early Modern Frankfurt, 73–84.
41 Schudt, Neue Franckfurter Jüdische Kleider-Ordnung, 48, § 35.

1754 the elders of the Frankfurt Jewish community stipulated, in a set of regulations consisting of 126 paragraphs concerning different areas of Jewish life, that Jewish bankrupts were not only banned from all honorary posts and from reading the Torah in synagogue, but were also prohibited from wearing a white collar or ruff and the Shabbes cloak.[42] Thus, both were honorary garments linked closely to one's position in the community and were invested with pride.

The importance of the Shabbes cloak as a sign of belonging had not vanished even by the late eighteenth century. Repeatedly, individuals complained that while their fathers had residential rights in Frankfurt, they as their sons would not receive the same rights automatically and thus were banned from wearing the Shabbes cloak. The magistrate, however, was less interested in this question and more concerned with the right to trade, which was likewise linked to residential rights. The magistrate remarked that many cases like this had been taken to the courts, but insisted that only Jews who have received residential rights themselves – irrespective of their fathers' status – were allowed to wear the cloak. The magistrate did not recognize the symbolic importance of these garments. A report concerning the issue stated, "as far as I am aware the Shabbes cloak, the Shabbes cap (*Schabbes Deckel*) and ruff are only worn in the [Jewish] street on their Shabbes and holidays".[43] Even in 1795 a certain Salomon Joseph Spiegel complained to the municipal authorities that the communal elders not only refused to grant residential rights to his future son-in-law Moses Schweitzer, but also withheld the right to wear the Shabbes cloak and ruff. The latter garments became the symbol for residential rights during the dispute that continued for many years.[44]

In Fürth, the Shabbes cloak (*Schul-Mantel*) and the ruff fulfilled a similar function. The Protestant theologian Andreas Würfel, who published a history of the Jews in Fürth in 1754, remarked that the elders of the community held the right to grant and withdraw residential rights, which were likewise tied to the right to wear the Shabbes cloak and ruff on Shabbat.[45] The sumptuary laws of the Fürth community from 1728, according to Würfel's translation, stipulated

---

42 Juden Akten 975, Reglement die hiesige Schutz Juden betr. 1754, 55 (Institut für Stadtgeschichte Frankfurt am Main). The regulations were penned following inner-communal conflict between two families. In this context, new sumptuary laws were also planned, but apparently never written or published. Isidor Kracauer: *Geschichte der Juden in Frankfurt a. M., 1150–1824*, vol. 2. Frankfurt am Main 1925, 205–211.
43 Juden Akten 458, no. 41 (Institut für Stadtgeschichte Frankfurt am Main).
44 Juden Akten 209 (Institut für Stadtgeschichte Frankfurt am Main).
45 Würfel, Historische Nachricht von der Judengemeinde in dem Hofmarkt Fürth, 5. Würfel's anti-Jewish tone is often harsher than that of Schudt. On the *takkanot* of Fürth see also: Litt, Jüdische Gemeindestatuten aus dem aschkenasischen Kulturraum, 133.

that "one needs to be able to distinguish men by their costume and thus one needs to be able to distinguish those who study from other men and servants". Therefore all students local and foreign had to wear ruffs. Würfel added here that all Jews wore big ruffs on Shabbat, while during the week students wore a small ruff, and those honored with the title *morenu* (our teacher) were always permitted to wear a big ruff.[46] Ruffs thus also functioned as a marker of internal difference within the Jewish community.

That typical Jewish Shabbat attire included the Shabbes cloak and a ruff is also confirmed by eighteenth-century engravings, many of which were engraved in Nuremberg, close to Fürth. The 1703 costume book *Neu-eröffnete Welt-Galleria* included an engraving of a "Frankfurt Jew and Jewess" produced by the Dutch engraver Caspar Luyken (1672–1708) and the Nuremberg engraver and publisher Christoph Weigel (1654–1725), who had worked together in Nuremberg since 1699.[47] For the spectator, the couple was probably to be identified as Jewish by the collar, the hat, and the cloak (though probably not a Shabbes cloak) of the male figure and the ruff and the winged bonnet of the female figure (Figure 2). The two female garments were mentioned, for example, in a 1785 inventory of possessions brought into marriage. When Rebecca Baruchen, the daughter of the communal leader Liebmann Baer from Breslau, was about to marry the Court Jew David Baruch in Bayreuth, she brought with her over 20 dresses, countless jewelry, many pieces of white cloth, and laces, but also one bonnet with "wings" (*Haube mit Flügeln*) and a ruff (*Halsfriess*) that together were worth more than 100 ducats.[48] Though the richness of her clothes was exceptional, these items seemingly belonged to a well-off family's closet.

The *Welt-Galleria*, like other early modern costume books, was a means to depict ideal types and to confirm a certain imagined order of early modern society.[49] Thus, in his introduction to the work, the Catholic Viennese preacher Abraham a Sancta Clara firmly pointed to the importance of dress as a marker of estate and origin and criticized the wearing of attire of other "nations". It is

---

46 Würfel, Historische Nachricht von der Judengemeinde in dem Hofmarkt Fürth, 151, § 110.
47 Abraham Sancta Clara, Christoph Weigel, and Caspar Luyken: *Neu-eröffnete Welt-Galleria worinnen sehr curios und begnügt unter die Augen kommen allerley Aufzüg und Kleidungen unterschiedlicher Stande und Nationen*. Nürnberg 1703, no 39. On the emergence of costume books see Ulrike Ilg: The Cultural Significance of Costume Books in Sixteenth-Century Europe, in: Catherine Richardson (ed.): *Clothing Culture, 1350–1650*. Aldershot 2004, 29–47. See also: Colding Smith: "Depicted with Extraordinary Skill". Ottoman Dress in Sixteenth-Century German Printed Costume Books, in: *Textile History* 44 (2013), 25–50.
48 Adolf Eckstein: *Geschichte der Juden im Markgrafentum Bayreuth*. Bayreuth 1907, 124–128.
49 Ilg, The Cultural Significance of Costume Books in Sixteenth-Century Europe, 43.

Figure 2: Frankfurter Jud und Jüdin, in: Abraham a Sancta Clara: *Neu-eröffnete Welt-Galleria: Worinnen sehr curios und begnügt under die Augen kommen allerley Aufzüg und Kleidung unterschiedlicher Stände und Nationen [. . .]*. Nürnberg 1703, Herzog August Bibliothek Wolfenbüttel © HAB http://diglib.hab.de/drucke/wt-4f-93/start.htm?image=00085.

therefore all the more interesting that the engraving of the Jewish couple was immediately preceded in the book by engravings of women and peasants from Regensburg and Nuremberg and was followed by a Dutch merchant and other Dutch figures but was not grouped together with the only other Jew in the volume, a Polish Jew (no. 71) who followed three other Polish figures: a nobleman, a hajduk (a foot soldier), and a peasant. Similar depictions of Fürth Jews can be found in the work of Johann Alexander Boener (1647–1720), a local engraver who produced a series of engravings of Nuremberg and Fürth, including the synagogue and the Jewish cemetery along with groups of Jews. In all of the engravings Jewish men and women were depicted with collars and ruffs and men with Shabbes cloaks. Although these garments were not worn daily, they marked the individuals as Jewish men and women (Figure 3).

Figure 3: Johann Alexander Boener: *Abbildung der Jüden und ihrer Weiber Trachten, in Fürdt, 1706.* Courtesy of Stadtarchiv Fürth, Bi 791, 13a.

It seems that non-Jews in Fürth and Frankfurt, and probably beyond, would have considered a Shabbes cloak, a ruff or collar and a beret, and a winged bonnet and a ruff for women as typical Jewish attire. Jewish authorities in both towns linked the permission to wear a Shabbes cloak and a ruff to residential rights. However, it is not entirely clear for how long the cohesive force of belonging really convinced Jews to wear these items. Already in the sumptuary laws of the Fürth community from 1770, the Jewish elders saw the need to emphasize that no Jewish burgher was allowed to leave the house on Shabbat and holidays without the Shabbes cloak.[50] Similarly, a 1786 source from Frankfurt debates the wearing of cloaks on work days and outside the Jewish street or synagogue. Here the magistrate instructed the Jewish inhabitants to always wear cloaks. A group of local Jews rejected this order and argued that they did not need such a cloak anymore to cover dirty or otherwise untidy garments, and that anyway these cloaks made them easily recognizable as Jews and thus vulnerable on the street. Moreover, there had never been an official municipal ordinance that obliged Jews to wear such a cloak.[51] The relation of this cloak to the Shabbes cloak is not entirely clear, but surely the complainants in this case had no interest in being recognized as Jews in the city of Frankfurt.

Conclusion

This comparative view of early modern Jewish dress in Poland and German-speaking lands has shown that certain garments turned into typical Jewish attire or into Jewish garments, at least among parts of the Jewish population. At the same time, the selective evidence has shown that sartorial distinction was a delicate issue. Though both Christian and Jewish authorities insisted on a regime of visual difference, Jews were not always easily recognized by Christians. Moreover, dress was a marker of difference also among Jews of different geographical origin and social status. For the German lands, we can assume that Jews developed distinctive regional variations of dress, though many apparently wore a typical attire distinct from that of local Christians by the eighteenth century. In the relatively conservative Jewish communities of Frankfurt am Main and Fürth, the black (Shabbes) cloak and the ruff (or collar) went back to sixteenth- and early seventeenth-century Spanish dress, which had fallen out of fashion. Jews of the Polish-Lithuanian Commonwealth, similarly, wore typical local garments, with differences in fabrics and embellishments, that became part of Jewish attire when they fell out of use among Polish noblemen.

---

50 Pinkas Fürth, D/Fu1/41, fol. 49v–50r (Central Archives for the History of the Jewish People, Jerusalem). Printed in: Litt, Jüdische Gemeindestatuten aus dem aschkenasischen Kulturraum, 265–266. Out of seven paragraphs on dress, only one pertains to men.
51 Juden Akten 171 (Institut für Stadtgeschichte Frankfurt am Main).

For all the particular differences between Jews from Poland and the German lands, one might describe the early modern emergence of a Jewish attire in similar terms, though with different garments. The developments diverged only in the nineteenth century, when at least larger segments of Jews in the German lands participated in the development of a bourgeois society and adopted the respective sartorial style, while Jews in the Kingdom of Poland remained legally unequal and maintained a strong group identity. The majority of the Polish Jewish population, with the exception of a small segment of integrationists, continued to wear distinctive Jewish costume in the nineteenth century and beyond, even when the Russian government sought to force the Jewish population to wear what they conceived as Christian or at least non-Jewish dress.

Beata Biedrońska-Słota and Maria Molenda
The Emergence of a Polish National Dress and Its Perception

Abstract: *This article examines the evolution of an early modern Polish national dress called the* kontusz *ensemble. It differed from the fashion of the West both in cut and look. The garment was mostly worn by the Polish nobility and was one of the distinguishing features of this estate and its ideology. It started forming in the sixteenth century, when knighthood was gradually abandoned and eventually replaced by an estate of landowners mainly involved in agriculture. These noblemen identified with the Sarmatian tradition and tried to prove their Sarmatian origins. Throughout the early modern period this garment was subject to modifications, but it retained its essential Eastern form.*

Introduction

The Polish national dress, the *kontusz* ensemble, differed from the fashion of Western Europe both in its cut and its accessories. It comprised a group of garments that might be defined as Eastern European. These garments belonged to the *szlachta* – the Polish nobility – and were one of the distinguishing features of this estate and its ideology. The term "national dress" first appeared only in the late eighteenth century, among the patriotic slogans of the Four-Year Sejm (1788–1792). However, it did not emerge out of nowhere: for more than two centuries the *kontusz* ensemble had functioned as the dress of the noblemen of the Polish-Lithuanian Commonwealth. To understand the significance of this attire it is necessary to consider some aspects of the *szlachta* habitus, the nobility's particular way of viewing the world and expressing emotions.

This article presents the development of the dress of the Polish nobility from the fifteenth to the nineteenth century. First, it describes the dress of medieval Polish knights; second, it discusses the emergence of the Sarmatian ideology and dress and the changes it underwent in the eighteenth century; finally, it concludes with a glance toward the nineteenth-century perception of the Sarmatian tradition. The article focuses on male dress, because female dress developed very differently, being strongly influenced by Western fashion.[1]

---

1 For more information on Polish female dress see: Maria Gutkowska-Rychlewska: *Historia ubiorów*. Wrocław 1968, 423–436, 529–541, 688–706, 768–804.

Medieval Forerunners

In medieval Poland, like elsewhere in Europe, it was important for people to show that they belonged to a certain estate, were of a certain social rank, or had a certain occupation. The *szlachta* was a direct successor of the knightly estate, so its essence was defined by the craft of war. In the Middle Ages, we find a number of examples of attempts at sartorial self-determination through a combination of Western and Eastern elements of fashion.

If we were to look for a garment that was representative of Polish elites already in the medieval period, we would have to point to the *szuba*, a kind of a long overcoat made from expensive textiles. The *szuba* came to Poland from the east in the fourteenth century, via Lithuanian and Ruthenian influences.[2] It was popular among European elites of the period generally to combine different regional garments: from the West (especially German and Italian fashion), from the East, and from the South (particularly from Hungary). Hungarian dress was relatively widespread and was recognized in Italy and elsewhere. In the eyes of some foreigners, Polish clothing was seen as something of a "corrupt" form of Hungarian attire.[3]

The Polish national costume began to acquire its main distinctive features already in the Middle Ages, when the mighty Byzantine Empire still thrived in the East. The Byzantine court in Constantinople, with its splendor inherited from the Roman Empire and enriched through relations with Persian Sasanians and Abbasid Muslims, became the source of cultural inspiration for Christians and Muslims alike.[4] Constantinople served for other countries as a source of conceptual models, such as forms of Oriental dress. As a result, the basic concept of a costume consisting of a modified tunic with a coat worn over it was established in the Byzantine Empire. The costumes made according to this basic form took on various shapes in different countries, depending on local tradition

---

2 Danuta Poppe: Szuba średniowieczna w Polsce i na Rusi, in: Maria Dembiński (ed.): *Szkice z dziejów materialnego bytowania społeczeństwa polskiego*. Wrocław 1989, 11–39.

3 Giulinao Passero: *Giuliano Passero cittadino napoletano o sia prima pubblicazione in istampa, che delle Storie in forma di Giornali, le quali sotto nome di questo autore finora erano andate manoscritte.* Naples 1785, 242; Władysław Pociecha: *Królowa Bona (1494–1557). Czasy i ludzie odrodzenia*, vol. 1. Poznań 1949, 203.

4 Beata Biedrońska-Słotowa: *Polski ubiór narodowy zwany kontuszowym*. Cracow 2005, 18–28; Ernst H. Kantorowicz: Gods in Uniform, in: id.: *Selected Studies*. New York 1965, 7–24; André Grabar, *L'empereur dans l'art Byzantin*. London 1971, 48, pl. IV; Elizabeth Piltz: *Le costume official des dignitaries byzantins à l'epoque Paléologue*. Uppsala 1994.

and the intensity of contacts with the East.[5] A notable distinction thus began to appear between the types of dress worn in Eastern Europe, particularly in Poland, and the completely different styles of dress worn in Western Europe.[6]

The Emergence of a Polish National Costume

The term "national costume" as used to describe the *kontusz* ensemble relates to the Polish nation in the early modern sense; that is, "nation" here refers exclusively to the Polish *nobility*. The emergence of a particular form of dress in Poland was closely connected to the development of the early modern Polish state, which was increasingly governed by a distinguished social group comprised of landowners of varying degrees of wealth. The sixteenth century was a period of profound transformations in Polish society. The knighthood was then being abandoned in line with the growth of landed estates established by those who preferred to occupy themselves with farming and the profits it generated. The group of landed gentry began to grow.[7] Nobles made up ten percent of the population, a much larger proportion than in most parts of Western Europe. With the emergence of a political system that had the nobility at the center of political representation, a need arose for a suitable ideology to reflect this group's growing power and influence. For the Polish nobility Sarmatism became such an ideology.

With the ideology of Sarmatism the *szlachta* defined itself as a group that was not only *better than* but also essentially *different from* the rest of the population. Following the theses put forward by certain Polish Renaissance authors, attempts were made to demonstrate the Polish gentry's historical origins in, and contemporary similarity to, the ancient Sarmatians, migrating pastoral

---

5 Patricia L. Baker et al.: *Silk for the Sultans. Ottoman Imperial Garments from Topkapi Palace.* Milan 1996; Tim Dawson: A Tunic from Eastern Anatolia, in: *Costume* 36 (2002), 93–99; Corina Nicolescu: *Istoria Costumului de Curte in Ţările Romane Secolete XIV–XVIII.* Bucharest 1970; Hermann Goetz: The History of Persian Costume, in: Alexander Upham Pope and Phyllis Ackerman (eds.): *A Survey of Persian Art, from Prehistoric Times to the Present,* vol. 3. New York 1938, 2227–2256.

6 It should be noted that Poland had trade, diplomatic and personal ties with the Byzantine state already in the twelfth century. Maria, the daughter of Sviatopolk Iziaslawich, the Grand Prince of Kiev and Byzantine princess Barbara Komnena, married Piotr Włostowicz (d. 1153), a palatine of the Polish prince Bolesław III Wrymouth and brought with her richly decorated costumes, see: Gutkowska-Rychlewska, Historia ubiorów, 276–277.

7 Ibid., 37.

tribes of Iranian origin.[8] The core tenet of the Sarmatian myth held that the ancestors of the Polish nobility conquered East-Central Europe in the "old times",
as Jan Długosz, a Polish chronicler of the fifteenth century put it. The *szlachta*
glorified its own way of living, fundamentally opposed to urban living and hos-
tile towards foreign influence.

With the emergence of Sarmatism the myth of a particular and ancient
Polish tradition was born. Although we do not really know how it evolved, its
consequences have lasted for centuries. In this way, the sixteenth century, the
time of flourishing humanist ideas, also saw the birth of a concept that provided
the basis for national chauvinism and, later, xenophobia. (It should be noted,
however, that the internally inconsistent Sarmatian humanism provided an example of openness to others, including people of other religions.) It was also at
this time that the Polish "Sarmatians", as the adherents of Sarmatism among
the gentry came to be called, discovered the appeal of the so-called "golden liberty", the political system of the Polish-Lithuanian Commonwealth after the
Union of Lublin (1569), in which all nobles, irrespective of their social status,
elected the king, controlled the legislature, and enjoyed substantial legal rights.
The concept may sound glorious, but some historians have argued that over
time it led to a growing anarchy in the country's political life.[9] The spirit of
knighthood still predominated at the beginning of the sixteenth century, but it
was not always ideologically compatible with the Sarmatian attitude, which was
expressed mainly in the desire to accumulate goods and to exercise political
power. Parallel with the Sarmatian tradition grew the concept of the Polish gentry as heirs of the citizen virtues of the ancient Romans. Some people, however,
lamented the loss of the knightly spirit and criticized "farmerization", the quiet
rural life away from the centers of humanism. This Sarmatian attitude, together
with the landlords' lifestyle, resulted in gradual changes of attire and the emergence of the distinctive male dress that later became known as the *kontusz* ensemble.[10] This gradual transformation of a knight into a member of the landed
nobility, fueled by the Sarmatian ideology,[11] resulted in male dress becoming

---

8 Tadeusz Ulewicz: Około genealogii sarmatyzmu (spóźnione podjęcie nieprzedawnionej dys-
kusji), in: *Pamiętnik Słowiański* 1 (1949), 101–114; Tadeusz Mańkowski: *Genealogia sarmatyzmu*.
Warsaw 1946; Tadeusz Ulewicz: *Sarmacja. Studium z problematyki słowiańskiej XV i XVI w.* Cracow
1950.
9 Maria Bogucka: *The Lost World of the "Sarmatians". Custom as the Regulator of Polish Social
Life in Early Modern Times.* Warsaw 1996.
10 Beata Biedrońska-Słota: *Sarmatism. Dreams of Power.* Cracow 2010.
11 See for example, Maciej z Miechowa (1456–1523): *Descriptio Sarmatiarum Asianae et
Europianae et eorum quae in eis continent.* Cracow 1521.

increasingly similar to that worn in the Persian and Ottoman Empires. This kind of costume soon became a distinctive tool of the gentry's consolidation. It marked its wearer's social affiliation and even, according to some observers, expressed the group's worldview. It testified to its wearer's outlook on life, and was also a means of propaganda. It declared one's attachment to tradition, which often meant benightedness and provincialism.

In Poland the spread of male attire sewn in accordance with Persian and Ottoman fashion was facilitated not only by the Sarmatian tradition but also by the presence of original Oriental costumes and their integration into the Polish lifestyle.[12] Original costumes from the Orient, mostly from the Ottoman Empire, were brought to Poland as honorary costumes, usually given to diplomats as a sign of respect. Known as *hilat*,[13] these costumes were sewn from the richest silk fabrics, with entwined gold and silver threads and decorated with sophisticated patterns, often designed by miniature-painters. An oft-cited example comes from a letter of 1549, written by the wife of Sultan Suleyman, Hurrem Sultan (also known as Roxelana), to King Sigismund II Augustus: "[…] To not leave the letter empty […] I sent two pairs of trousers with a shirt, with a belt for them, six scarves and a towel."[14] An envoy of King Sigismund II Augustus noted in 1557 that during the farewell ceremony "a gold-threaded lower dress was brought and another broad one to put over, also gold-threaded, accompanied by several pieces of *kemkha* [silk textile]".[15] He further remarked that "after the banquet Chaush Pasha assisted the envoy and a couple of his men to a separate room where, as a sign of favor, they are dressed in varicolored gold-threaded kaftans, with various figures of birds and other creatures".[16] In a similar way, Sefer Muratowicz, a diplomat sent to Persia by King Sigismund III in 1601, was given a green damask *żupan*, with a gold-threaded dress on top.[17] One may assume that ready-made Oriental costumes, brought to Poland and used on certain important occasions to demonstrate

---

12 Przemysław Mrozowski: Ubiór jako wyraz świadomości narodowej szlachty polskiej XVI–XVIII wieku, in: Anna Sieradzka and Krystyna Turska (eds.): *Ubiory w Polsce. Materiały III Sesji Klubu Kostiumologii i Tkaniny Artystycznej przy Oddziale Warszawskim Stowarzyszenia Historyków Sztuki*. Warsaw 1994, 19–27.

13 Patricia L. Baker: *Islamic Textiles*. London 1995, 93.

14 Zygmunt Abrahamowicz and Ananiasz Zajączkowski (eds.): *Katalog dokumentów tureckich: dokumenty do dziejów Polski i krajów ościennych w latach 1455–1672*. Warsaw 1959, 103.

15 Józef Ignacy Kraszewski: *Podróże i poselstwa polskie do Turcji*. Cracow 1869, 20.

16 Łukasz Gołębiowski: *Ubiory w Polsce od najdawniejszych czasów aż do chwil obecnych, sposobem dykcjonarza ułożone*. Cracow 1861, 132.

17 Sefer Muratowicz: *Relacya Sefera Muratowicza, obywatela warszawskiego, od Zygmunta III, króla polskiego, dla sprawowania rzeczy wysłanego do Persyi w r. 1602. Rzecz z starego rękopisma wybrana y teraz dopiero do druku podana*. Warsaw 1777.

splendor and magnificence, had an impact on the preferences and tastes of Polish noblemen.

In addition to textual and visual sources confirming the influx of Oriental costumes to Poland, we find also material remains. When brought to Poland, Oriental costumes were often reworked into liturgical vestments and adapted for the Church's needs, though we cannot be sure whether these costumes were first worn or were turned right away into liturgical vestments. This adaptation, however, probably explains why original Oriental costumes from before the nineteenth century have not been preserved in any Polish collection. What is preserved, however, are original precious textiles in secondarily-assembled paraments.[18]

The richness of Persian and Ottoman textiles, costumes, armor, and jewelry appealed to the Sarmatians' taste. Colorful clothing, furs, and jewels were also calculable capital investments for the *szlachta*. Contacts with neighboring countries had had a significant influence on this taste. Clergyman and writer Szymon Starowolski (1588–1650) mentions that wide and sweeping fur coats (lined with sables and ermines) were borrowed from the Russians, coats for soldiers from the Tatars, and short, very tight jackets, wide shoes, leather greaves, and coats from the Swedes.[19] In France, England, or the Netherlands such exotic items as fur coats were most often a decorative element, having the status of an oddity; in Old Poland, by contrast, Oriental garments and accessories were present as an integral part of everyday life.

Among Western observers, Polish fashion and love of exotic things evoked rather critical reactions. Frenchmen found it was odd to wear such long, heavy garments lined with fur, given the climate. In France, fashion was dictated by the court centered around the king. In the eyes of foreigners, the Polish lifestyle, in its fashion and its feasts, resembled Persian customs. In this era of European expansion, Europeans felt superior to "savage, uncivilized" people. For masquerades and balls it was common to dress up as exotic figures, and alongside Indians, Arabs, Chinese, Persians, and Turks, there were Polish and Muscovite costumes, too, an expression of the negative assessment of Sarmatian fashion and taste.[20] Karol Ogier, a French writer and diplomat, wrote in 1635 that praying Polish voivodes wearing national clothes reminded him of Eastern magi bowing before baby Jesus "with great grandeur and in a long suite of courtiers

---

18 Magdalena Piwocka: A Turkish Hilat at Jasna Góra, in: *Arma Virumque Cano. Profesorowi Zdzisławowi Żygulskiemu jun. w osiemdziesięciopięciolecie urodzin.* Cracow 2006, 343–350.

19 Janusz Tazbir: *Kultura szlachecka w Polsce. Rozkwit-upadek-relikty.* Poznań 1998, 158.

20 Ibid. 169; Larry Wolff: *Inventing Eastern Europe. The Map of Civilization on the Mind of the Enlightenment.* Stanford 1994, esp. chapter 1.

and camels".[21] Jakub Sobieski had an audience with Pope Paul V in 1612, during which his servant was terribly drunk and eventually tripped, scattering devotional items. Allegedly, the pope was amused and asked who the servant was: "a baptized Turk or Tatar?"[22] An account of the arrival of the Polish envoy to Paris in 1645 by a French woman, Francesca de Motteville, also expresses a Western person's view of Sarmatian pomp: "it has shown the ancient glory that was taken by the Persians from the Medes [...] Although Scythians were never famous for indulging pleasures, their descendants, close neighbors of the Turks today, seem to be striving to imitate the grandiosity and richness of the Turkish sultan."[23] Polish lords were

> wearing silks interwoven with gold and silver. The textiles of their clothes were so costly, so beautiful, in such vivid colors, that they tore the eyes. On the caftans jewels shimmered. It has to be said however that among all of this richness the splendor was very close to the great barbarism; they do not wear underwear at all, they sleep not on bed sheets but on animal hides, which they wrap themselves with [...] their heads are shaven, only on the top is a small flock of hair hanging down to the back.[24]

The Polish national costume that developed in the seventeenth century was highly ornate, colorful, and richly adorned with jewelry. It consisted of a *żupan*, a long front-buttoned garment, most often crimson in color, similar to Turkish and Persian dress, and a *delia*, a long overcoat, whose shape – with its long, dangling, decorative sleeves reaching to the floor, thrown to the back and hanging along the line of the back – closely imitated the dress used at the sultan's court. The *delia* was often lined with fur and had a wide fur collar. In the front it was often braided with haberdashery tapes. The *kontusz*, a kind of caftan worn over the *żupan*, first appeared in the seventeenth century and grew steadily in popularity thereafter. The head was dressed in a *kołpak* – a high hat with a wide fur band and a decorative bundle of heron or ostrich feathers fixed in a *szkofia*, a kind of brooch. The whole ensemble was decorated with jewelry in the form of golden or silver haw-shaped or hazelnut-shaped buttons, meticulously decorated with granulation and filigree, and set with gems. A necessary addition to this Sarmatian costume was a *karabela* – a Turkish-style saber – hanging on straps at the left side. Expensive Polish calf-length shoes, made from yellow or red leather, indicated the nobleman's wealth. The haircut was

21 Karol Ogier: *Dziennik podróży do Polski 1635–1636*, vol. 1. Gdańsk 1950, 173.
22 Jakub Sobieski: *Peregrynacyja po Europie (1607–1613). Droga do Baden (1638)*, edited by Józef Długosz. Wrocław 1991, 206.
23 See Françoise de Motteville: *Anna Austriaczka i jej dwór*. Warsaw 1978, 90.
24 Ibid., 91.

also distinctive: fashionable Sarmatians shaved their heads high, leaving only a central strip of hair running along the skull (Figure 1). This haircut quickly became a principal sign of belonging to the social group, much as facial hair was shaped according to fashion. Jędrzej Kitowicz (1728–1804), a historian and memoirist, wrote: "one who dressed as a Pole had to wear a moustache, and could not shave it without making a clown of himself."[25]

Figure 1: *Votive painting of Albert Stanisław Borkowski of Borków*, c. 1631, St. Thomas and St. Stanisław Church in Piotrawin. Photo by Beata Biedrońska-Słota.

The dress of Krzysztof Zbaraski, as represented in his portrait in the Lviv Painting Gallery, is a good illustration of this phenomenon. Zbaraski (ca.1580–1627) acted in various roles as a statesman of Poland, including being sent abroad as a diplomat on various missions (Figure 2). The best known of these is his mission to Istanbul to the court of Sultan Mustafa I in 1622–1624 to negotiate the liberation of Polish knights who had been taken captive, together with their commander, field hetman Stanisław Koniecpolski, after the defeat at Cecora (in Moldavia) in 1620. Zbaraski also wanted to convince the Turkish side that Poland had not

25 Jędrzej Kitowicz: *Opis obyczajów za panowania Augusta III*. Wrocław 1951, 465.

Figure 2: *Portrait of Krzysztof Zbaraski*, c. 1627, Lviv Painting Gallery. Photo by Beata Biedrońska-Słota.

promised to pay a war tribute. He departed from Końskowola on September 9, 1622, and returned there on Easter, 1623, having successfully completed the mission that would later grow into a legend.[26] As part of his efforts to make the mission effective, Zbaraski had gone to the Sultan's court wearing a costume that demonstrated his high rank and his noble stance, as shown in his painted image. Zbaraski is shown in the portrait in a long white *żupan* of mid-calf length, girded with a soft red silk sash and a narrower leather belt supporting saber slings on which a *karabela* hangs. The *żupan* is buttoned under the neck, with a clasp adorned by a large red gem. A splendid *delia* worn on the *żupan* is made of Turkish gold lamé and silver lamé fabric of the type known as *serâser*, with

---

26 Samuel Twardowski: *Przeważna legacyja Krzysztofa Zbaraskiego od Zygmunta III do sołtana Mustafy*. Warsaw 2000, 295.

a large-scale pattern of golden peacock feathers on silver background. The whole *delia* is lined with fur and has a large straight fur collar and very long sleeves thrown to the back and is fastened with decorative large buttons placed on the margin of one fly. Short shoes made of yellow leather reach above the ankles. The dress is complete with a splendid *kołpak* on the head, which has a wide fur surround and a rich *szkofia* decorated with rubies and supporting a very high bunch of feathers. According to a written description by Samuel Twardowski,[27] the magnificent crest especially attracted attention, so that even the sultan himself wanted to buy it. It deserves special attention that the costume worn by Zbaraski in the portrait today may be considered at first glance a Turkish dress. His attire suggests that in the seventeenth century this costume was already such an integral element of Polish tradition that the Polish envoy had chosen to wear it on his diplomatic mission to the Ottoman Empire. The picture presents a synthesis of all the distinctive characteristics of the epoch and provides evidence that Oriental costumes had become part of Polish tradition.

Another episode in the royal court demonstrates the extent to which Polish costumes inspired by Oriental fashion were seen both as Oriental dress and as typically Polish, already in the seventeenth century. When Tatar troops were expected to join the Crown's army in 1654, the Court decided to fund and prepare costumes for these Tatars and their commanders. These costumes, which were given to the Tatar envoys, appeared as typically Polish: *kontuszes, żupans, ferezjas* (long overcoats), and hats, all made to Oriental fashion of expensive western materials.[28] Another example was the preparation, at the wish of the king, of a *żupan* and a *ferezja* from exquisite cloths for the Tatar envoy Dedesh Aga and his numerous retinue, who were sent by the Crimean Khan in 1655.[29] Similar gifts were given to the Tatar envoy Alisz Aga, sent to the king in 1655. He received magnificent dresses from Venetian velvet lined with fur and a *kontusz* with golden loops and braiding.[30] A dress assembled in this way also made a strong impression on foreign observers already in the seventeenth century. The Irish physician of John III Sobieski, Bernard O'Connor, recorded in his memoir: "Sobieski used to wear a native dress and this is different from other European dresses and incomparably more solemn."[31]

---

27 Ibid.

28 Archiwum Główne Akt Dawnych (Central Archives of Historical Records in Warsaw) [AGAD], Archive of the Treasury of the Crown III, vol. 5, 680–681.

29 Ibid., 699a.

30 Ibid., 701.

31 Quoted from Julian Ursyn Niemcewicz: Zbiór pamiętników o dawnej Polsce, in: Julian Ursyn Niemcewicz (ed.): *Dzieła*. Cracow 1883–1886, vol. 4, 395.

The form of the Polish costume underwent modifications during subsequent centuries, but its basic form as influenced by Oriental dress was maintained. By the middle of the eighteenth century it attained its classical form, consisting of a *żupan*, a *kontusz*, and a *delia*. The form of the *kontusz* had changed and acquired its distinctive split sleeves. The *kontusz* was invariably girded at the waist with a decorative silk sash, gold lamé or silver lamé, woven using a large amount of golden and silver threads (Figure 3). Like most elements of the costume, the sash was of Oriental provenance too.

Figure 3: *Kontusz costume*, c. 1770, National Museum in Cracow.

Differences within Polish Nobility: The Myth of Equality

The Polish costume described above appears mostly to be that of an ideal type of the wealthy Polish nobility. However, one should not forget that the nobility was not a homogeneous group. The *szlachta* proclaimed the equality of its estate in the sixteenth century and never created any formal hierarchy; thus, in theory, every nobleman had the same status, including the wealthiest magnates, and this alleged equality was regarded as the foundation of the nobility's democracy and free elections. However, social differences among Polish noblemen remained, which were also visible in their costumes, though less in terms of styles than in the embellishments that were added and the quality of the fabrics that were used.

In the seventeenth century, another line of conflict emerged, between the *szlachta* and the king. The conflict between the *szlachta* and King Sigismund III Vasa, which lasted from 1606 to 1608, was called the war between *czupryna* and *ponta*, that is, between the Polish hairstyle described above and the Spanish style of beard trim. Sigismund III, who usually dressed in western (Spanish) fashion, had a pointy goatee. One foreign observer remarked that the king's Spanish attire distinguished him from his subjects, the Polish *szlachta*, who did not like this attempt at distinction. The king was supposed to be the king of kings after all, meaning a member of Polish nobility. The king's trusted man Marcin Wolski was also criticized for wearing foreign clothing.[32] Sigismund III wore Polish dresses in certain situations to gain the support of the *szlachta*, as for example during the siege of Smoleńsk (1609–1611).[33] A similar story is told of Jan II Kazimierz (1609–1672), who is said to have changed his clothing at a critical point in the Zborów battle of 1649, during the Khmelnytsky Uprising, when Ukrainian Cossacks and their Crimean Tatar allies fought against the Polish-Lithuanian Commonwealth. At one point, while cheering on the Polish troops to hold ground, the king changed from French into Polish dress. After the settlement with the hetman of the Cossacks was signed and the king had returned to Warsaw, he went back to wearing French clothes, again to the displeasure of the *szlachta*.[34]

The question of visual belonging to the Polish *szlachta* must have been even more serious for foreign kings elected to the Polish throne. To win the favor of the *szlachta*, these monarchs used their image in a particular way. A remarkable illustration of this phenomenon is a portrait of August III from Saxony painted by Louis de Silvestre (1737) (Figure 4). August III is presented in Polish clothing, wearing a red *kontusz* with lapels, a *żupan* tied with a sash

---

32 Walter Leitsch: Strój i naród w Polsce w trzeciej tercji XVII wieku, czyli jak spodnie nabrały znaczenia politycznego, in: *Barok. Historia–Literatura–Sztuka* 12 (1999), 11–31, esp. 18–19.
33 Ibid., 17–18.
34 Jan. K. Ostrowski: Myśli o portrecie staropolskim, in: Anna Marczak-Krupa (ed.): *Portret. Funkcja – forma symbol, Materiały sesji Stowarzyszenia Historyków Sztuki, Toruń, grudzień 1986.* Warsaw 1990, 171–185, esp. 174.

Figure 4: Louis de Silvestre: *Portrait of King Augustus III in a Polish costume*, c. 1737, National Museum in Cracow.

and a ribbon with the badge of the White Eagle order; in addition, he has a star of the White Eagle order on his chest and a Golden Fleece order on his neck. His hair is cut in accordance with Polish fashion. Before him, August III's father, August II, had also utilized portraits that styled him as a Polish nobleman, an image modeled on Jan III Sobieski and to the liking of the Polish *szlachta*.

While in the seventeenth century, in independent Poland, wearing a Polish costume expressed belonging to and self-identification with the *szlachta,* the eighteenth century, when Poland was divided, saw an in-creasing politicization of dress and fashion. The presence of Western fash-ion, perceived as foreign to Poland, was a point of heated dispute in the worldview of Polish elites, as disagreements over frock or *kontusz,* wig or moustache, entered the language of politics. Used as an identifying sign of "true patriots", traditional Polish costume enriched the repertoire of im-ages that were drawn upon in ideological and patriotic disputes, far be-yond the question of *szlachta* identities alone. The choice of clothing became an element of political play, as is finely illustrated by the example of Jan Potocki, who in 1788 planned to gain a seat in the Sejm as a delegate of the Poznań voivodeship. Potocki was raised abroad, and spoke better French than Polish. Nevertheless, he appeared in a *kontusz,* first at *kontrakty,* an annual local meeting of the *szlachta* in Poznań, then at a *sejmik* in Środa, eliciting an enthusiastic reaction among the *szlachta* (Figure 5).[35] The decision to appear in what was perceived by members of the *szlachta* as both noble and patriotic dress was a well-taken step.

Figure 5: *Kontusz sash,* Słuck, c. 1780, National Museum in Cracow.

This new and more political perception of dress, however, did not mean that dis-tinctions among members of the Polish nobility disappeared. The historian

---

35 Jarosław Dumanowski: *Świat rzeczy szlachty wielkopolskiej w XVIII wieku.* Toruń 2006, 194.

Jędrzej Kitowicz notes that the magnates did not know how to stand out from the common crowd of nobility, because every time they created a new style or trend the *szlachta* immediately imitated it.[36] A great illustration of this is the example of Piotr Sapieha (1701–1771), born in Dresden, voivode of Smoleńsk, owner of huge parts of land in Lithuania, and an heir of the Opaliński family and successor to their real estate in Great Poland. According to Kitowicz, Sapieha was since the years of his youth characterized by a love of tasteful and exquisite attire and was often very irritated by the *szlachta*'s tendency to imitate his clothing. On one occasion, he ordered a *czechman*, a long overcoat with sleeves, sewn from white multan (a light woolen textile of long, fluffy hair), lined with blue velvet and with an order badge attached to it.[37] Sapieha managed to present himself brilliantly in Poznań courts, being the only one wearing a multan white *czechman* with an order badge. But when he came to the courts the next time almost all the noblemen of Poznań were wearing multan *czechmans*, hemmed if not completely lined with velvet. "And he was even more surprised, when this year in Warsaw he saw plenty of multan *czechmans*. He presented his own to the cook; and immediately multan *czechmans* from the lords have gone to the stablemen and administrators."[38]

The Perception of the Polish National Costume in the Eighteenth Century

The Polish national costume gained its final shape in the middle of the eighteenth century. It still bore political meaning, as it distinguished the members of the nobility, the estate whose leading role in the state was manifested in the election of kings and in the *liberum veto* rule that gave each member of the noble assembly the right to nullify any legislation. During skirmishes between the *szlachta* and the Saxon army in 1715, clothing was seen as an expression of national, ideological, and religious identity: "nobody who wore a German garment could have been sure of his life."[39] The increasing influence of Western fashion on the Polish

---

36 Jędrzej Kitowicz: *Opis obyczajów za panowania Augusta III*, vol. 2, ed. by Roman Pollak. Wrocław 2003, 528.
37 Irena Turnau: *Słownik ubiorów. Tkaniny, wyroby pozatkackie, skóry, broń i klejnoty oraz barwy znane w Polsce od średniowiecza do początku XIX w*. Warsaw 1999, 119.
38 Kitowicz, Opis, 528–529.
39 See Józef A. Gierowski: *Między saskim absolutyzmem a złotą wolnością. Z dziejów wewnętrznych Rzeczypospolitej w latach 1712–1715*. Wrocław 1953, 303.

szlachta was accompanied by a tempestuous discourse about the role of clothing in upholding the tradition of the nobility and in defining national identity. Already in the second half of the seventeenth century, the poet and satirist Wacław Potocki (1621–1696) had described the presence of foreign attire in the *szlachta*'s wardrobe in a very negative light: "We have renounced everything along with our ancestors' dress, when we covered ourselves in foreign [dress] out of contempt [for our tradition]."[40] The acceptance of foreign fashion in this way was perceived as being contrary to the essence of Polish nobility: to history, tradition, and the ancestral cult. It would have evoked the outrage of the ancestors if they could have seen it. The author and poet Jakub Kazimierz Haur wrote in his "Ekonomia ziemiańska" ("The economy of landed noblemen"): "As then the old good habit dies, the same way new fashions of today's century are raised, as often and everywhere they change into different shape, model, and kinds not stolid. If people of old rose from the dead, they would gather that mad Shrovetide ceremonies are constantly held in this world."[41]

The contemporary historian Jędrzej Kitowicz (1728–1804) presented a detailed account of eighteenth-century costumes: "At the beginning of the rule of Augustus III (King of Poland 1733–1763) few gentlemen wore foreign attire, except for members of Czartoryskis' house, Lubomirski, the Voivode of Krakow, and a couple of others, who already under Augustus II (1670–1733, elected King of Poland 1697–1706, 1709–1733) had switched to German attire." Though the Saxon court was dressed according to French fashion at the time, it was perceived as German fashion in Poland. The same author further relates how during the coronation of Augustus III all participants were dressed like the king, according to the Polish fashion. Nevertheless, immediately after the ceremony, when the king put on "German" clothing again, Polish aristocracy immediately changed into Western European fashion.[42]

During the time of the Four-Year Sejm the question of a uniform for the non-existent army was discussed, prompting interesting reflections of the satirists: "What do sharovary [a wide kind of trousers, associated at that time in Poland with Turks or Cossacks] have in common with the Polish heart, or does one put on and take off vices along with clothes [...]. Does a cubit of cloth make one braver?"[43] On the other hand, the problem of proper dress for the Polish nobility

---

40 Quoted from: Jan S. Bystroń: *Dzieje obyczajów w dawnej Polsce wiek XVI–XVIII*, vol. 2. Warsaw 1933, 443.
41 Quoted from: Ibid.
42 Kitowicz, Opis, 475–478.
43 Irena Turnau: Rozwój ubioru narodowego od około 1530 do 1795 roku, in: *Kwartalnik Historii Kultury Materialnej* 34 (1986), 413–424, esp. 417.

was important enough to be taken up by satirical Sarmatian writers of the eighteenth century, who ridiculed foreign fashion. A nobleman who submitted to the demands of foreign fashion was described as being like an eagle turned into an owl: "Oh, youth you are fashionable so! / Long kontusz cut to frock / Barber sprinkled head with powder / Made him such an ugly cut."[44] In the eighteenth century, the *szlachta* wanted to limit travel and legally prohibit young people from going abroad, "because those who came back from these voyages seemed as though they were members of some other nation".[45] This generational change was reflected by inventories, such as that of Biechów chatelain Bartłomiej Szołdarski and his son Ludwik from 1755. The father owned only national clothing and the son only Western dress, wigs, and stock ties. The chatelain's parade ensemble consisted of a crimson *kontusz* lined with stoat fur and a pink satin *żupan*, while for grand occasions the son wore a non-sheared velvet dress with golden loops braided along the ribs, a white vest decorated with silver and with golden buttons, and blue velvet trousers with golden buttons.[46]

This development implied not only a generational but also a social change. The gradual rejection of Sarmatian fashion in favor of Western European fashion during the eighteenth century implied a social devaluation of Sarmatian ideology. Among members of the *szlachta* who favored Western fashion, the *kontusz* became a costume for servants, a livery. This was the case, for example, among the servants of the Czernichów voivode Józef Potulicki at an early point in 1735.[47]

Satirists and moralists criticized the abandonment of national dress, and prophesied that the foreign fashion would bring along with it cultural practices from Spain or Italy. Some thought that the disappearance of the *kontusz* ensemble would cause the disappearance of the Polish language as well.[48] Stanisław Witkowski, a poet and satirist active in the early seventeenth century, wrote: "Today you cannot recognize a Pole anymore; Italians, Frenchmen, / All over the princely courts, the Polish language is sure to perish. / The common garments are to perish too, because today *stradyjoty*, / *Rubany*, such capes with golden lace, / *Saltebrety*, *kolety* and other inventions."[49]

---

44 Zbigniew Kuchowicz: *Obyczaje staropolskie XVII–XVIII wieku.* Łódź 1975, 252–253. English translation by Maciej Walasek.
45 Sowa, Fantomowe, 265.
46 Dumanowski, Świat, 200.
47 Ibid., 192.
48 Janusz Tazbir: *Kultura szlachecka w Polsce. Rozkwit–upadek–relikty.* Poznań 1998, 45.
49 Stanisław Witkowski, *Złota Wolność Koronna Seymom y Ziazdom na potomne czasy służąca. Z Deklaracyą krótką ku zatrzymaniu Staropolskiey Wolności po zawarciu Zgody y Miłości Braterskiey przez Seym Warszawski w Roku 1609.* Cracow 1609. n.p. Stradyjota/stradyjotka, ruban, saltebret/saltembret and kolet are garments.

During the reigns of Augustus II and Augustus III, Polish costume was long, nearly to the floor. After the middle of the eighteenth century it changed markedly. *Kontusz* and *żupan* became shorter, reaching only slightly below the knees. Details of the dress also changed: the sleeves became much wider and longer, and wider-split. Near the end of the eighteenth century the details of the *kontusz* style changed again, giving the costumes a rather modest, classical look. Shirt collars appeared which covered the *żupan's* collar; shirt cuffs emerged from the *żupan* sleeves. These changes were modifications of the cuts' details, which resulted from general changes in Polish male fashion. However, the *kontusz* and *żupan* did not disappear, but still kept their position as basic elements of the *szlachta* dress. Over all these periods winter dresses, called first *szuba* or *delia*, then *bekiesza* and later *kierezja* or *opończa*, were made of fur, often lined with velvet, typically crimson in color, and tied under the neck with a thick silver or golden string.

Polish dress and its adaptations to western fashion also drew the attention of foreigners, who recorded their impressions in their memoirs. Foreigners saw a lack of taste and unfamiliarity with the rules of elegance in the Polish habit of freely combining Polish and foreign fashion. Nathaniel William Wraxall (1751–1831), an English diplomat and traveler, described Polish dress as follows: "There is something martial, rude, and characteristic in the Polish habit, which by no means displeases. It breaks that tame and insipid uniformity of external appearance, which, in the course of the present century, has almost entirely supplanted the ancient national distinctions of Europe."[50] Another foreigner visiting Poland, Friedrich Schulz, a traveler from Livonia, noted that

> saber, smallsword, jacket, French dress, national dress and frock, haircut and style, headdress or hat, everyone puts on what they like, these things are even mixed in the weirdest way. Often younger and older people of high estates are seen in a round hat, haircut, sharovars, English frock and French smallsword; or Polish saber, French attire, embroidered vest [...] nankeen trousers and English shoes with leggings; or finally English frock, vest, leather trousers, bootees with garters, head curled all over and a Polish four-edged hat on it. These are peculiarities that no one is offended with here, even though they show a lack of taste and the greatest negligence.[51]

50 Nathaniel William Wraxall, *Memoirs of the Courts of Berlin, Dresden, Warsaw and Vienna in the years 1777, 1778, and 1779*, vol. 1. London 1800, 399–400.
51 Fryderyk Schulz: *Podróże Inflantczyka z Rygi do Warszawy i po Polsce w latach 1791–1793*. Warsaw 1956, 246.

An example of such a combination can be found in a portrait of the Kalisz voivode Ignacy Działyński from around 1765. He is wearing a *kontusz* and a *żupan* combined with a wig on his head.[52]

Social Distinction and Dress Regulation

From the sixteenth to the eighteenth century, clothes were valuable movable property.[53] They were usually placed at the beginning of post-mortem inventories or right after silverware and jewelry. Polish researchers, especially since the 1950s, have made frequent use of the inventories as a source for the history of material culture. Among the surviving documents are inventories of possessions of noblemen as well as burghers and even peasants. Historian Jarosław Dumanowski has studied items listed in the inventories focused mainly on *szlachta* from Greater Poland, and based his publication on 300 inventories.[54] Alicja Falniowska-Gradowska in turn published 41 last wills of *szlachta* from Krakow from the years 1650 to 1799.[55] The descriptions of the clothes in the inventories usually include the origin of the textile and its color, for which a very rich vocabulary was used, drawn for example from the world of cuisine (cinnamon, pepper, rosemary, caper, olive, clove, orange, peach, and lemon). This kind of description was closely connected with the formation and defense of an elite identity for the *szlachta*, for whom the abundance and variety of spices was a defining feature of elite old Polish cuisine, resistant to French culinary influences.[56] Use of porcelain resulted in the appearance of the word "porcelain" from the middle of the eighteenth century to name a certain shade of white textile. Such colors alluded to the common feasting of the Polish nobility, an element of an insider, initiate culture. But for a long time it was crimson and

---

52 Barbara Dolczewska: Galeria portretów rodzinnych w Kórniku. Obrazy z XVII i XVIII wieku, in: *Pamiętnik Biblioteki Kórnickiej* 25 (2001), 267–292, here 286–287.

53 See: Ibid., 284; Andrzej Pośpiech: Miejsce ubioru w wielkopolskich pośmiertnych inwentarzach szlacheckich XVII wieku, in: *Kwartalnik Historii Kultury Materialnej* 34 (1986), 433–449.

54 Dumanowski, Świat. An extensive query of the inventories was also done by Irena Turnau when she was working on the book "Ubiór narodowy".

55 Alicja Falinowska-Gradowska (ed.): *Testamenty szlachty krakowskiej XVII–XVIII w. Wybór tekstów źródłowych z lat 1650–1799*. Cracow 1997.

56 Dumanowski, Świat, 185. A characteristic feature of *szlachta* customs was the significance given to the formulation of all forms of outside presentation, including clothing and jewelry. It was an existence based on a model of a spectacle – hence the appreciation of fashion, spectacular enterprises and feasts: Sowa, Fantomowe, 267.

shades of red that were held in greatest favor for the clothing of the *szlachta*. In the invaluable seventeenth-century memoirs of Jan Chryzostom Pasek, marshal of the Rawa Sejm and chamberlain of the Krakow land, there is an anecdote about a Ruthenian man captured during battle by Pasek, who was wearing a grey *kontusz* at the time. The prisoner, later seeing another Pole wearing a crimson *kontusz* – despite the attire being worn out – preferred to be taken by him, whom he understood to be more prominent because of the color of his dress.[57]

In the eighteenth century every member of the *szlachta* owned at least one set of parade clothes, which indicated the estate to which he belonged. A poorer nobleman could give up furniture, glassware, and books, but he had to have his national dress. There appears to be a great gap between stereotypes of the Polish nobility's lavishness and ostentation in dress and the reality expressed in the inventories. The inventories scrupulously list also items of clothing that are tattered, worn-out, old, threadbare, moth-eaten, or re-sewn. The *szlachta* paid close attention to how others looked and closely guarded its exclusivity, but Adam Gdacjusz, a seventeenth-century preacher, noted: "We see what excesses there are in dress, one cannot see who is a nobleman, who is a burgher, who is a merchant, and who is a craftsman."[58]

Clothing, which was one of the most valuable elements of the *szlachta*'s movable property, was typically inherited from generation to generation.[59] It helped form intergenerational bonds and traditions. Leaving a garment in a last will could be a part of familial strategy, as there are instances of clothes being given by a grandfather to a grandson, like in the case of Kazimierz Strobiszewski, a nobleman, who bequeathed a *kontusz* in green and navy blue to his grandson, as he was in conflict with his son and thus appointed also his grandson as successor. Clothing remained valuable well into the eighteenth century, especially after the destruction and pauperization caused by war in its early decades. That changed, however, at the end of the century, when items were deemed "old" after several years. Clothing lost its value as a tool of intergenerational communication.[60]

During the Sejm of 1776, which introduced a number of reforms, an attempt was undertaken to codify outward appearance, and it was recommended that noblemen in each voivodeship decide on a uniform dress, to be made of domestic cloth, that would serve to distinguish each region's deputies. This attempt was part of wider reforms aimed at limiting excessive luxury

---

57 Jan Chryzostom Pasek: *Pamiętniki*, ed. by Roman Pollak. Warsaw 1987, 63.

58 Bystroń, Opis, 454.

59 Dumanowski, Świat, 203.

60 Ibid.

in dress, which was deemed immoral and wasteful, in line with the European Enlightenment's critique of luxury. The regulations were tightened in 1780, but even then the *szlachta* was not particularly limited. Textiles deemed acceptable included *Gros de Tours*, cheap silks, satins, gauzes, muslins, and *blond* laces. In a novel by Michał D. Krajewski from 1785, the protagonist wears the voivodeship uniform of a different voivodeship every day, thus satisfying his need for splendor.[61]

Though the Sejm's resolution did not define the details of the uniforms and did not make them mandatory, individual local assemblies almost immediately selected their own colors for *kontuszes, żupans*, and sashes. The Sejm of 1778 saw the gentlemen already in their voivodeship uniforms. Some voivodeships (e.g. those of Brześć-Kujawy and of Inowrocław) introduced also separate Sejm uniforms, different from those worn at the local assemblies. In 1778, an amaranthine *kontusz* and a white *żupan*, silver epaulets with gold and with colored fringes on the left shoulder were obligatory in the Krakow voivodeship; two years later the *kontusz* was to be navy-blue with an amaranthine collar and a *żupan* of the same color. Hats with quadrilateral head and fur trim were worn with the voivodeship uniforms. On the other hand, knights of the two most important orders (White Eagle and Saint Stanislaus) wore red-and-white or white-and-crimson ensembles. The law on voivodeship uniforms was confirmed by the Sejm in 1780, which at the same time prohibited the use of any decorations with them.

These considerations concerning national dress during the second half of the eighteenth century, and especially during the Four-Year Sejm (1788–1792), despite the previous leaning towards Western fashion, were an indication of the rise of patriotic attitudes in the troubled country. The national dress was now worn not only by the magnates and the *szlachta* in general, but also by the bourgeoisie in the capital and in smaller towns, who wore *kontuszes* and *żupans*, even though they were not allowed to wear a sash tied on a *kontusz* like the *szlachta*.[62] The regulations of the Sejm were supposed to stop the spread of Western fashion. These attempts were surely unsuccessful, and, moreover, some of the voivodeship uniforms were given the shape of western attire. Such was the case with Wschowa chamberlain Józef Radoliński, who owned seven voivodeship uniforms, all of them three-part ensembles consisting of a uniform,

---

61 Michał D. Krajewski, *Woyciech Zdarzyński, życie i przypadki swoje opisuiący* 15. URL: *https://wolnelektury.pl/katalog/lektura/krajewski-woyciech-zdarzynski-zycie-i-przypadki-swoje-opisuiacy.html* (30 Sept. 2018).

62 Turnau, *Rozwój ubioru narodowego*, 417; Małgorzata Możdzyńska-Nawotka: *O modach i strojach*. Wrocław 2005, 82.

a vest, and trousers. The second camlet uniform of the voivodeship came with a vest and goose-skin trousers.[63] The change of national dress into foreign in the second half of the eighteenth century was also a generational change; the youth dressed in accordance with Western fashion, despite attempts to turn the traditional dress of the *szlachta* into a patriotic attire.

National Dress at the Time of the Partition of Poland

Apart from *kontusz* and *żupan*, new items that were viewed as national dress emerged during the nineteenth century, for example the *czamara*, a long garment often lined with fur and decorated with braiding, and the *sukmana*, a peasant's coat made of woolen cloth. Participants in the Polish uprisings were not indifferent to the problems of fashion: during the November uprising of 1830–31 the *czamara* gained patriotic meaning. "Warsaw man/Took off the frock/Against the czar/There is *czamara*", wrote Polish poet and independence fighter Rajnold Suchodolski.[64] When the national bard Adam Mickiewicz wanted to describe a defender of the homeland, he wrote that for "the soldiers of homeland uprising" only *czamara* were fitting and not red French hats, English ermines, or German togas and berets. "You shall wear insurgents' *czamary*, you old and young; because you are all soldiers of the homeland uprising. As in Polish *czamara* is a name of the dying man's clothes. And many of you will die in the insurgents' clothes. And all of you shall be ready to die."[65] The stock of national dress was further augmented by the peasant's coat, the *sukmana*, which had already gained importance during the time of the Kościuszko uprising in 1794. Even earlier, in the time of the Bar Confederacy of 1768, the confederate hat had become popular.[66] When the Polish nation in its modern form first began to emerge in the nineteenth century, the *kontusz*

---

63 Dumanowski, Świat, 199.

64 Tazbir, Kultura szlachecka, 45.

65 "Wy nośce Czamary powstańskie, i starsi, i młodsi; bo wszyscy jesteście żołnierzami powstania Ojczyzny. Czamarą zaś nazywa się po polsku strój, w który ubiérano umierającego. A wielu z Was umrze w stroju powstańskim. Wszyscy zaś niech będą gotowi umrzéć." Adam Mickiewicz, *Księgi narodu polskiego i pielgrzymstwa polskiego.* URL: *https://wolnelektury.pl/katalog/lektura/ksiegi-narodu-polskiego-i-pielgrzymstwa-polskiego.html* (4 Dec. 2018); Zofia Stefanowska (ed.): *Swojskość i cudzoziemszczyzna w dziejach kultury polskiej.* Warsaw 1973, 211.

66 Maria Molenda-Berkowicz: Moda w czasach konfederacji barskiej, in: *Zeszyty spisko-sądeckie* 3 (2008), 89–94, esp. 92.

ensemble, which belonged mostly to the *szlachta* in the days of the Polish-Lithuanian Commonwealth, turned into a symbol of belonging to the newly imagined Polish nation. In the time of Galician autonomy, for example, it was eagerly worn by the bourgeoisie, particularly in Krakow.

The nineteenth century saw a renaissance of the Sarmatian idea. The threat of the Russification and Germanization of the local population in the partitioned territories by the neighboring empires made people look to the past for support. Sarmatism served as firm ground for an endangered tradition in the time of the motherland's bondage. This tradition gained special meaning after the defeat of the November Uprising in 1831, when the wearing of national costumes was prohibited by law, most strictly under Russian and Prussian rule.[67] Thus, wearing the *kontusz* costume became a form of patriotic demonstration; the *kontusz* ceased to be daily attire. At the same time the *czamara* turned into a symbol of national grief: a long simple, dark-colored dress, with braiding as the only decoration. Only in Galicia, under Austrian rule, did the citizens of Krakow receive from the Emperor Franz Joseph I in 1861 the privilege of carrying a *karabela* with the "full ancient Polish costume, consisting of the outer clothing called *kontusz* and the lower called *żupan*". Four years later an analogous privilege was extended to the citizens of Lwów. *Kontusz* costumes were ordered and worn at traditional national celebrations, at sessions of parliament in Lwów and Vienna, and during weddings, family congregations, and jubilees.[68] The *kontusz* costume became an icon, but was not worn as casual dress.

Conclusion

The development of a national dress of the Polish nobility continued throughout the early modern period and saw several modifications and changes. The form of the particular Polish dress was influenced by the Sarmatian tradition and by the incorporation of textiles and styles from the East, mostly the Ottoman Empire. The early modern dress of the Polish nobility was also characterized by the desire to distinguish itself from other European nations. In its different forms, materials, and embellishments, it was also a means of expressing high status and wealth, both in the context of the whole society and within the *szlachta*, despite the declared and theoretical equality of Polish nobility. This attire displayed the splendor of the wearer and became one of the symbols

---

67 Adam Buława: Pejzaże konspiracji. Kod patriotyczny, in: *Polityka* 1 (2013), 37– 45.
68 Turnau, Ubiór, 162.

determining and presenting the essence of the character and worldview of the masculine part of Polish nobility.

By the eighteenth century new garments like the *czamara* and the *sukmana* were incorporated in the national dress as a way to display patriotism. In the second half of the eighteenth century the national costume, apart from being a symbol of belonging to the nobility, gained patriotic value under the worsening political conditions of the country. This patriotic significance was especially important during the time of the partitions, when wearing these specific garments was an evident manifestation of Polish patriotism. Their nature, however, had already changed, and they were more of a costume, a symbolic outfit, than an everyday dress.

Constanţa Vintilă-Ghiţulescu

Shawls and Sable Furs: How to Be a Boyar under the Phanariot Regime (1710–1821)

Abstract: *Wallachia and Moldavia, as peripheries of the Ottoman Empire, were ruled by Phanariot princes throughout the eighteenth century. These "Greeks" were dragomans at the sultan's court or high dignitaries of the Greek Orthodox Patriarchate in Constantinople and governed the two Danubian Principalities in the name of the sultan. My article examines how the local nobility, the Orthodox elite of the countries, reacted and adapted to the Oriental ways of the Phanariot courts. It reveals how the local elites adhered to the Phanariot political regimes and tacitly adopted the new fashions and lifestyles, which would eventually be instrumental in the fashioning of their identity. The available primary sources consist of dowry lists, probate inventories, sumptuary laws, and visual documents (engravings and prints published in travelogues, paintings, and costume books), and they show in great detail the process of self-fashioning and self-display through clothes and costumes.*

After the Ottoman advance on Vienna in the late seventeenth century, the Christian elites of Central and Southeastern Europe embarked on a game of appearances using Ottoman fashion as a model. Ottoman cultural influence was visible in the two principalities of Moldavia and Wallachia already in the seventeenth century, but it became more dominant after 1711, when the Ottoman grip on the region tightened. Until that year, members of the local nobility, the boyars, had had the right to choose native-born rulers from amongst their own political elite. But after the battle of Stănileşti by the River Prut in 1711 and the self-imposed Russian exile of the prince of Moldavia, Dimitrie Cantemir, the rulers of the Danubian principalities were directly appointed by the sultan, selected from among the dragomans or high officials of the Orthodox Patriarchy of Constantinople residing in the Phanar district of Istanbul.[1] Known

---

[1] My special thanks for the English translation of this study are addressed to Dr. James Christian Brown (University of Bucharest). This study was supported by the project *Luxury, Fashion and Social Status in Early Modern South-Eastern Europe (LuxFaSS)*, with number ERC-2014-CoG no. 646489, financed by the European Research Council and hosted by New Europe College, Bucharest. I would like to thank Denise Klein, Cornelia Aust, Thomas Weller for their insightful reading of earlier drafts of this paper. I am also grateful to Costina Anghel, curator of the National Museum of Art in Bucharest, who has always helped me find me way in the

as Phanariots, these new rulers arrived in the Romanian lands with a host of other "Greeks" from the imperial capital, and they transformed the princely courts of Bucharest and Iași according to their tastes.

Along with the princely courts, local society, too, became more and more Ottomanized. The native elite rapidly imitated the new fashion of the Phanariots[2] and, in most cases, adopted also the original Greek and Ottoman names together with the objects.[3] Dowry lists, wills, tax assessments, probate inventories, and votive portraits in churches reflect this Ottomanization of the local elites' fashion. Anton Maria del Chiro, the Italian secretary of Prince Constantine Brâncoveanu (r. 1688–1714) and Prince Stephen Cantacuzino (r. 1714–1716), describes a Wallachian society adept at copying Ottoman models in the fields of fashion, manners, and culinary tastes.[4] Indeed, the upper levels, at least, of Romanian society seem to have been Ottomanized. However, the boyars did not borrow only from the Ottomans; they also followed other models provided by their Christian religion and heritage and by their connections to Eastern and Western Europe.

This article investigates how "Ottoman" the Romanian boyars were during this period of multiple affiliations, between 1710 and 1821, by analyzing the ways in which they dressed. I begin with a brief outline of the ambivalent status of the boyars at the Phanariot court and then focus on certain clothing items, such as the boyars' special headgear, shawls, and furs, as symbols of their Ottomanization and as means of social distinction. The discussion shows, for example, how the işlic hat turned from a costume accessory into a political instrument that was used in the internal competition for precedence on the political stage. The second part of the article discusses the Phanariots' reaction to the local elite's ostentatious display of luxury and its practices of social distinction, based in particular on a study of sumptuary laws.

---

museum collections. After the fall of Constatinople in 1453, many Orthodox Christians settled in the Phanar district. On this topic see Christine Philliou: *Biography of an Empire. Governing Ottomans in an Age of Revolution*. Berkeley 2011.

2 Adam Jasienski: A Savage Magnificence. Ottomanizing Fashion and the Politic of Display in Early Modern East-Central Europe, in: *Muqarnas* 31 (2014), 174–176; Michał Wasiucionek: Conceptualizing Moldavian Ottomanness. Elite Culture and Ottomanization of the Seventeenth-Century Moldavian Boyars, in: *Medieval and Early Modern Studies for Central and Eastern Europe* 8 (2016), 39–78.

3 Ștefan Greceanu: *Viața lui Constantin vodă Brâncoveanul*. Bucharest 1906, 278–313.

4 Anton Maria del Chiaro: *Istoria delle Moderne Rivoluzioni della Valachia*. Venice 1718.

Boyars and the Princely Court

Only boyars who belonged to the upper class of the *evgheniți*[5] and held important office had access to the Phanariot court and, thus, by extension to the cultural model mentioned above. These so-called "great boyars" were the descendants of old families with considerable wealth, which gave them access to high office. To appear at the princely court and participate actively in court life, they also had to acquire a certain etiquette. The "petty boyars", by contrast, did not have access to the court. They were one level lower in the social hierarchy and did not have the financial means necessary to gain positions in the princely council; they had to content themselves with lesser posts in the secondary administrative apparatus, even if they came from old families.[6]

Even though the great boyars saw in the princely court a source of power and income and a model style of life, they considered themselves superior to the Phanariots and the people they brought with them from Istanbul. They were proud of their long ancestry and tried under all circumstances to affirm the priority they believed it granted them. Luxury and fashion were important means for the local elites to display their claim to precedence as well as their political opposition. Indeed, the boyars used shawls, furs, robes, and jewelry to emphasize both their social belonging and their superiority over the Phanariots and, especially, their princely entourage of "Greeks".[7]

The boyars took inspiration from both Ottoman and European clothing trends, which they saw at the Phanariot court and during their travels, as well as in books and magazines. At the Phanariot court the influence of Turkish fashion was strong and affected even foreigners, but there was also a presence of Europeans and European dress. Doctors, cooks, and men of letters came

---

5 The term became current in the eighteenth century, with the installation of the Phanariot regime, as a replacement for the Slav term *blagorodnic*. *Evghenit* derives from the Greek *evgenia* and means "noble, boyar" as does *blagorodnic*. Some boyars underlined their belonging to the *protipendadă* (great boyar class) by describing themselves as "boyar *evghenit* and *blagorodnic*". The term *protipendadă* came into use in the same period, through the intermediary of the Greek spoken both in the princely chancery and at court, from the Greek *próti pendáda*.

6 Constanța Vintilă-Ghițulescu: *Evgheniți, ciocoi, mojici. Despre obrazele primei modernități românești (1750–1860)* [Boyars, Upstarts, Peasants. Romanian Faces of the Modernization]. Bucharest 2013.

7 "Greeks" is the generic name used in the period to denote all Orthodox Christians coming from the other side of the Danube, from the Ottoman Empire, who monopolized commercial activity and the skilled trades. Some of them came in the suite of the Phanariot rulers and received important offices in the princely divan, while others came in search of a better life, pursuing various occupations: teachers, artisans, merchants, mercenaries, etc.

from across Europe to be at the service of the Phanariot rulers. Some of them kept their European clothes while others adopted the local variety of Turkish fashion. One of the latter was the French painter Jean-Etienne Liotard, who in 1742–1743 was called to the court of Prince Constantine Mavrocordat in Iaşi to make portraits of the princely family.[8]

The boyars requested "gazettes" and fashion magazines from Europe, not only to be informed about political changes, but also to stay up-to-date with the latest developments in matters of fashion.[9] For instance, on 7 April 1777, Grand *Vistier* (treasurer) Ioan Canta bought four volumes of the *Encylopédie*, the famous French dictionary of Enlightenment edited by Denis Diderot.[10] The boyar Iordache Slătineanu read the British magazine of politics and culture *The Spectator* and the French women's literary almanac *Almanach des Dames*.[11] In Iaşi, in 1806, Charles Frédéric Reinhard, Consul General of France in the two principalities, encountered boyars reading the French fashion magazine *Le Journal des modes*.[12]

The boyars' interest in various European periodicals suggests that they also purchased Ottoman costume books. These albums, with illustrations of the different peoples living in the sultan's realm, were a principal source of inspiration for the European nobility.[13] They were "produced by European artists for

---

8 On Liotard's presence in Iaşi: Remus Niculescu: Jean-Etienne Liotard à Jassy, 1742–1743, in: *Genava* 30 (1982), 127–166. See also his portrait of the Moldavian princess Ekaterina Mavrocordat, 1742–1743, Kupferstichkabinett, Staatliche Museen zu Berlin, inv. KDZ 1626.

9 In the correspondence of the boyar Barbu Ştirbei with the Constantin Hagi Pop commercial house in Sibiu, the insistence with which German, Greek, and Italian "gazettes" are requested may be observed. See the letters of 22 March 1784, 26 July 1784, 24 February 1793, 20 November and 25 December 1795, 28 January 1798, 18 November 1799, Nicolae Iorga: *Scrisori de boieri şi negustori olteni şi munteni către casa de negoţ sibiiană Hagi Pop*. Bucharest 1906, 8–9, 27, 32, 35, 37. The journals published in Leipzig at the time were: *Damenjournal von einer Damen-Gesellschaft* (1784); *Journal, Fabrik, Manufakturen und Handlung, Kunst und Mode* (1792); *Charis. Ein Magazin für das Neueste in Kunst, Geschmack und Mode, Lebensgenuß und Lebensglück* (1801); *Zeitung für die Elegante Welt* (1801).

10 Serviciul Judeţean al Arhivelor Naţionale, Iaşi [Departmental Archives, Iaşi] (hereafter SJAN), Colecţia Documente P. 1023/2, "Sama lui Şerban logofăt pentru cheltuiala casii dumisale Ioan Canta biv vel vistier pe anul acesta, precum arată anume înăuntru, leat 1777 ghenuar 1".

11 Alexandru Alexianu: *Mode şi veşminte din trecut*, vol. 2. Bucharest 1987, 147.

12 Paul Cernovodeanu et al (eds.): *Călători străini despre ţările române în secolul al XIX-lea: serie nouă*, vol. 1. Bucharest 2004, 273–274.

13 Giulia Calvi: Across Three Empires. Balkan Costumes in 16th-Century Europe, in: Constanţa Vintilă-Ghiţulescu (ed.): *Traditional Attire to Modern Dress. Modes of Identification, Modes of Recognition in the Balkans* (*XVIIth–XXth Centuries*). Newcastle 2011, 29–52; Robert Born: Mapping Transylvania as a Multiethnic and Multiconfessional Region in Costume Books (17th–19th Centuries), in: ibid., 53–83.

a European public" and also used by foreign diplomats in the course of their missions in order to identify Ottoman officials. In the eighteenth century, the Ottoman elite also became interested in the production and acquisition of such albums.[14] However, sources on the principalities are scarce and, to date, I have not discovered a "costume book" in the Wallachian and Moldavian archives.

Vestimentary Signs and Social Distinction

There were a number of easily recognizable elements that made up what contemporaries in the principalities perceived as Turkish dress. The following discussion focuses on several of these clothing items and accessories, which the boyars adopted in a very specific way that left room for their individual strategies of social distinction. I begin with different forms of men's headgear, then examine shawls and other luxurious clothes and accessories for women, and finally turn to consider valuable furs worn by both elite men and women in the principalities.

The Boyar's Headgear

The *işlic*, a high hat that derived its name from the Turkish *başlık*, was a typical feature of a boyar's dress and offered visual evidence of his rank, social position, and status [Figure 1].[15] This headwear was permitted to all Christians in the Ottoman Empire; yet in the Romanian lands especially it took on a symbolic dimension. There was a great variety of *işlic* available in the principalities. The Moldavian Grand *Vistier* Ioan Canta in his chronicle *Record of Expenses* mentions the following varieties: "*işlic* of sable for the groom"; light grey *işlics* (of lambskin); "Moldavian *işlics*"; "Nogai *işlics*"[16]; night *kavuks*; and *kalpaks*, made and adorned by Ştefan the *işlic*-maker or Păun, the head of the *kalpak*-makers' guild (*kalpakci-başa*).[17] The guild of *işlic*-makers in Bucharest

---

14 Suraiya Faroqhi: Introduction, or why and how one might want to study Ottoman clothes, in: Suraiya Faroqhi and Christoph K. Neumann (eds.): *Ottoman Costumes. From Textile to Identity.* Istanbul 2005, 20.
15 On clothes with regard to rank and social status in the Ottoman Empire see Donald Quataert: Clothing Laws, State, and Society in the Ottoman Empire, 1720–1829, in: *International Journal of Middle East Studies* 29 (1997), 406.
16 From the name of the Tatar tribe.
17 SJAN, Iaşi, Colecţia Documente P. 1023/2, accounts for 17 January 1777 and 12 April 1777.

Figure 1: Auguste de Henikstein: *High-Ranking Boyars*, 1825, drawing, 199 × 250 mm. Courtesy © Library of the Romanian Academy.

was very powerful and often appealed to the prince for the punishment of leather-workers or furriers who did not respect the guild members' exclusive right to make *işlics*.[18] The guild's repeated appeals also attest to the considerable income to be obtained by practicing this trade, as the demand for *işlics* was nearly universal.

The features of this particular headgear were strictly regulated. Depending on its size, form, material, and color, the *işlic* told the story of its wearer. The Phanariot prince and his sons, the *beyzade*s, as well as the five foremost office-holders of the ruler's divan, wore *işlics* covered with sable fur. But while the prince was entitled to a *gugiuman* (Turkish *gücemin*) of sable fur with a white top, the great boyars were entitled only to sable *gugiumans* with red tops. And while the great boyars in high offices wore large round *işlics*, the petty boyars wore small round *işlics* topped by a felt square colored according to their rank and office.[19]

---

18 Vasile Alexandrescu Urechia: *Istoria românilor,* vol. 1. Bucharest 1891, 439–443.

19 Furnică, Industria, 213. For a discussion of the social and political signification of headgear in the Ottoman Empire see Patricia L. Baker: The Fez in Turkey. A Symbol of Modernization?, in: *Costume* 20 (1986), 72–85.

The *işlic* and *kalpak* of boyars lower down the social hierarchy were covered with fur of lower quality, namely marten, lamb, fox, or polecat.

The type of *işlic* a man wore also indicated his proximity to the center of power. Investiture to high office took place in a public ceremony, in which the newly appointed boyar was given a new *işlic* and caftan, and, agreeing to respect his elevated position, thus "put on" the identity of the social group he had entered. With high office, that is, came a new costume, one that maintained the official's position in the social hierarchy, underlined his prestige and grandeur, brought recognition in public, and induced submission and fear. Indeed, when a great boyar appeared in public, displaying his *işlic*, his caftan with furs, and his beard, it called for an immediate recognition of his power. In the 1820s, the boyar, author, and member of the prince's council, Grand *Logofăt* (chancellor) Dinicu Golescu, described the effects of this visibility of his social status as follows: "Seeing me with my beard they recognized that I was of divan rank." He then goes on to tell of the complete submission he induced when he appeared on the roads of Wallachia in the garb of an *ispravnic* (county prefect): the common people threw themselves on the ground, he says, with "their heads bare, as if condemned to death".[20]

Of course, the significance of the *işlic* was renegotiated as the men wearing them transgressed social boundaries, misused their privileges, and carried the form of the headgear to excess. According to legend, boyars owned two sets of hats: one that was permitted by their rank and office, and another one for their own pride, which was worn especially among friends and which tended to be much larger and more richly ornamented.[21] Possibly, this "fashion for *işlic* grandeur" was inspired by the example of the viziers of Sultan Mustafa III (r. 1757–1773), who "pressed for turbans grander than those worn by more illustrious forerunners".[22] The fashion for immense *işlics*, however, gave rise to pamphlets and caricatures in which the hats and their wearers were mocked. In the *Gromovnic*, a book of astrological predictions from 1795, the anonymous author sketched several boyars' heads, adding an ironic note to each sketch: "boyar with a *gugea* on his head"; "boyar with a lamp on his head"; and "boyar with breadcrumbs on his head" [Figure 2].[23] From there, it

20 Dinicu Golescu: *Însemnare a călătoriii mele, Costandin Radovici din Golești făcută în anul 1824, 1825, 1826.* Bucharest 1977, 137.

21 Radu Rosetti: *Amintiri. Ce am auzit de la alții.* Bucharest 1996.

22 Madeline Zilfi: Whose Laws? Gendering the Ottoman Sumptuary Regime, in: Faroqhi and Neumann, Ottoman Costumes, 135.

23 Library of the Romanian Academy, Fond Carte Rară, CRV 587, *Gromovnic al lui Iraclie împărat carele au fost numărătoriu de stele, acum a doua oară tipărită la leat 1795.* [hereafter BAR]

Figure 2: Detail of a boyar headwear, in: *Gromovnic al lui Iraclie împărat carele au fost numărătoriu de stele, acum a doua oară tipărită la leat 1795*. Courtesy © Library of the Romanian Academy.

is but a short step to the negative image of the *işlic* "as tall as the obelisk in the public gardens", which certain modern scholars have seen as proof of the vanity of the boyars, who were proud of their ornaments but unashamed that they could not read or write.[24]

To foreigners who passed through Moldavia and Wallachia on the way to Istanbul at this time, the boyar's *işlic* was a source of amusement in its extravagant shape and size. Considered "odd", and as such noteworthy, the *işlic* became the subject of a series of narrative and visual depictions. The Scottish diplomat, traveler, and painter Robert Ker Porter, for instance, left an account of boyar *işlics*, accompanied by several sketches. In 1818, during his stay at the Wallachian court in Bucharest, he was invited by Prince Scarlat Callimachi to attend a concert, which gave him the opportunity to observe and to draw the locals and their headgear. He writes:

> I amused myself in silently sketching some of their figures. The general costume was Turkish, and of every-coloured brocade, embroidered, and befurred; so far all was well, till the huge Whalachian cap turned the whole ridiculous. It is of a pumpkin form, nearly three feet in circumference, and of an equally enormous height. The material, a grey silvery Bucharian lamb-skin, with a tassel at the top, to assist the wearer in taking it off

---

24 Alecu Russo: *Cântarea României*. Bucharest 1980 [first edition 1850], 82–83.

when he means to salute an acquaintance. This little appendage is green with every person, excepting the royal family, and they have it white. The cap of the lower orders is of the same shape, but not quite so large; and a square cushion covered with dark cloth is its enormous crest; in fact all these people appear so top-heavy it is painful to look at them, after the first risible impression of the absurd passes away.[25]

The boyars did not wear only the *işlic*; they also wore turbans and other garments from the Ottoman Empire. Yet while there are various sources on dress in Istanbul and other places of the empire, including regulations concerning the color of turbans,[26] evidence with regard to the Romanian lands is scarce: a series of portraits, a couple of written sources, and the terminology used for specific items. Nevertheless, these sources indicate that, like other Christians in the Ottoman Empire, the Romanian boyars also wore striped *taklids* and *çalmas*. *Taklid*, or *taclit*, was a shawl worn around the waist, holding the typical *anteri* coat tightly. *Çalma*, or *cialma*, were shawls worn around the head as turbans. For instance, in the 1820s, the Serbian painter Pavel Djurcovic made portraits of the young boyars Constantine Cantacuzino and Iancu Manu wearing the *çalma* turban. [Figure 3, Figure 4]. While *taklids* and *çalmas* were worn by the great boyars with important offices in the divan, lesser boyars and servants of the princely court wore *donluks* around their heads, a turban of cloth of inferior quality.[27] The *Customs Catalogue* from 1 January 1792 specifies that "*taklids* of *alagea* (linen silk)" came from Aleppo, while *donluks* were brought from Istanbul.[28] At a safe distance from the imperial center, the Romanian lands escaped the more rigorous dress codes of the empire, where – as Matthew Elliot has shown – Christians at some point lost the right to wear turbans and were prescribed to wear only the *işlic* and the *kalpak*.[29] In the principalities, by contrast, a boyar could put a *çalma* or *taklid* on his head without fearing for his life. However, if he were to have traveled in the Ottoman Empire, he would have had to catch up on the latest dress regulations in advance, because wearing the wrong clothes could have cost him his head. This is what happened, for instance, to the young boyar Aleco Vlahuţi at the beginning of the nineteenth century. When he arrived in Istanbul he had a *sarık* (silk cloth) wound around

25 Sir Robert Ker Porter: *Travels in Georgia, Persia, Armenia, Ancient Babylonia & c. During the Years 1817, 1818, 1819*, vol. 2. London 1822, 787–788.
26 Matthew Elliot: Dress Codes in the Ottoman Empire. The Case of the Franks, in: Faroqhi and Neumann, Ottoman Costumes, 105–106.
27 Arhivele Naţionale Istorice Centrale [National Historical Central Archives], Bucharest (hereafter ANIC), Fond Manuscripts, Ms. 1773, fol. 19–20.
28 Urechia, Istoria românilor, 246.
29 Elliot, Dress Codes, 106.

Figure 3: Anonymous: *Portrait of Iancu Manu*, oil on canvas, 0,755 x 0,630 m. Courtesy © National Museum of Art, Bucharest.

his head, not knowing that this particular form of headgear had just been forbidden. It was enough to be spotted at the window of a house in the village of Therapia on the Bosporus by the *bostancıbaşı*, the head of the palace guards, who happened to be passing, for him to be condemned to death.[30]

Shawls and Textiles for the Boyar Ladies

Female members of the Romanian elite also were influenced by fashion trends from the Ottoman Empire and similarly used certain clothing items, such as shawls, as a means of social distinction. Giulia Calvi has emphasized how cashmere shawls connected "material modernity, distinction, and taste" to construct hierarchy and status.[31] Having arrived in Istanbul from India, cashmere shawls quickly spread throughout Europe. They were considered a highlight in

---

30 Nicolas Soutzou: *Mémoires du Prince Nicolas Soutzo, grand-logothète de Moldavie, 1798–1871.*Vienna 1899, 55–59.

31 Giulia Calvi: Translating Imperial Practices, Knowledge, and Taste Across the Mediterranean. Giulio Ferrario and Ignatius Mouradgea d'Ohsson, in: Constanța Vintilă-Ghițulescu (ed.): *Women, Consumption, and the Circulation of Ideas in South-Eastern Europe, 17th–19th Centuries.* Leiden 2017, 20. See also Giulia Calvi's contribution to this volume.

Figure 4: Pavel Djurcoviciu: *Constantin Cantacuzino*, 1820, Wikimedia Commons
https://en.wikipedia.org/wiki/File:Pavel_Đurković_(attrib.)_-_Constantin_Cantacuzino.png.

a woman's appearance and were soon adored by Italian noblewomen[32] and found in the wardrobes of ladies of French high society.[33] This can be seen in paintings of the time, such as the portrait of "Frau Luise Mila" by the German painter Johann Erdmann Hummel, which shows an elite woman with a red cashmere shawl draped over her shoulders in the 1810s.[34]

---

[32] Giulia Calvi: Luxury comes from the East. Fashioning "à l'indienne" between the Ottoman Empire and Italy (XVIII–XIX), unpublished paper read at the international workshop *People, Trade, Gifts and Beyond. The Circulation of Goods and Practices between the Ottoman Empire and Europe (16th–19th Centuries)*, Berlin, 4–5 July, 2016.

[33] For the fashion for shawls, which became a ubiquitous accessory, see the recommendations in the illustrated magazines of the day: *Journal des Dames et des Modes* and *Costumes parisiens*, 1798–1812. URL: *http://gallica.bnf.fr/ark:/12148/bpt6k57090g/f18.image* (30 Nov. 2017).

[34] Alte Nationalgalerie, Berlin, Johann Erdmann Hummel, *Frau Luise Mila*, 1810.

The shawl also served as an important accessory in the visual representation of upper-class women from the Danubian Principalities. Almost all the portraits of female members of the Romanian elite produced between 1780 and 1840 show a seated woman and her shawl. These shawls are presented in the finest detail, and are not simply left on couches awaiting their mistress but cover her shoulders, are haphazardly thrown over her body – which is also adorned by other luxury items and insignia of power – or decorate an item of furniture in the background of the picture.[35] [Figure 5]

Figure 5: Eustaţie Altini: *Portrait of a woman*, 1813–1815, oil on canvas, 0,865 x 0,640 cm. Courtesy © National Museum of Art, Bucharest.

To cover their shoulders, the wealthy ladies of the boyar elite cherished cashmere shawls and shawls made of *giar*, a valuable fabric made from camel hair and decorated with flowers and embroidery in gold or silver thread. Moreover, both cashmere and *giar* were the preferred material for other valuable garments as well. The soft and velvety cashmere was often used for Turkish-style trousers, which were worn by women and men alike and which appear in the sources as

---

35 See the portraits in the Gallery: Romanian Modern Art, Romanian National Museum of Art, Bucharest.

"*çaksır* of shawl" or "*cintieni* of shawl".[36] For instance, the dowry of a boyar lady from 1775 lists a "*cübbe* (overcoat) of shawl cloth with laces of gold thread, without fur".[37] *Giar* was used for overcoats as well. The dowry of a boyar lady from 1797 lists among her belongings "a *cübbe* of *giar*, fur-lined with polecat".[38] On their heads boyar ladies wore *sanks*, a sort of silk cloth adorned with numerous precious stones or embroidered flowers. There are descriptions of this particular type of head-covering by Andreas Wolf, a Transylvanian Saxon doctor at the princely court of Moldavia between 1780 and 1783,[39] and by the naturalist Balthazar de la Motte Hacquet, who provides an engraving of a *sank* and writes: "a boyar's wife usually wears a *sank* of thin silk or muslin, in the form of a sugar loaf, adorned with pearls and other jewels and with all sorts of ribbons and flowers. Her hair is twisted over it in one or more plaits, or plaited into a long pigtail. At the peak of this head ornament is a tassel, and on one side or in front it is adorned with two ostrich feathers."[40]

The *Customs Catalogue* published on 1 January 1792 indicates the provenance and price of several of these clothes and accessories, underlining their value as luxury items vis-à-vis similar products. Ordinary shawls imported from Egypt and sold in the shops of Romanian towns, for instance, were not of great interest to the wealthy boyars.[41] Instead, they chose the expensive shawls, some of them "adorned with jewels and pearls", which were brought from India, Damascus, Aleppo, or Chios, first to Istanbul and from there to the principalities.[42] The correspondence of a commander of the princely guard, *Delibaşa* Gheorghe Constantin, who was involved in the luxury trade selling

---

36 BAR, Fond Episcopia Buzău, LXXXV/53, 26 January 1791.

37 BAR, Fond Documente Istorice, CCXLVII/182, 13 September 1775.

38 BAR, Fond Documente Istorice, MLXXXVI/34, 19 September 1797.

39 Andreas Wolf came to Moldavia in 1780 and stayed at the court until 1783. In 1784 he was in Wallachia, returning to Moldavia in 1788–1790 and 1796–1797. He wrote *Beiträge zur einer statistisch-historischen Beschreibung des Fürstenthums Moldau*. Hermannstadt 1805. See Cernovodeanu, Călători străini, vol. 10:2, 1277.

40 Balthasar la Motte Hacquet: *Hacquet's neueste physikalisch-politische Reisen in den Jahren 1788 und 1789 durch die Dacischen und Sarmatischen oder Nördlichen Karpathen*, vol. 1. Nürnberg 1790, 138f., see Cernovodeanu, Călători străini, vol. 10:2, 830. See also the engraving 'Boyarin aus der Moldau', Balthazar de la Motte Hacquet, 1790, in the French edition of his book *L'Illyrie et le Dalmatie, ou mœurs, usages et costumes de leurs habitants et des ceux des contrées voisines*. Paris 1815.

41 See the list of prices in *Catalogul vămilor* (The customs catalogue) for the taxing of goods entering Bucharest in 1792. Urechia, Istoria românilor, vol. 4, 1891, 246.

42 La Motte Hacquet, Hacquet's neueste physikalisch-politische Reisen, vol. 2. Nürnberg 1791; See Cernovodeanu, Călători străini, vol. 10:2, 844.

shawls and gold jewelry with diamonds, hints at the market value of cashmere and *giar* products from India. It suggests that a *giar* was worth 500 silver coins (*groschen*), which was a considerable sum of money. On 17 December 1813, Constantin noted that, from among the goods he had received from Lahore via Constantinople, he had sold fifteen shawls and five *giars* in Bucharest and sent another six shawls and one *giar* to Moscow, because they could not be sold locally. The deal brought him and his associates, Greek merchants in Constantinople, no less than 10,803 *groschen*.[43] Indeed, although a sumptuary law from 1778 (discussed in more detail below) stated that cashmere and *giar* shawls were "useful against the cold and durable",[44] and the fabrics were therefore not forbidden, the use and visual depiction of luxury items made of these materials shows that there was obviously more to it than the practical aspects alone.

The Boyars' and Boyaresses' Furs

Following the Ottoman model, the Romanian boyars and their wives wore rich and varied furs, regardless of the season.[45] Constantine Caracaș, a Greek doctor in Bucharest at the beginning of the nineteenth century, notes that the boyars wore many furs "one on top of the other", both in winter and in summer, and moreover adorned many other items of clothing with furs, while "the elegant bodies of the ladies were wrapped in light furs and heavy dresses of material from India, silk or goldwork."[46] Certain furs were very expensive and therefore traditionally formed part of ceremonials. They featured in the investiture of rulers, including the enrobing of boyars, and in the reception of diplomatic missions, as well as in the ritual exchange of gifts. Particular furs were also associated with a distinct position within the political hierarchy and with specific occasions. For instance, silk overcoats (*cübbe*) with ermine fur were worn only by the Grand *Vistier* and only on official occasions at the princely court. His everyday garments were adorned with squirrel or fox fur.[47]

It is no wonder that the boyars and their wives saw in furs an important means of social distinction and spent huge sums of money in order to buy

43 ANIC, Fond Achiziții Noi, LXXVII/7, 9, 10, 11, 12–17 December 1813.
44 BAR, Fond Carte Rară, CRV 443A, fol. 12r.
45 Hülya Tezcan: Furs and Skins owned by the Sultans, in: Faroqhi and Neumann, Ottoman Costumes, 63–79.
46 Constantin Caracaș: *O veche monografie a Munteniei de dr. Constantin Caracaș (1800–1828)*. Bucharest 1937, 107.
47 SJAN, Iași, Colecția Documente P. 1023/2.

expensive furs and fur adornments for their overcoats, headwear, and robes. There was a great variety of furs of different quality and price they could choose from. The *Customs Catalogue* of 1 January 1792 lists the furs available in the principalities according to their market value: furs of "black fox" were the most valuable, followed by "the good sables of Russia", so-called to distinguish them from "the poorer sables that come from Russian Lehia [Poland]" and "the sables of Beciu [Vienna]". For the less wealthy, the market also offered furs from ermine; black and Siberian polecats; red, white, and "Cossack" foxes; martens; and lynx, down to the everyday furs of rabbits and foxes.[48] The most expensive furs arrived every spring from Russia,[49] and those were the ones on which the elite spent most of their money. Alexandre d'Hauterive, the French secretary of Prince Alexander Mavrocordato Firaris (r. 1785–1786), saw how "Moldavians ruined themselves by buying expensive textiles and pelisses."[50] For example, the former Grand *Vistier* Ioan Canta spent considerable sums on cubits of silk fabric called *ghermeşut* silk (from Turkish *germsud*) imported from Damascus and Istanbul and on a silk fabric embroidered with silver or gold thread called *sevai* (from Turkish *sevayi*)[51]; these materials were then turned into "a *cübbe* lined with sable", "a red *cübbe* of *altân* [felt cloth with gold thread] lined with sable", and coats well adorned with the sable of "Mosc[ow]", Russian polecat (*sângeapi*), and the furs of squirrels, foxes, and mink.[52]

Dress and Politics: The Phanariot Reaction to Boyar Luxury

The opulent luxury of the boyars was not only a recurrent theme in the eye-witness accounts of the period.[53] It was also a phenomenon to which the

---

48 Urechia, Istoria Românilor, vol. 4, 248–249.
49 Ignatius Stefan Raicevich: *Observazioni Storiche, naturali e politiche intorno la Valachia et la Moldavia*. Naples 1788, 134. The author was the Ragusan secretary of Prince Alexander Ypsilantis.
50 "Les moldaves se ruinent en étoffes et en pelisses," Alexandre Maurice Blanc de Lanautte comte d'Hauterive: *Mémoire sur l'état ancien et actuel de la Moldavie (1787)*. Bucharest 1902, 322.
51 From the Turkish *sevayi*, silk fabric embroidered with silver or gold thread.
52 SJAN, Iaşi, Colecția Documente P. 1023/2, f. 52. The purchases are listed for 10 December 1776, 7 April 1777, and 5 April 1777.
53 See for instance the account written by Charles-Marie d'Irrumberry conte de Salaberry, who travelled to Istanbul in 1796 and made a long stop in Bucharest. He is amazed by the "opulent luxe" of the Wallachian boyars dressed up in "Indian fabrics, shawls and sable

Phanariot rulers had to pay attention, and they did so in a number of ways. Some Phanariot rulers supported the boyars' appetite for luxury. The chronicler Ion Neculce (1672–1745), a very wealthy boyar of early eighteenth-century Moldavia, writes that the Phanariot prince Gregorios Ghika (r. 1726–1733) "desired" that the court of Iaşi "be well dressed".[54] He asked the boyars, regardless of their material condition, to put on rich garments when they made an appearance at court.[55] At the opposite extreme was Prince Constantine Mavrocordato, who ruled several times over both Wallachia and Moldavia between 1726 and 1752.[56] A "rational" erudite, the ruler promoted moderation in all things. His own public appearances were lessons in modesty and simplicity. He also adopted an austere lifestyle: "He would get up early in the morning at five o'clock of the night and would stand in the church with great attention and piety, together with all the boyars and princely servants who dwelled at the princely court." The prince despised luxury and "the pleasures and pastimes of life", exiling music from the princely court and adopting fasting, prayer, and humility, thus presenting an example that could not be ignored. Indeed, according to the chronicler of the time, the boyars felt they had to remodel their public appearances according to the princely model: "Many of the great boyars were obliged to imitate the harsh fasts that he kept", give up tobacco, and "keep a rein on their bodily desires".[57]

However, the Phanariot rulers were often reluctant to curb the luxury and opulence of the local elites, because of their short reigns (only three years at a time) and the difficulty of implementing regulations regarding boyar lifestyle. For instance, Prince Gregorios Alexander Ghika (r. 1777–1782) of Moldavia reportedly "considered giving the command not to wear all sorts of garments", but did not have the courage to issue such a law, because "it might be that many [boyars] would not take this command into account." He knew that he would have to impose any such measure by force and did not dare punish the powerful boyars loved by the people. Instead, in order to not "look bad before the common people", he followed the above-mentioned model of Prince

---

furs". M. le Comte de Salaberry: *Essais sur la Valachie et la Moldavie, theatre de l'insurection dite Ypsilanti*. Paris 1821, 35.

54 He ruled several times: in Moldavia 1726–1733, 1735–1739, 1739–1741, 1747–1748; in Wallachia 1733–1735, 1748–1752.

55 Ion Neculce: *Letopiseţul Ţării Moldovei*. Chişinău 1990, 436.

56 He ruled several times: in Wallachia, 1730, 1735–1741, 1744–1748, 1756–1758, 1761–1763; in Moldavia, 1733–1735, 1741–1743, 1748–1749.

57 Nestor Camariano and Ariadna Camariano-Cioran (eds.): *Cronica Ghiculeştilor. Istoria Moldovei între anii 1695–1754*. Bucharest 1965, 621–623.

Constantine Mavrocordato. The chronicler of the time writes: "His Highness made for himself alone a suit of clothes of felt, *libade* and *cübbe*, and one day, without announcement, he came out dressed in them to the divan." Faced with the modest and frugal image presented by the ruler, the boyars could not but conform, at least when they were guests at the princely court: "Seeing this, the native boyars began also to make themselves *libades* and *cübbes* of felt."[58] Still, the felt coats were probably cast aside as soon as Prince Gregorios Alexander Ghika lost his throne and another prince, much more indulgent in matters of clothing, was installed.

This example underlines how fragile were the power relations between the native elite and the Phanariots. As has been mentioned, the boyars' social status had previously been based on birth rights: their belonging to an ancient family had given them the right to rise to the top of the social hierarchy, a social ascent that showed in their clothing, carriages, country houses, and heraldic insignia.[59] But with the arrival of the Phanariot rulers and their entourage, the Romanian boyars became excluded from direct access to high office. They entered a fierce competition for the most prestigious positions, investing in a "culture of appearances"[60] that proved ruinous to all sides. Moreover, a new social group emerged and made its appearance on this stage: the merchants who had enriched themselves from trade in luxury products. Profiting from this fluid redefinition of social groups, some of them bought ranks and offices, executed skillful matrimonial strategies, and entered the privileged group of the great boyars.

It is in this context that sumptuary laws appeared in the principalities. They testify to the Phanariot rulers' efforts to control state and society and regulate social mobility within the elite, whose composition changed with every change on the throne. Sartorial regulations existed in many places and were a common means by which authorities tried to control the wealth of the elite and regulate social distinction.[61] These sources therefore tell us about the competition between rulers, members of the elite, and those who tried to enter

---

58 Pseudo-Enache Kogălniceanu and Ioan Canta: *Letopisețul Țării Moldovei de la domnia întâi și până la a patra domnie a lui Costandin Mavrocordat vv. (1733–1774)*, ed. by Aurora Ilieş and Ioana Zmeu. Bucharest 1987, 117–118.
59 Claire Sponsler: Narrating the Social Order. Medieval Clothing Laws, in: *Clio* 21 (1992), 265–283, here 266.
60 An allusion to Daniel Roche: *La culture des apparences. Une histoire du vêtement XVIIe–XVIIIe siècle*. Paris 1989.
61 On Europe, see Alan Hunt: Governance of the Consuming Passions. A History of Sumptuary Law. New York 1996; Graeme Murdock: Dressed to repress? Protestant Clerical Dress and the Regulation of Morality in Early Modern Europe, in: *Fashion Theory* 4 (2000), 179–199; Catherine Kovesi Killerby: Sumptuary Law in Italy 1200–1500. Oxford 2002; Kate

these privileged circles. But they do not only "narrate the social order"[62]; they also highlight the need to affirm power relations through consumption and social practices. Because although luxury was often stigmatized as "the source of the devil", as for instance by Rousseau in his *Discourses*,[63] it nevertheless proved indispensable in the display of social identity. In most parts of Western Europe, sartorial regulations became sporadic in the eighteenth century.[64] In the Ottoman Empire, such regulations appeared in the context of an increased social mobility, a "social opening",[65] and continued to exist until late in the nineteenth century.[66] In the Romanian lands, clothing laws were promulgated only during a short period, belated in relation to Western Europe but not to the Ottoman Empire: the first sumptuary law dates from 1778, the last from 1815.[67]

The Romanian clothing laws were inspired by the Ottoman model. The Phanariot princes, as high officials in the Ottoman administrative system, were familiar with such texts, and the boyars travelled often enough to the empire's main cities to know about Ottoman sartorial regulations. The Wallachian high official and diplomatic agent Ianache Văcărescu (1740–1797) writes in his *History of the Most Powerful Ottoman Empire* about the reforms of the sultan of his time, Sultan Mustafa III (r. 1757–1773): "He changed the debauched clothes both of the subjects (re'ayas), with the command that all should wear black clothes in Istanbul and elsewhere, excepting only Vlaho-Moldavia, and of the Turks, both with a command to wear simple clothes and by example, for the Emperor himself wore them." The author underlines that while these dress regulations did not apply in the territory of the tributary principalities, they still served the Phanariot ruler Constantine Mourouzis (r. 1777–1782) as an example and made him appear in public in "plain clothes".[68]

Dimitrova and Margaret Goehring (eds.): Dressing the Part. Textiles as Propaganda in the Middle Ages. Turnhout 2014.

62 Sponsler, Narrating.

63 Jeremy Jennings: The Debate about Luxury in Eighteenth and Nineteenth-Century French Political Thought, in: *Journal of the History of Ideas* 68 (2007), 81.

64 Ulinka Rublack: *Dressing Up. Cultural Identity in Renaissance Europe*. Oxford 2010, 265–270.

65 Quataert, Clothing Laws, 406.

66 Ibid., 403–425.

67 In Romanian historiography, sumptuary laws have been more often cited than analysed. See: Alexianu, Mode și veşminte; Adrian-Silvan Ionescu: *Modă şi societate urbană în România epocii modern*. Bucharest 2007; Ioan-August Guriță: *Gavril Callimachi. Mitropolitul Moldovei (1760–1786)*. Iași 2017, 322–325.

68 Ianache Văcărescu: *Istoria Othomanicească*, critical edition, introductory study, notes, and glossary by Gabriel Ştrempel. Bucharest 2001, 94. The author held the positions of grand

The first sumptuary law in the principalities was issued in 1778 by Prince Constantine Mourouzis, but it was crafted by the head of the Orthodox Church in Moldavia, Metropolitan Gavril Kalimaki. It also includes the signature of Patriarch Avram of Jerusalem, as well as a curse on all men and women who would not submit to the command of these political and religious authorities. The law did not prohibit a particular fashion or color but rather certain rich fabrics and ornaments that added value to men's and women's garments: "taffeta, *cumaş* (from Turkish *Kumaş*, silk fabric), *ghermeşut* from India, Şam [Damascus], Ţarigrad [Istanbul], or Europe woven with wire (*fir*), braid (*peteală*), gold and silver thread (*sârmă*), or flowers of silk." The latter ornaments were all forbidden. Clothes had to be "plain", made of fabrics without other threads added and without adornments, braid, or lace. However, as mentioned above, cashmere shawls and *giars* did not come under the interdiction, with the explanation that they protected from the cold. Also excluded were the valuable caftans used by rulers to invest new officials, those offered to brides, and other textiles used at weddings.[69]

The text of the law mentions economic and moral concerns as the motives behind the legislation. This line of argumentation reappears in later sumptuary laws, including, for instance, one promulgated in 1794, which prohibited the import of expensive fabrics, and one promulgated in 1796, which forbade the import of carriages in order to support local manufacturers.[70] The 1778 law condemned "the grand houses of the great boyars" who went into debt "out of pride", wasting their fortunes on the "vanity" of appearances, ruining the country and corrupting the morals of the society. The text argues that the interdiction of the aforesaid fabrics and ornaments was necessary on the grounds of their precarious nature: brought from far off and purchased with extraordinary financial efforts, these clothes were kept in conditions where they deteriorated quickly, damaged by the "smoke" in boyar houses or eaten by moths during the long winters.[71] The clothes therefore could not accumulate wealth or become a secure capital for the family estate or form part of the inheritance, which was critical for the family's survival. If the boyars wanted adornments,

---

spătar [minister of the army], grand *vistier* [treasurer], and grand *ban* [governor of the province Oltenia]. He authored his history between 1788 and 1794.

69 BAR, Fond Carte rară CRV 443A, ff. 1r–13v. See also Dumitru Furnică: *Din istoria comerţului la români mai ales băcănie, 1593–1855.* Bucharest 1908, 45–57.

70 Urechia, Istoria românilor, V, 306–307, X/1, 575.

71 Boyar houses were heated in the winter with stoves that produced thick smoke, in rooms that were not well ventilated. Clothes and other items were kept in chests and coffers, sprinkled with tobacco leaves or lavender flowers.

the text argues, they should adorn themselves with jewelry and other "items of gold", that is, "things that do not spoil" and "are an enduring fortune, which is kept down to the sons of sons".[72] Indeed, the last wills of contemporaries show that clothes mostly vanished while those other items survived. The will of Maria Văcărescu, for instance, the divorced wife of grand *ban* Nicolae Brâncoveanu, notes that many of the "fabrics" she had received as dowry have been "lost", while a considerable amount of her jewelry passed to her heirs. Unlike clothing, such items of gold, diamonds, rubies, sapphires, or emeralds could indeed be used as currency to purchase estates, deposited as security, or offered as gifts.[73]

Still, "prestige expenses" (Norbert Elias) were indispensable for maintaining rank,[74] and the 1778 law explicitly recognized the need for luxury in highlighting and displaying rank, office, and social status in public. It distinguished between the adequate consumption habits of different groups and of individuals of different financial means within these groups. It targeted the "new men", those rich merchants who bought themselves a place in the social hierarchy by the display of opulent luxury, and it acknowledged that the boyars generally believed they were "doing their duty" when they "adorn[ed] themselves with valuable and expensive clothes" and ruined themselves in "glittering ornaments" out of "the love of honor".[75] Therefore, the text argues, such extravagant expenses should be incurred only by those who can afford them; "those who are lacking and do not have are not obliged to become indebted beyond what is permissible for clothes, which it would be fitting for them to have in common with those of their own sort."[76]

It is uncertain to what extent these sumptuary laws were followed or enforced. This is a typical problem in the study of legal texts, which has been discussed with regard to other regions.[77] Prince Constantine Mourouzis' sumptuary law of 1778 apparently was immediately made light of. After the text was read aloud to the public in the main square, to the sound of drums, pamphlets spread in the alleyways of Iași mocking the ruler's efforts:

---

72 BAR, Fond Carte rară CRV 443A, ff. 12v–13r.

73 BAR, Fond Documente Istorice, MLXXXVI/34, 19 September 1797.

74 Norbert Elias: *La société de cour*. Paris 1974, 49.

75 BAR, Fond Carte rară CRV 443A, f. 7r–v.

76 BAR, Fond Carte rară CRV 443A, f. 7r.

77 On the Ottoman Empire see Zilfi, Whose laws?, 127. On contemporary Italy see Diane Owen Hughes: Sumptuary Law and Social Relations in Renaissance Italy, in: John Bossy (ed.): *Disputes and Settlements. Law and Human Relations in the West*. Cambridge 1983, 69–99.

Contantine *Vodă* Mourouzis / Being a very grumpy man / Gave an order firmly / That all
should wear homespun / Oh, my poor *cübbe* / With *artaname*[78] and heavy / I had lined it
with sable fur / To wear it at Christmas / But now woe is me / I'll never put it on again.[79]

Indeed, it seems as if the law could not temper the boyars' desire for social recognition. They seem to have continued playing out their prestige on the public
stage through luxury consumption. The sanctioned textiles and ornaments appear prominently among the purchases of members of the boyar elite of the
time. For instance, in the same year the law was promulgated, 1778, several
such items appear in the dowry received by Măriuța Cantacuzino-Deleanu, the
daughter of the great boyar and former Grand *Spătar* Iordache Cantacuzino, on
her marriage to the former Grand *Agă* Constantine Ghica: "a *cübbe* coat of *altân*
[felt cloth with gold thread], a dress, and an *anteri* coat, all of them similarly
furred: with a lining and edging of sable and with heavy laces." The dowry list
includes also other items of clothing as well as many other "items of gold". The
wedding itself was held with great pomp at the country house of Deleni, outside
of Iași.[80]

Conclusion

When in 1711 Phanariot Greeks from Istanbul replaced the local boyars as rulers
of Moldavia and Wallachia, this accelerated the process of the Ottomanization
of Romanian society, a process that found expression in the clothing and consumption patterns of the local elites. The great boyars with access to the court
partly adopted the dress and lifestyle introduced by the new rulers and their
entourage. In particular, they started wearing certain Ottoman-inspired headgear, such as the *işlic*, while their wives admired shawls. Elite members of both
sexes also invested heavily in expensive textiles, furs, and other luxury items in
accordance with the Phanariots' model. However, the local elites did not simply
copy Ottoman clothing items but also found inspiration in European fashion
trends. They used these new textiles, garments, and accessories purposefully,
in order to fashion their own identity and assert what they saw as their superiority over both the Phanariots and their Greek entourage.

---

78 Probably *altâl, altânbaş*, a felt cloth woven with gold thread. See the explanation in
Alexianu, Modă și veșminte, vol. 2, 370.
79 Ibid., 103.
80 BAR, Fond Documente Istorice, CCCCXXVII/53, 2 April 1782.

Moreover, expensive Ottoman-style clothes and luxury items also served for the boyars as key instruments in the competition for high office and rank among themselves and for the newly rich in their efforts to acquire high office and enter such elite circles. Obtaining and maintaining high social status involved a considerable consumption and public display of luxury goods. To show his rank, a high-ranking boyar had to appear at the princely court in specific attire: a sable *işlic* accompanying a lavishly decorated *cübbe* with sable lining and a cashmere *taklid*. He was forced to spend great sums of money or even to go into debt in order to purchase those items that guaranteed him political visibility and a prestigious position in the social hierarchy. Indeed, Ottoman material culture had a profound impact on identity formation in the Danubian Principalities, as it did for Christian elites elsewhere in the Ottoman Empire; it provided social markers of difference and was of utmost importance for the elite's self-representation and self-fashioning.

Consumption, luxury, and the construction of social identity were intrinsically linked, and this applied to both men and women. The wives of the great boyars followed Ottoman fashion trends no less than their husbands, and participated with them in the public display of luxury items. The Romanian sumptuary laws, which were issued by the Phanariot rulers in collaboration with the religious authorities between 1778 and 1815, therefore almost never referred to women as a separate social category.[81] Rather, they addressed the whole society, singling out men in the upper elite of society for promoting extravagant expenses. However, it seems that expensive clothes and luxury items remained a key means of social distinction. The fragile balance of power made most of the Phanariot rulers hesitant to curb the luxury and ostentation of the local elite by issuing or rigidly imposing clothing laws. Instead, some of them decided to provide a model of modesty themselves, putting pressure on the great boyars to follow suit.

---

[81] Compare the clothing regulations in the Ottoman Empire referring to women, seen as important figures in the propagation of luxury and immorality, Zilfi, Whose laws?, 135–136.

Giulia Calvi
Imperial Fashions: Cashmere Shawls between Istanbul, Paris, and Milan (Eighteenth and Nineteenth Centuries)

Abstract: *Descriptions of material culture offer a point of entry into the circulation of textual and visual knowledge from the Ottoman to the French Empire and Italy in the late eighteenth and early nineteenth centuries. This article analyzes, discusses, and connects three different sources: Ignatius Mouradgea d'Ohsson's* Tableau général de l'Empire Ottoman *(1787–1820), Giulio Ferrario's* Il costume antico e modern *(1817–1834) and Carolina Lattanzi's* Il Corriere delle Dame *(1804–1874). The texts shed light on the fashion for cashmere shawls and cashmere cloth imported from India to the Ottoman Empire and Europe in the Napoleonic era. They also outline the crucial role of translation from Turkish to French and Italian as well as the role of dragomans, printers, engravers and editors in spreading the culture of fashion.*

In recent years and in connection with the growth of global history, the notion of *fashion* has attracted several critical assessments in view of its Eurocentric leanings.[1] The study and classification of fashion should be more globally inclusive – so goes the argument – and not centered on the notion of style change, which generally coincides with a process of westernization across the globe, equating fashion with Western modernity and labeling all other clothing practices as traditional and static. Attention has shifted to differences of time and place and to the interrelated dynamics that contribute to the making of fashion. These comprise groups of manufacturers, designers, retailers, journalists, promoters, and consumers – groups that are in communication with each other and common to all fashion systems. From this perspective, the system of

---

1 Arti Sandhu: *Indian Fashion. Tradition, Innovation, Style.* London 2015, 8; Tereza Kuldova: *Luxury Indian Fashion. A Social Critique.* London 2016.

Note: This study was supported by the project *Luxury, Fashion and Social Status in Early Modern South-Eastern Europe (LuxFaSS)*, with the reference number ERC-2014-CoG 646489, financed by the European Research Council and hosted by New Europe College, Bucharest.

fashion becomes a "hybrid subject" characterized by the interconnecting networks of various forms of production, consumption, and demand.[2]

In this chapter I will focus on some hybrid practices of clothing consumption, tracing the ways through which Eastern cashmere patterns and shawls acted as a source of inspiration across the Mediterranean. Between the second half of the eighteenth and first half of the nineteenth century these patterns and shawls were imported, imitated, selectively appropriated, and adapted, from India to Istanbul, Paris, and Milan.[3] I will focus on the role of mediators: intellectuals, institutions, printing firms, artists, journalists, and magazines for a female audience. All of them shaped the fashion for cashmere, spreading it across borders, languages and social classes, and turning it into a widespread popular phenomenon of hybrid and gendered clothing practices.

Trading with the Levant

Since the second half of the sixteenth century, the Levant had been a crucial gateway for printed cottons flowing from Indian centers of manufacture into Europe. Portugal was the first European country to open the trade, which also flourished along the route connecting Cairo or Alexandria to Venice and from there to all of Europe.[4] From the seventeenth century, Genoa, Livorno, and especially Marseille were importing Indian textiles and producing local imitations.[5] In Marseille and in Venice production was in the hands of Armenians from the Ottoman Empire. The circulation of Asian patterns and textiles was part of the migration of Christian minorities, Greeks and Armenians, fleeing to Venice from the Ottoman conquest of Byzantine territories and taking with them know-how, technology, and innovations. In 1733 the Venetian Senate

---

2 Sandhu, Indian Fashion, 9; Beverly Lemire: Domesticating the Exotic. Floral Culture and the East India Calico Trade with England, c. 1600–1800, in: *Textile History* 34 (2003), 65–85.

3 This paper is an enlarged and throughly revised version of an earlier publication. See Giulia Calvi: Translating Imperial Practices, Knowledge and Taste Across the Mediterranean. Giulio Ferrario and Ignatius Mouradgea d'Ohsson, in: Costanta Vintilă-Ghiţulescu (ed.), *Women, Consumption, and the Circulation of Ideas in South Eastern Europe, 17th-19th Centuries*, Leiden 2017, 12–46.

4 Maria Joao Ferreira: Asian Textiles in the Carreira da India. Portuguese Trade, Consumption and Taste, 1500–1700, in: *Textile History* 46 (2015), 147–168.

5 Margherita Bellezza Rosina and Marzia Cataldi Gallo: *Cotoni stampati e mezzari dalle Indie all'Europa*. Genoa 1993, 69; Olivier Raveux: Fashion and Consumption of Painted and Printed Calicoes in the Mediterranean during the later Seventeenth Century. the Case of Chintz Quilts and Banyans in Marseilles, in: *Textile History* 45 (2014), 49–67.

granted the Armenian weaver Elia d'Alessandri a twenty-year monopoly for the production of cotton cloth with gold and silver thread and natural flowers "in the Indian style of Basdar and Suratt". As it was difficult to import Indian cotton due to the "extreme" distance, he was allowed to use cotton from the Greek islands of Kefalonia and Zante. The Armenian also exported to Istanbul shawls woven with Spanish wool and decorated with natural flowers, gold and silver that "sell well in the Turkish lands".[6] For 40 years, until 1773, the Armenian family d'Alessandri carried on the production of different types of textiles for the domestic and Turkish markets, receiving public financial support and tax exemptions. The designs as well as the brilliance and fastness of color of Indian textiles attracted early modern European and Ottoman consumers, setting the stage for the later fashion of cashmere patterns and shawls.

Historians of material culture generally underestimate the non-Western side of this phenomenon, as well as the importance of colonialism in establishing trade routes and networks. Eurocentric accounts have often assumed that cashmere shawls became fashionable only through being displayed in Europe, based on the claim that fashion is a purely Western phenomenon.[7] From India, these precious items of clothing were exported to Istanbul, Alexandria, and Russia, and to the Romanian principalities, where painters portrayed men and women from the boyar dynasties wearing shawls, sashes, and turbans in a variety of striped and floral patterns. In Trieste, the popular portrait artist Giuseppe Tominz used cashmere shawls in a variety of colorful patterns to portray high-status Habsburg ladies, women in Greek and Slav merchant households, as well as Turks living in the city.[8] Napoleon and his officers brought cashmere shawls back from the 1798–1801 French Egyptian campaign, and Empress Josephine (1804–1809) started the fashion of wearing them in Paris. Her collection consisted of 300 to 400 cashmere shawls.[9] French consumers obtained the shawls from resident agents in Istanbul and Moscow, as well as from Alexandria and Smyrna via Marseille.[10]

---

6 Roberto Berveglieri: *Inventori stranieri a Venezia (1474–1788)*. Venice 1995, 233–249.

7 Carlo Marco Belfanti: Was Fashion a European Invention?, in: *Journal of Global History* (2008), 3, 419–443; Michelle Maskiell: Consuming Kashmir. Shawls and Empires, 1500–2000, in: *Journal of World History* 13 (2002), 1, 27–65.

8 Fabrizio Magani: Giuseppe Tominz ritrattista goriziano, in: Giuseppe Esposito and Annalia Delneri (eds.): *Ottocento di frontiera. Gorizia 1780–1850. Arte e cultura*. Milan 1995.

9 Annemarie Kleinert: Le *"Journal des dames et des modes" ou la conquête de l'Europe féminine (1797–1839)*. Stuttgart 2001, 86.

10 Monique Lévi-Strauss: *Cashemire. La Création française 1800–1880*. Paris 2012; Susan Hiner: Lust for Luxe. Cashmere Fever in Nineteenth Century France, in: *Journal of Early Modern Cultural Studies* 5 (2005), 1, 76–98.

Luxury Comes from the East

In the second half of the eighteenth century, the fashion for cashmere shawls was spreading in Istanbul. The following text comments on Ottoman civil society at the time, where luxury textiles coming from the east encouraged practices of social distinction and the creation of different markets for elites and ordinary people and where consumption often transgressed religious norms:

> Under Ottoman rule a widespread deviation from the traditional clothing norms of the Quran has taken place. Except for the *ulema* and a few lay devotees, all well-to-do families manage to procure silk clothes and the richest textiles. Those coming from India are the most sought after. They come in single colors; striped; with flowers and in every kind of silk; in golden and silver thread for the gentle sex; for servants in wealthy households; and for some administrators at the Court. Highly-priced shawls of extremely fine wool are in great fashion. Price is of no concern, as the Ottomans love to have those measuring twelve feet by four and of such fine weave that they can pass through a ring. Men and women wear them all year long. In winter, men wear them to walk the streets and go horse riding. They cover their heads with these shawls in bad weather, as in those countries people have no umbrellas and carriages are reserved for the delicate sex. Women cover their heads and shoulders and some make winter clothes that cost more than the finest muslins and the more exquisitely embroidered textiles. People of the lower orders wear locally produced shawls.[11]

The Itschs Agassy, domestic servants in wealthy households, could wear silk and Indian shawls, and officers at the court were followed by a laquais "chargé d'un schal des Indes", whose charge was to carry an Indian shawl to cover their masters' heads in case of rain.[12]

This detailed description of the inclination for precious Indian textiles and cashmere shawls in Istanbul contrasts with the practices of less wealthy Christian minorities in provincial towns, who follow the dictates of Ottoman and western fashion in a flexible way:

> Christian women, especially the Greeks, enjoy more freedom and sometimes follow European fashions and use makeup. If they leave the house, they have to conform to Muslim rules and wear the veil, a dark *feredjé* and black shoes. All women from other nationalities must follow the same rules, and in all urban districts police officers from

---

11 Giulio Ferrario, *Il costume antico e moderno, o storia della milizia, della religione, delle arti, scienze ed usanze di tutti i popoli antichi e moderni, provata coi monumenti dell'antichità e rappresentata cogli analoghi disegni. Europa, vol. 4: Dell'Impero Ottomano. Degli Slavi moderni a cura di Carlo Magnetti*, Milan 1827, 385 (my translation).
12 Ignatius Mouradgea d'Ohsson: *Tableau général de l'Empire Othoman*, vol. 2. Paris 1790, 160–161.

time to time read out loud these sumptuary regulations. Such rigid codes of dress are not enforced in the provinces, and in the islands of the Greek archipelago there is the greatest freedom. Here women keep to their ancient customs and go unveiled. Therefore, European women who have settled in the provinces of the Empire are less restless. Their clothing is indeed a bizarre mixture of many costumes: some wear the *feredjé* and an Indian shawl in lieu of a veil.[13]

Both quotations introduce the reader to crucial features of luxury goods, whose main rhetorical and social use was embedded in a web of values and norms. Religion, ethnicity, class, and gender affected the level of demand for both locally-produced and imported goods, constructing the social codes that defined consumption, sociality, and appearance: wealthy Muslim families broke the monopoly of Islamic law and adopted transgressive clothing practices; elite men and women wore original textiles from India, while ordinary people bought locally-produced imitations; rigid sumptuary codes in Istanbul contrasted with the more tolerant *milieu* of provincial towns; and for both Muslims and Christians religion played a central role in the construction of consumption practices.

Ignatius Mouradgea d'Ohsson

The new preference for long and light cashmere shawls imported from India to Istanbul traces a *fil rouge* connecting material modernity, distinction, and taste. This can be seen in two beautifully illustrated folio volumes published for the educated elite of Europe: Ignatius Mouradgea d'Ohsson's *Tableau général de l'Empire Ottoman*, printed in Paris in three volumes by Didot between 1787 and 1820; and Giulio Ferrario's *Il costume antico e moderno*, published in Milan between 1827 and 1834. Ignatius Mouradgea d'Ohsson (1740–1807) was the first Ottoman to publish in French an illustrated history of the Ottoman Empire. An Armenian dragoman (interpreter) in the service of the Swedish consul in Constantinople, Ignatius Mouradgea was born to a French mother and a Catholic Armenian father already in the service of the Swedish diplomatic representative as an interpreter.[14] In this cosmopolitan milieu, the Mouradgeas, father and son,

---

13 Ferrario, Il costume, 358.
14 Elisabeth A. Fraser: "Dressing Turks in the French Manner". Mouradgea d'Ohsson's Panorama of the Ottoman Empire, in: *Ars Orientalis* 39 (2010), 199–229; Carter Findley: Writer and Subject, Self and Other. Mouradgea d'Ohsson and his Tableau générale de l'Empire Othoman, in: Sture Theolin et al. (eds.): *The Torch of the Empire. Ignatius Mouradgea d'Ohsson and the Tableau*

were cultural mediators, having good knowledge of languages and being well integrated in the court hierarchy and in the political networks of the Empire. Ignatius added the name d'Ohsson in 1787, when the king of Sweden Gustave III gave him noble status as reward for his services to the crown. In 1784 he left for Paris to publish his celebrated work, printed by Pierre Francois Didot "the younger", a central figure of the Parisian luxury book trade. A subscription aimed at an aristocratic readership financed a deluxe *elephant folio* edition, illustrated with 233 engravings, 41 of which are full-page or double-page foldouts. In the opening discourse to the reader, d'Ohsson sketches a short biography: "I was born and grew up in Constantinople, and during my entire life I was employed in the service of a court intimately connected to the Sublime Porte. More than anybody else I had the means to overcome all difficulties and to accomplish the task that I have now decided to complete."[15] The *Tableau général* is divided into two parts: the first on Muslim jurisprudence and the second on the history of the Ottoman Empire, which d'Ohsson never completed. In the second volume, the section on morality comprises two books: the first is entitled "food" (*de la nourriture*), and the second, "dress" (*du vetement*), which includes sumptuary norms, interior decoration, styles of clothing, shoes, furs, colors, perfumes, and carriages.

Among a wealth of images showing major religious practices (pilgrimage to Mecca, mosques, burial sites, ceremonies, processions) and some secular entertainments (libraries, music, and dance), a few plates represent the clothing of men and women from different ethnicities. Long cashmere shawls drape the bodies of elite European women, distinguishing them from Muslim women and slaves who wear the veil. A team of at least 28 artists (painters, designers, and engravers) produced most of the prints, under the direction of Charles Nicolas Cochin (1715–1791), a major figure in the eighteenth-century art world in Paris. Recent research has shed light on the Ottoman and Persian sources of the *Tableau général* and the French adaptation of the paintings and drawings that d'Ohsson brought with him from Constantinople, which the French disliked and transformed, hiring painters to redraw the "clumsy" figures of the originals to meet western aesthetics and taste.[16] Still, d'Ohsson insists that, because of a long-standing iconoclastic tradition, only extreme caution, lengthy and expensive procedures, and painstaking research enabled him to acquire the

générale de l'Empire Othoman in the Eighteenth Century. Istanbul 2002, 27–28; Elisabeth A. Fraser: *Mediterranean Encounters. Artists Between Europe and the Ottoman Empire 1774–1839*. University Park, PA 2017.

15 Ignatius Mouradgea d'Ohsson: *Tableau général de l'Empire Othoman*, vol. 1, Paris 1788, *Discours préliminaire*.

16 Fraser, Dressing Turks, 213.

collection of paintings and drawings he brought to Paris. Ottoman painters had produced them with great difficulty and in secrecy, working either on their own or in d'Ohsson's home. He argues that there were no great artists in the Empire, at least none that compared to painters in Italy, France, or the Netherlands:

> How could they advance in this sublime art in a nation that does not care about it, where there are no models and where even the Christians have no taste for paintings, nor the habit of getting portrayed, and where Greek and Armenian painters have no other resources for their talent but painting holy images in churches or in private chapels? [...] It is useless to talk about Muslim painters: there are perhaps twenty in the whole Empire and they limit themselves to landscapes, maps, and drawings [...] some paint animals, but rarely human figures.[17]

Partial translations of the *Tableau général* in German, Russian, Swedish, and English (the latter published in Philadelphia in 1788) were put on the market. However, a further editorial circulation in Italy has not yet been acknowledged. I will now turn to this unexplored connection between Istanbul, Paris and Milan, the capital of Napoleon's Regno d'Italia (kingdom of Italy) and one of the main urban hubs of the French Empire where information on fashion was produced and disseminated.

Fashion, Books, and Giulio Ferrario

Little is known of the spread of cashmere shawls in Italy, which seems to have occurred via importation from France, in the period during and after the Napoleonic regime. The decade between 1805 and 1815 witnessed an important modernizing thrust in Italian society, and consumption was part of a larger cultural transformation shaped by print and mass media. Fashion was not just a matter of expanding markets or imitation. It was also shaped by "a culture in which print was central, and it was the printing of information – visual as well as textual – that spread practices of fashion that could be fully communicated".[18] In the first decade of the nineteenth century, the editorial business in Milan was expanding rapidly.[19] Napoleon was crowned king of Italy in Milan's Duomo in 1805, and the capital of the kingdom, where the court and administration resided,

---

17 Mouradgea d'Ohsson, Tableau générale, vol. 2, 456–458.
18 Beverly Lemire and Giorgio Riello: East & West. Textile Fashions in Early Modern Europe, in: *Journal of Social History* 41 (2008), 887–916, quotation on 888.
19 Marino Berengo: *Intellettuali e librai nella Milano della Restaurazione*. Milan 2012 repr. Milan 1980.

offered many opportunities for employment and entrepreneurship. Important innovations, such as compulsory primary education and public subsidies for publishers, sparked the growth of an editorial market that catered to a widening readership.

In this vibrant cultural atmosphere Giulio Ferrario published a monumental collection of world history, *Il costume antico e moderno* (Ancient and modern costumes of the peoples of the world), published in 21 volumes between 1817 and 1834 in parallel Italian and French editions.[20] The fourth of his nine volumes on Europe was dedicated to the Ottoman Empire, for which Ferrario used Mouradgea d'Ohsson's *Tableau général* as his main textual and only visual reference. The two authors have never been studied in connection to one another, and this analytical angle sheds light on the translating capacities of two public intellectuals, who, in different geopolitical centers of the Mediterranean, worked as mediators across imperial boundaries, spreading fashion, prints, and books.

Giulio Ferrario (1767–1849) was an erudite ecclesiastic, a sophisticated philologist and a cultural entrepreneur, librarian and then director of the Biblioteca Braidense, the main public library in Milan. He lived through Napoleon's reign in Italy and its demise in 1814. He then became a faithful subject of the Austrian monarchy and dedicated his major work to the Habsburg Emperor Franz I.[21] His *Il costume antico e moderno* built upon the tradition of early modern costume books in a world perspective, which in the early modern period were printed in Italy, Europe, and in some non-Western countries.[22] This encyclopedic work was also part of a developing editorial production, in which compendiums of contemporary travel literature gained increasing success.

Ferrario's volume on the Ottoman Empire contains water-colored prints picturing the costumes of the different ethnic groups in the Empire's lands, with a last section on the "modern Slavs". 85 illustrations were readapted from the *Tableau général*. Ferrario's small team of artists readjusted the visual apparatus, which had already gone through a Westernizing process of translation. Vittorio and Francesco Raineri, Leone Giacomo Bussi, and Giacomo Gallina colored the black-and-white plates by hand, and at times condensed the representation of figures in the space of the page, as Ferrario's edition was not an *elephant folio*. On the whole, however, the plates are faithful reproductions of Mouradgea

---

20 Ferrario, Il costume.
21 Stefano Nutini: Ferrario, Giulio, in: *Dizionario Biografico degli Italiani*, vol. 46. Rome 1996. http://www.treccani.it/enciclopedia/giulio-ferrario_(Dizionario-Biografico)/ (6 July 2019).
22 Giulia Calvi: Cultures of Space. Costume Books, Maps and Clothing Between Europe and Japan (Sixteenth to Ninetenth centuries), in: *I Tatti Studies in the Italian Renaissance* 20 (2017), 331–363.

d'Ohsson's images, which focus on the vivid representation of ceremonies, mosques, burial sites, libraries, the Bosporus, music, and dance. The images of women's and men's clothing repeat the original visual apparatus, portraying European women wearing cashmere shawls in contrast to the veiled Muslims. Throughout his work, Ferrario systematically looks at civil society ("civil customs", the customs of "private people"), outlining the practices that shape "the active consumer" who participates in taste formation, responding to new goods and combining goods in new ways to create a social identity and lifestyle. In this context, Ferrario translates the section on "morality" in the second volume of d'Ohsson's work.

In the longstanding Western tradition of costume books, the meaning of custom comprises social norms and bodily practices as well as the material culture of clothing and fashion across genders, ethnicities, and ages. Ferrario delves into d'Ohsson's text for cuts, shapes, and colors of dress, shoes, furs, turbans and hats, detailing how men and women use perfume, smoke tobacco and opium, drink coffee, listen to music and, when inebriated by alcohol and opium, dance. Translating d'Ohsson, who wrote for a European audience, Ferrario mirrors his perspective on the Ottoman's widespread private transgression of sumptuary laws shaped by Islamic moral codes. The description of the passion for cashmere shawls is repeated word for word from the *Tableau général* but is not confined to the immense city of Constantinople, which "mixes foreigners of different nations with the local inhabitants, Muslim and Christian, offering the most striking diversity of costumes and languages, and infinite nuances of customs and practices".[23] Tracing the route of Indian textiles across the Levant into the manufacturing centers of the Asian subcontinent, Ferrario acknowledges the high quality of Indian production, its global export, and the transformation of this process as a result of European technology. His attention focuses on the imitation and hybridization encouraged by the circulation of Western products in the East, and vice versa.

> Indian artisans with great skill and intelligence copy Europe's most refined products and they do it using simple tools. No artisan in our countries could do this [. . .] In some productions, such as printed textiles, Indian craftsmen are absolutely superior to Europeans. Manufactures in Europe cannot reach the lively and long-lasting colors of Indian textiles. The same is true for precious stones and golden filigree. Indian silk and cotton production is universally acclaimed. Their woven cotton is incredibly fine and they can mend a broken piece of muslin with such dexterity that no human eye would ever detect it. They weave 4 meters long muslin pieces of cloth that can fit into a snuff-box or pass through a ring. Indians are the most skilled weavers in the whole world and have

---

23 Mouradgea d'Ohsson, Tableau générale, vol. 2, 429.

exported their products since Roman times to distant lands [...]. Our famous machines in Manchester produce cotton and woolen textiles at great speed; but Indian patience is superior to European efficiency in delicacy and finesse.[24]

Ferrario emphasizes Asian trade networks and downplays the quality of European manufactures, echoing contemporary aesthetic trends that valued authentic patterns of handloom weaving over the Western rational organization of mass-produced copies "from our famous Manchester machines". He traces the routes of Indian cloth from the Coromandel Coast to Europe, and from other Indian regions to Africa and America. Golden and silver woven textiles are sold to China and are much preferred to those produced in Lyon for their unequalled light texture. From the mountainous Kashmir region come the shawls, scarves and woolen cloth that Italians call *Casimir*.[25] Asian imports and European-made copies were integrated into European fashion cycles – Chinoiserie, orientalism, japonisme, Indian style – creating different markets for different consumers: consumers of the middling sort bought European-made items, while elites distinguished themselves by wearing the high-priced originals.

Ferrario's work shows that cashmere soon spread to Western Europe and Milan. In part two of the third volume of *Il costume*, which focuses on urban society in contemporary Italy, he writes that, in winter, women wear cashmere with differentently decorated patterns: "We have seen cashmere dresses adorned with three rows of tulips [...] large merino shawls with borders woven into large bunches of flowers or long merino woolen scarfs with high borders like the ones you can see in the illustration. The price of these varies according to their quality and fine texture."[26] (Figure 1) For a complete picture of fashion in Milan, however, Ferrario advises his readers to read the *Corriere delle Dame*, one of the first magazines for women to be issued in Italy. In the preceding 24 years, he notes, this journal had issued 20 volumes that popularized the changing Parisian fashions in detailed colored plates, adding to it the local styles of dress worn by Italians who refused to follow passively Imperial French whims.[27]

---

24 Ferrario, Il costume, Asia, vol. 2, 206–208.
25 Ibid., 208–209.
26 Ibid., Europa, vol. 3, pt. 2, 931.
27 Ferrario, Il costume, Europa, vol. 3, 117.

Figure 1: Giulio Ferrario: *Il costume antico e moderno, Europa*, vol. 3, pt. 2, 929, fig. 139. Courtesy of the Biblioteca Braidense, Milan.

Il Corriere delle Dame (1804–1874)

The *Corriere delle Dame*, from which Ferrario draws his information on contemporary urban fashion and lifestyle in Milan, was the most up-to-date fashion journal addressed to a female readership. Modeled after the French *Journal des Dames et des Modes* (1797–1839),[28] it reproduced fashion plates of women's and

---

28 Kleinert, Journal des dames et des modes.

men's clothing, mostly from Paris, and later from London and Vienna, with some Italian dresses and accessories, too. The journal began its weekly publication in 1804, profiting from the unique opportunity provided by Napoleon's coronation. Preparation for the sumptuous ceremony extended to the new kingdom of Italy, where French regulations on furnishings and gala dresses for the court were introduced. Fashion dealers, tailors, hairdressers, and embroiderers invaded Milan, putting on the market a wide variety of products for the elites who were waiting to take part in the coronation.

The *Corriere delle Dame* was owned and directed by Carolina Lattanzi, née Arienti (1771–1818), an energetic intellectual with feminist leanings, who took advantage of the opportunity and quickly established good relations with members of the new government.[29] She managed to obtain the monopoly for publishing the prints of all uniforms of the highest charges and magistrates of the kingdom, as well as 25 subscriptions to the *Corriere delle dame* from members of the viceregal court. The journal expressed strong support for Napoleon and his entourage, celebrating, as Lattanzi wrote, the rising of the new Empire in Europe in contrast to the decline of the Ottomans.

The colored fashion illustrations, which could also be printed separately, were the key assets of the journal, which was not only an editorial but also a financial success, owing to the innovative commercial enterprise launched by Lattanzi. All items in the prints – clothing for men and women, as well as accessories such as cashmere shawls and cashmere gilets for men – were described in detail, priced and sold, and shipped through the mail service to the subscribers who requested them. The prints reproduced French and, to a lesser degree, Italian fashion (Figures 2 and 3). The use of cashmere was not exclusively focused on women's shawls, scarves, cloaks, and dresses, but also included clothing for men: cashmere trousers and gilets. Several of the journal's February, March, and April issues of 1807 reproduced and sold madras shawls and scarves with decorated and colored woven patterns as well as long white cashmere scarves with woven, colored borders. The May issues advertised dresses made of Indian muslin, large embroidered muslin shawls, and Turkish colored handkerchiefs as both French and Italian fashion. One July issue advertised a "huge" embroidered cashmere shawl with a long fringe that made it "heavier than a monk's cloak", anticipating the winter fashion that would inevitably make this item more expensive.[30] Paper models of the dresses could also be ordered via mail, so that women could cut and sew the clothing at home for a much lower price. This

---

29 Silvia Franchini: *Editori, lettrici e stampa di moda*. Milan 2002, 40–41.
30 *Il Corriere delle Dame*, 1807, 19 July, 247.

Figure 2: *Corriere delle Dame,* no. 43, 26 October 1806, 831, fig. 140. Courtesy of the Biblioteca del Senato 'Giovanni Spadolini', Rome.

created a viable and reciprocally empowering commercial connection between artisans, producers of fashion, and the weekly journal, and the availability of paper models was an essential element in the popularization of style not only for the elites, but also for a wider consumer public.

Research on the *Corriere delle Dame* has focused on its editorial fortunes from the perspective of a gendered nation-building culture. No attention has been given to the international information it provided, which has been dismissed as merely a taste for exoticism. In fact, the *Corriere delle Dame* had an interesting political column, "Termometro politico", with news and comments on the military and political initiatives of the French, Habsburg, Ottoman, and Russian powers. In addition,

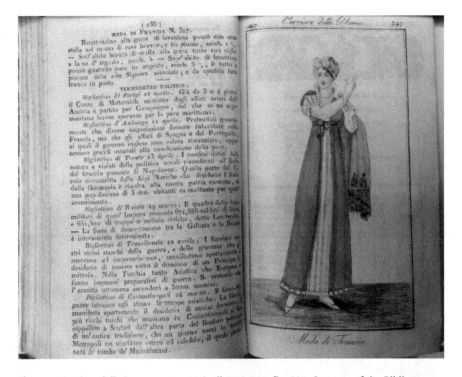

Figure 3: *Corriere delle Dame*, no. 17, 28 April 1810, 137, fig. 327. Courtesy of the Biblioteca del Senato 'Giovanni Spadolini', Rome.

weekly installments on material culture and books spread knowledge about the Ottoman Empire. For instance, *Il Corriere delle Dame* published excerpts from Ferrario's third volume on the Ottoman Empire, introducing its female readership to nineteenth-century Italian travelogues. The journal also published the chapters on food, diet, and coffee from Giovan Battista Rampoldi's *Annali Musulmani*, printed in Milan in twelve volumes between 1822 and 1826,[31] a work that also served as a source for Ferrario. Rampoldi (1761–1836) was not a scholar, but he learned Arabic and traveled extensively across Turkey, Egypt, Syria, and North Africa between 1780 and 1790, apparently without official charges. His *Annali musulmani* is essentially a compilation modeled on Barthélemy d'Herbelot de Molainville's *Bibliothèque Orientale* (1777–1779), and although not considered part of the Orientalist canon, it was the first attempt in Italy to write a widely encompassing history of the Islamic states based on a collection of Oriental sources and on the author's personal

---

31 Giovan Battista Rampoldi, *Annali musulmani*, Milano 1822–1826.

experience and knowledge of local languages. The printing of selected chapters of the work in *Il Corriere delle Dame* provides an example of how information on non-Western people was popularized by means of journals and travelogues. Addressing a middle-class, urban, female readership, *Il Corriere delle Dame* disseminated popular and entertaining narratives on the use of tobacco and the sociality surrounding the consumption of coffee in Istanbul, avoiding all references to local styles of dress and the veiling of women. In the journal, Oriental fashion was shaped by the consumer desires of European women and men, and in 1825 turbans of all sorts and with silver decorations were advertised as the craze of the moment. Turquerie was the cultural framework for the vogue for long cashmere shawls, turbans, and the loose, open garments that were to be worn in private.

In 1825, the journal advertised the launching of a new collection of calendars entitled *The Gallery of the World*. Calendars were printed at the beginning of each year and were the cheapest type of publication for a popular readership of men and women. *The Gallery of the World* aimed at describing the history, costume laws, and products of all nations, in a highly readable style. In 1826, the journal published excerpts of Ferrario's work on the costumes of the world and offered thirteen of its prints as a separate calendar. Prices advertised six different types of bindings, from cheap paper to expensive silk and Moroccan leather. Indeed, Ferrario's encyclopedic work on the costumes and customs of world, initially aimed at an aristocratic cosmopolitan readership and issued by a team of artists and collaborators in the Biblioteca and Accademia of Brera, eventually became the product of an expanding, urban editorial market. The work as a whole was printed in cheaper editions, and parts of it circulated in *Il Corriere delle Dame*. Both served to popularize visual and textual information addressed to different audiences and disseminating a culture of appearances in which print was central. They both also shared the non-academic Orientalism propagated in travelogues and journals that publishers were eager to put on the market. Chapters from Ferrario's *Il Costume* could now circulate among middle-class readers and especially among women, for whom the original luxury edition paid by a subscription of royalty, aristocrats, and well-to-do professionals and businessmen was unattainable.

Concluding remarks

This article has used several descriptions of material culture as a point of entry into the circulation of textual and visual knowledge from the Ottoman to the French Empire and to Italy. Three different sources have been discussed and connected: Ignatius Mouradgea d'Ohsson's *Tableau général de l'Empire Ottoman*,

Giulio Ferrario's *Il costume antico e moderno*, and Carolina Lattanzi's *Il Corriere delle Dame*. Building upon one another and viewed from different analytical angles, the sources shed light on the fashion for cashmere shawls and cashmere cloth imported from India to the Ottoman Empire and Europe from the eighteenth through the nineteenth centuries.

Ignatius Mouradgea d'Ohsson's *Tableau général* offered a firsthand systematic study of Ottoman society, in which dress and the consumption of clothing was framed in the context of Islamic law and religion. Giulio Ferrario's *Il costume antico e moderno* pursued an ethnographic approach to dress practices across the centuries from the viewpoint of an armchair traveller in the tradition of early modern costume books. Ferrario addressed an elite readership of royalty, nobility professionals, and merchants in Italy and Europe. *Il Corriere delle Dame*, directed by Carolina Lattanzi, was one of the main and longest-lasting weekly magazines for women, initially under the influence of French fashion and Napoleonic rule. It put cashmere shawls and scarfs on the fashion market. The prints it displayed in its weekly issues advertised garments that women could buy or sew at home. *Il Corriere delle Dame* was part of a system of fashion developing in Milan, the capital of the French Empire in Italy, where retailers, designers, journalists, promoters, and consumers were in communication with each other. In this sense, it marks a turning point in the process of cultural transfer that this paper has reconstructed, as it democratized the spread of information on politics, theatre, literature, medicine, hygiene, and fashion beyond the circles of the elites whose names are listed in the catalogue of 211 associates who financed Ferrario's volumes.

The article's focus on descriptions and prints of cashmere shawls sheds light on the different intellectual styles, editorial contexts, and changing audiences that go into the making of a system of fashion in which the media are a key element of communication. Translation is a crucial feature of the whole process, as each of these texts selected, appropriated and re-invented the hybrid languages of clothing across borders and Empires.

Forum

Bernhard Gissibl

Everything in its Right Place?

The Macron Moment and the Complexities of Restituting Africa's Cultural Heritage

Abstract: *In November 2017, French President Emmanuel Macron pledged to re-turn African cultural heritage stored in French public collections to their original owners. One year later a working group around Senegalese economist Felwine Sarr and French art historian Bénédicte Savoy produced a widely received report proposing how this process of restitution could be put in practice. Both speech and so-called restitution report provided a vital stimulus to the ongoing debates across European countries about the appropriate handling of objects and arte-facts acquired in territories under European colonial domination. This essay sit-uates the current Macron moment within the longer international controversies on colonial restitution that had already gained momentum in the late 1970s. It queries the cultural diplomacy behind Macron's speech and addresses both the Afrotopian potential that informs much of the optimism of the report and the ten-sions between the righting of historical injustices and the historical complexities of colonialism that arise from the report's privileging of restitution over prove-nance research. Charting the reverberations of the report across the European world museum world, the essay analyses how the report has shifted the moral pa-rameters of the debate about colonial objects in Germany and discusses how the aims of restitution and in-depth provenance research could possibly be reconciled.*

"Starting today, and within the next five years, I want to see the conditions put in place so as to allow for the temporary or definitive restitution of African cul-tural heritage to Africa." With these words French President Emmanuel Macron pledged to make restitution a priority of his country's cultural politics in front of an audience of some 800 students at the University of Ouagadougou, the capital of Burkina Faso, in November 2017. Ever since this announcement, the self-im-posed five-year-countdown has been ticking. As a first step towards turning the promise of restitution into practice, the French President commissioned a work-ing group around Senegalese economist Felwine Sarr and French art historian Bénédicte Savoy to compile a report how to implement this pledge. One year after Macron's announcement, in November 2018, the two scholars published their report on "The Restitution of African Cultural Heritage".[1] Even more than Macron's speech, the report he commissioned provided a vital stimulus to ongoing debates across European countries about the appropriate handling of objects and artefacts acquired in territories under European colonial domination. The following essay charts this debate triggered by the French President, first by situating the current "Macron Moment" within the longer international controversies on colonial restitution that had already gained momentum in the late 1970s. Then, it discusses Macron's speech as an attempt at personal distinctiveness within the inherited politics of *Françafrique*, using cultural politics as a symbol of change within an African policy that is otherwise marked by stark continuities as well as competition with China. In a third step, the Sarr/Savoy-report is analysed as a political document written by scholars trying to hold the President accountable to his pledge. Afterwards, the essay addresses the varying reverberations the report has had in the world of world museums across Europe, finally focussing on the enormous and polarizing influence it has exerted in Germany. Here, it pitted the project of restitution against the investigation of provenances that was already under way in many museums, raising the question of how these projects could possibly be reconciled.

Restitution for Authenticity – Forward to the 1970s

The restitution report by Felwine Sarr and Bénédicte Savoy has fanned and instilled a new urgency into a debate over decolonization, displaced heritage, and cultural sovereignty that had been lingering for about half a century. If not longer, given the fact that, at least since 1935, each Oba of Benin has demanded the restitution of at least some of the artefacts a notorious British punitive expedition had looted from the West African kingdom in 1897.[2] Despite the obvious, yet complicated case of the Benin objects, it was not until the early 1970s that a broader international debate emerged about the return,

---

1 Felwine Sarr and Bénédicte Savoy: *The Restitution of African Cultural Heritage. Towards a New Relational Ethics.* November 2018, URL: http://restitutionreport2018.com/sarr_savoy_en.pdf (last accessed 30 May 2019).
2 See e.g. Audrey Peraldi: Oba Akuenza II's Restitution Requests, in: *Kunst & Kontext* 2017/1, 23–33; Barbara Plankensteiner: The Benin Treasures. Difficult Legacy and Contested Heritage, in: Brigitta Häuser-Schäublin and Lyndel V. Prott (eds.): *Cultural Property and Contested Ownership. The Trafficking of Artefacts and the Quest for Restitution.* London 2016, 133–155.

repatriation or restitution of objects and artefacts displaced under colonial rule. At that time, African leaders and intellectuals realized that decolonization was incomplete if restricted to political independence, having to encompass elements of economic and cultural sovereignty, too. It was the president of the then Republic of Zaïre, Mobutu Sese Seko, who drew the world's attention to the fact that the majority of his country's artistic patrimony was located outside Africa due to "systematic pillage" conducted under European colonialism. Therefore, "the rich countries, who possess the artworks of the poor countries", should at least "return part of them".[3] Understanding restitution as a core element of his decolonial cultural politics of *authenticité*, Mobutu used the United Nations and its cultural organization UNESCO as stages for claims-making, especially in order to gain leverage in bilateral debates with Belgium as the former colonial power.[4] His initiative, backed by other African states, sections of the Third World movement and the occasional museum director or curator within Western European societies, resulted, in December 1973, in UN-resolution 3187, which directly referred to the "restitution of works of art to countries victims of expropriation". The issue was advanced by the first African Director-General of UNESCO, the Senegalese Amadou-Mahtar M'Bow, who pushed the "return of cultural assets to their countries of origin" as a "legitimate claim" within the framework of his organisation.[5] In October 1978, UNESCO installed the *Intergovernmental Committee*

---

3 Mobutu Sese Seko addressing the Congress of the International Association of Art Critics in Kinshasa in September 1973, quoted in Sarah van Beurden: *Restitution or Cooperation? Competing Visions of Post-Colonial Cultural Development in Africa* (Global Cooperation Research Papers 12). Duisburg: Käte Hamburger Kolleg/Centre for Global Cooperation Research (KHK / GCR21) 14 (2015) (doi: 10.14282/2198-0411-GCRP-12). For the broader context, see van Beurden: *Authentically African. Arts and the Transnational Politics of Congolese Culture.* Athens/OH 2015.
4 Sarah van Beurden: The Art of (Re)possession. Heritage and the Cultural Politics of Congo's Decolonization, in: *Journal of African History* 56 (2015), 143–164. On the broader context of 1970s international debates about authenticity, see Andrea Rehling and Johannes Paulmann: Historische Authentizität jenseits von "Original" und "Fälschung". Ästhetische Wahrnehmung – gespeicherte Erfahrung – gegenwärtige Performanz, in: Martin Sabrow and Achim Saupe (eds.): *Historische Authentizität.* Göttingen 2016, 91–125, esp. 121–123; Winfried Speitkamp: "Authentizität" und Nation. Kollektivsymbolik und Geschichtspolitik in postkolonialen afrikanischen Staaten, in: Klaudia Knabel, Dietmar Rieger and Stephanie Wodianka (eds.): *Nationale Mythen – kollektive Symbole. Funktionen, Konstruktionen und Medien der Erinnerung.* Göttingen 2005, 225–243.
5 An Appeal by Mr. Amadou-Mahtar M'Bow, Director-General of UNESCO: A Plea for the Return of an Irreplaceable Cultural Heritage to Those Who Created It, in: *The Unesco Courier* 31, July 1978, 4.

for Promoting the Return of Cultural Property to its Countries of Origin or its Restitution in Case of Illicit Appropriation with the task to mediate and facilitate bilateral interstate negotiations for the return of specific objects. By 1979, sympathetic experts within the International Council of Museums (ICOM) regarded "the reassembly of dispersed heritage through restitution or return of objects which are of major importance for the cultural identity and history of countries having been deprived thereof" as an "ethical principle recognized and affirmed by the major international organizations".[6]

This optimistic assessment may have been true for organizations like UNESCO and ICOM, but not necessarily for all of their members. As it turned out, principled recognition did not pertain to Western governments and museums. It still awaits in-depth and source-based historical investigation into how exactly, in the interplay of various levels from international organizations down to individual museums, the impetus for restitution was refused, deferred, watered down and deflected into political deals or culture- and museum-related development cooperation.[7] Already the 1973 UN-resolution went no further than registering a "special obligation" of former colonial powers in this matter.[8] The former colonial powers, including France and Western Germany, were successful in defending the non-retroactive character of any international convention that related to displaced cultural heritage. They managed to transform a terminology of legitimate and rights-based restitution into a language of voluntary return and cooperation; victims of expropriation became communities of origin. The repatriation of artefacts was depoliticized and integrated into broader policies of development cooperation in the field of culture. The Intergovernmental Committee faced a mission as cumbersome and complicated as its name. Its importance lies not with the respectable number of objects it managed to return after often years-long negotiations, but with the fact that it existed at all. Like the UN system in general,[9] the Committee has provided a forum in which formerly colonized

---

6 Herbert Ganslmayr et al.: Study on the Principles, Conditions and Means for the Restitution or Return of Cultural Property in View of Reconstituting Dispersed Heritages, in: *Museum International* 31, 1 (1979), 62–66, here 66.

7 Bénédicte Savoy: Die verdrängte Debatte, in: *Süddeutsche Zeitung*, 3 March 2019. A revealing controversy between German museum directors has recently been reconstructed by Anna Valeska Strugalla: Ein Ding der Unmöglichkeit, in: *taz*, 11/12 May 2019, URL: http://www.taz.de/Rueckgabe-von-geraubter-Kunst/!5591215/ (30 May 2019).

8 For a survey, see Thomas Fitschen: 30 Jahre Rückführung von Kulturgut. Wie der Generalversammlung ihr Gegenstand abhanden kam, in: *Vereinte Nationen* 2004/2, 46–51.

9 See the latest resolution A/RES/73/130 on the Return or restitution of cultural property to the countries of origin adopted by the UN-General Assembly on 13 December 2018, URL: https://www.un.org/en/ga/search/view_doc.asp?symbol=A/RES/73/130 (30 May 2019).

countries could articulate their claims and create awareness for the problem. But generally, the international law regarding cultural heritage has remained under-developed, especially when compared to booming policy fields like the environment or human rights. "There is no denying", Australian legal scholar Ana Filipa Vrdoljak concluded in 2008, "that there had been a sustained resistance in certain quarters to the formulation and implementation of an international legal framework in the cultural heritage field, especially in respect to the removal and return of cultural objects."[10] Sarr and Savoy state the same in more scathing terms: There has been "no progressive movement [towards restitution] for the past 40 years".[11]

The Macron Moment

One must bear this long prehistory in mind in order to understand the extraordinary hope and promise associated with the Macron moment. For the first time in the long history of claims and negotiations between global North and global South, the highest representative of a former colonial power has called his country's colonial rule a crime against humanity and proactively pledged restitution. Commentators across the political spectrum were astonished by the "brilliant recklessness" of Macron's initiative and the report it produced,[12] which was likened to taking a wrecking ball to the quaint and tranquil world of ethnographic and anthropological museology.[13] Sceptical and critical observers shiver at this recklessness, fearing for the dilapidation of Europe's museum collections and their universal character, and warning against selling the objects as indulgences for the wrongs of colonialism.[14] Activists for restitution, on the other hand, tend

---

10 Ana Filipa Vrdoljak: *History and Evolution of International Cultural Heritage Law. Through the Question of the Removal and Return of Cultural Objects.* Seoul 2008, 4–5.

11 Sarr/Savoy: Restitution of African Cultural Heritage, 21.

12 Peer Teuwsen: Experten in Frankreich empfehlen die sofortige Restitution zahlreicher Kulturgüter aus der Kolonialzeit (21 November 2018), in: *NZZ*, URL: https://www.nzz.ch/feuille ton/in-frankreich-fragt-man-bang-werden-jetzt-unsere-museen-geleert-ld.1438527 (30 May 2019).

13 Alexander Herman: Legal challenges remain for restituting African artefacts from French museums (28 November 2018), in: *The Art Newspaper*, URL: https://www.theartnewspaper.com/comment/french-report-calls-for-massive-restitution-of-african-artefacts-while-macron-promises-return-of-26-items-to-benin (30 May 2019).

14 See e.g. Bahners: Französisches Ausleerungsgeschäft; Hermann Parzinger: Zeitenwende oder Ablasshandel?, in: *Frankfurter Allgemeine Zeitung* 29 November 2018, URL: https://www.faz.net/aktuell/feuilleton/debatten/wie-sollte-man-mit-kolonialen-kulturguetern-umgehen-15914615-p2.html?printPagedArticle=true#pageIndex_1 (30 May 2019); Erhard Schüttpelz: Everything must go. Looting the Museum as Compensation for Looting the World. Raubkunstforschung als angewandte

to regard Macron as the long-awaited Alexander determined to untie the Gordian knot of displaced cultural heritage. Just a few days after the speech, Ghanaian columnist Kwame Opoku, who has commented on issues of cultural restitution for the online media portal *Modern Ghana* in more than two hundred articles since 2008,[15] hailed Macron's declaration as "historical", for it set a new moral yardstick for restitution. He enthusiastically announced the advent of a "post Ouagadougou period" in which the universal claim of Western museums was on the defensive.[16] In another article, Opoku invoked "our African gods and ancestors to bless Bénédicte Savoy, Felwine Sarr and their team" for restoring "part of the self-respect and dignity" that had been lost as a consequence of colonial conquest and rule.[17] In a similar vein, postcolonial activist groups and advocates of restitution in Europe discerned a sea change and a radical new beginning in Euro-African relations effected by the report.[18] However, the long history of deferred restitution should caution against too great expectations regarding swift or wide-ranging action. Back in 1979, the ICOM working group was equally convinced that the restitution of objects with core cultural significance for their communities of origin would "soon become an element of *jus cogens* of international relations".[19] But international law, itself a product of imperial expansion and in significant ways developed to enable and legitimize it,[20] did not develop as expected. In order to enact restitution as wholesale as

---

Wissenschaft, URL: https://boasblogs.org/humboldt/everything-must-go-looting-the-museum-as-compensation-for-looting-the-world/ (27 July 2019).

15 See https://www.modernghana.com/author/KwameOpoku (30 May 2019).

16 Kwame Opoku: Humboldt Forum And Selective Amnesia: Research Instead Of Restitution Of African Artefacts (21 December 2017), URL: https://www.modernghana.com/news/824314/humboldt-forum-and-selective-amnesia-research-instead-of-re.html (30 May 2019).

17 Kwame Opoku: Further Comments On Sarr-Savoy Report On Restitution (31 January 2019), in: *Modern Ghana*, URL: https://www.modernghana.com/news/912541/further-comments-on-sarr-savoy-report-on-restitution.html (30 May 2019).

18 See, for example, Jürgen Zimmerer's interview with Dieter Kassel: Ein Vorschlag von 'globaler Tragweite', in: Deutschlandfunk Kultur, 22 November 2018, URL: https://www.deutschland funkkultur.de/koloniale-raubkunst-ein-vorschlag-von-globaler-tragweite.1008.de.html?dram:arti cle_id=433866 (30 May 2019). Cf. already the open letter of several postcolonial activist groups to Chancellor Angela Merkel concerning the restitution of cultural objects and human remains to Africa, 18 December 2017, URL: http://www.no-humboldt21.de/offener-brief-zur-rueckgabe-von-afrikanischen-kulturobjekten-und-menschlichen-gebeinen/ (30 May 2019).

19 Herbert Ganslmayr et al.: Study on the principles, conditions and means for the restitution or return of cultural property in view of reconstituting dispersed heritages, in: *Museum International* 31, 1 (1979), 62–66, here 66.

20 See e.g. Anthony Anghie: *Imperialism, Sovereignty, and the Making of International Law.* Cambridge 2012; further the legal scholarship conducted under the label of Third World

recommended by their report, Sarr and Savoy propose to use bilateral agreements as a lever to facilitate an exception to the principle of the inalienability of cultural objects in public ownership. If Macron followed this proposal, he would, if not abandon, definitely undermine the legal tradition of the inalienability of public collections that dates back as far as the Edict of Moulins in 1566.[21] Given the historical reach of the French Empire into the Middle East, Asia and Oceania, this would have ramifications far beyond the restitution of African cultural heritage currently under discussion.

So far, the radical rhetoric of the report still awaits corresponding action. But the radical potential of Macron's pledge, the expectations it raised and the transnational debates it fanned, created a discursive situation in which the French president's motives behind his motion have hardly been questioned. After all, the opportunity of the Macron moment needed to be seized, not interrogated for the purity of his intentions. Yet neither the verbal pledge nor the restitution it promised have happened in a political vacuum. Macron's remarks on the restitution of Africa's cultural heritage were but a few sentences towards the end of a verbose speech that lasted about two hours. It was Macron's first speech on the African continent, and as such, it was a signal to both the millions of citizens with electoral rights and family ties to the African colonies, and to the citizens of Francophone Africa. According to political scientist Oumar Ba, first African speeches by French Presidents habitually contained an obituary of the *Françafrique* as we knew it, the promise of a new departure for a common future with Africans on African terms, a proud comment on shared Francophonie, and a list of present challenges in which France will aid Africans.[22] Among the challenges enumerated were terrorism, climate change, overpopulation, urbanization and migration. The speech also did not fail on the usual pledge regarding the percentage of the gross national income to be dedicated to development aid. (This time it was 0,55%, back in 1995 Jacques Chirac still promised 0,7%.) But these were standard issues. The pledge to restitution was Macron's personal endowment, a markedly different policy than all his predecessors in office pursued. Indeed, if there was one word that stood out throughout his speech, it was "generation". Macron used the term twenty

Approaches to International Law (TWAIL): Makau W. Matua: What is Twail?, in: *American Society of International Law, Proceedings of the 94th Annual Meeting 2000*, 31–39.
21 Marc Weber: *Unveräußerliches Kulturgut im nationalen und internationalen Rechtsverkehr.* Berlin 2002.
22 Oumar Ba: Should Africans care for Emmanuel Macron's "African speech" in Ouagadougou? (29 Nov 2017), URL: https://africasacountry.com/2017/11/should-africans-care-for-emmanuel-macrons-africa-speech-in-ouagadougou (30 May 2019).

times, most heavily during the opening paragraphs of the speech in which he claimed he and his audience both belonged to a post-colonial, future-oriented generation that refuses to perpetuate the perceptions of the past. Invoking the shared belonging to the same generation is supposed to create commonality across the colonial divide. For Macron as representative of the French side, belonging to this generation involved accepting the "crimes of European colonization" as part of his country's history. Macron explicitly placed himself in a long line of French intellectual criticism of Empire since the 1920s by directly referencing writer André Gide and investigative journalist Albert Londres.[23] Among all the policy fields addressed during the speech, the return of cultural artefacts displaced during the decades of French colonial rule constituted the most concrete, tangible and radical form of putting the announced departure of an entangled French-African postcolonial generation into practice.

Of course, even this departure would only be a departure of sorts, addressing some legacies of colonialism while leaving others intact. It only speaks to the irresolvable complexities of decolonization that the majority of these objects would have to be returned to the very political entities that European colonialism itself created. Macron's speech as well as the report are predicated upon a bilateral logic of restitution, which is informed by both state-centrism and political realism. Political elites accustomed to the practices of gatekeeping states would certainly not fail to tap the political potential of such cultural transactions, even, or perhaps especially, in cases in which minorities or marginalized groups within their states are concerned.[24] Interestingly, it also went without comment that the very speech that promised to redress one colonial legacy indulged in the extension of another, for Macron wished for a "strong, influential Francophonie" to make French "the number one language in Africa and maybe even the world". In both cases, the (re-)appropriation of French cultural universals by Africans – "our" heritage and "our" language – is based upon the expectation that this means the tightening and perpetuation of Afro-French entanglements, and the securing, if not extension, of France's cultural and political influence in Africa. To be sure, the pledge of grand-scale restitution would not have happened without Macron and his individual style of doing politics. However, its timing is significant beyond the whim and will of a President intent

---

23 Cf. Lilyan Kesteloot: Albert Londres et André Gide. Deux témoignages sur l'Afrique des années vingt, in: *Revue des litératures du Sud* 153 (2004), 88–95; Irene Albers, Andrea Pagni, and Ulrich Winter (eds.): *Blicke auf Afrika nach 1900. Französische Moderne im Zeitalter des Kolonialismus.* Tübingen 2002.
24 On the gatekeeping postcolonial African state, see Frederick Cooper: *Africa since 1940. The past of the present.* Cambridge 2002.

on putting his personal stamp on French policies. It comes at a political moment when France and other Western countries are on the defensive on the African continent – a development that has been described as a transformation from *"Françafrique"* towards *"Chinafrique"*.[25] Macron never addresses Chinese invest-ment in Africa directly, but it is present throughout his speech, most obviously in a passage in which he advertises a new African-youth-oriented investment policy that is sensitive to the failures of the past. Translated from diplomatese, he begs his audience to trust the former colonizers, for they have erred in the past but learnt from it. The colonizers of today, however, the "new investors, with companies which provide billions but not one job for Africans, which pro-vide billions while repeating the same mistakes as in the past and which may appear to be easy solutions for today" were bound to "replicate the turmoil, mis-takes and sometimes crimes of the past". Such a warning does not sound too convincing, however, if one considers recent developments in the field of art and museum politics in West Africa. In December 2018, the Museum of Black Civilizations was opened in Dakar, the capital of Senegal – a state-of-the-art mu-seum on African soil, subscribing to a decolonial agenda and providing ample space for African artefacts, erected with substantial funding from China. Such an intrusion of Chinese cultural diplomacy into French-speaking West Africa obvi-ously constitutes a challenge to France, and it may well have promoted the redis-covery of artworks and cultural artefacts as the useful diplomatic tools they have been in the past, during colonial rule and after.[26] At a time of intense competition and renewed scramble over investments and influence in Africa, Macron wants "Africa to be a priority of French economic diplomacy". In such a situation it is surely no disadvantage to have thousands of objects available for potential resti-tution as supple tools for a cultural diplomacy that prepares, supports, eases, and complements more material French and European interests in Africa. Such awareness to the context of the pledge should caution against taking restitution as, above all, a disinterested moral politics of decolonization. It still forms part of the cultural and political economy of *Françafrique* and its transformation into a relationship on more coeval terms.

---

25 Brian Tourré: *De la "Françafrique" à la "Chinafrique". Quelle place pour le développement africain?* Paris 2012.

26 See e.g. Sarah van Beurden: The Art of (Re)possession. Heritage and the Cultural Politics of Congo's Decolonization, in: *Journal of African History* 56 (2015), 143–164. See also the theme issue of the European History Yearbook 2016 on the material culture of modern diplomacy, espe-cially Harriet Rudolph: Entangled Objects and Hybrid Practices? Material Culture as a New Approach to the History of Diplomacy, in: *European History Yearbook* 17 (2016), 1–28.

Pressure on Presidential Demand: The Sarr/
Savoy-Report

Concerning the scope and practice of restitution, the Ouagadougou speech had left several backdoors open, which the Sarr/Savoy-report intended to slam shut. Macron restrained his promise "to do everything possible to bring them back". Further, he considered temporary return and "circulation"[27] a viable option and emphasized that the objects' safety and care after return would be matters of serious consideration. Felwine Sarr and Bénédicte Savoy seized the opportunity of their mandate to render these three options as non-viable as possible. They used the report to increase moral pressure and commit Macron to his pledge, rein in the potential for diplomatic bargaining and "think of restitutions as being something more than a mere strategic maneuver".[28] Sensitive to the late 1970s terminological quarrels over the legal, historical, and political implications of "restitution" versus "return", Sarr and Savoy leave no doubt that restitution implies "the recognition of the illegitimacy of the property". Consequently, speaking of restitution means speaking of "justice, or a re-balancing, recognition, of restoration and reparation". The "circulation" of objects, envisioned by Macron in his letter of mission and benevolently offered by major European museums under the guise of "shared heritage",[29] is rejected as a strategic manoeuver that avoids the necessary transfer of legitimate ownership and merely perpetuates European control over the objects and the status of the "dispossessed cultures" as supplicants of Europe.

Sarr and Savoy remove the ambiguity contained in the oxymoron of "temporary restitutions" by accepting this practice only as a preliminary solution until the legal and institutional prerequisites for definitive restitution of cultural heritage back to Africa are put in place. Their report further disputes the entrenched objection that African states lacked the knowledge and institutional

---

27 See the preamble of his letter of mission to Sarr and Savoy, which reiterates the aim of "restitutions temporaires ou définitives du patrimoine africain" already mentioned in the speech and favours "une action déterminée en faveur de la circulation des oeuvres", facsimilated in Sarr/Savoy: Restitution of African Cultural Heritage, 107–108.

28 Sarr/Savoy: Restitution of African Cultural Heritage, 22.

29 See e.g. Hermann Parzinger: Geteiltes Erbe ist doppeltes Erbe, in: *Frankfurter Allgemeine Zeitung*, 16 October 2016, URL: https://www.faz.net/aktuell/feuilleton/shared-heritage-geteiltes-erbe-ist-doppeltes-erbe-14481517.html?printPagedArticle=true#pageIndex_0 (30 May 2019); Sarah van Beurden: The pitfalls of "shared heritage", URL: https://blog.uni-koeln.de/gssc-humboldt/the-pitfalls-of-shared-heritage/ (30 May 2019); Thomas Thiemeyer: Kulturerbe als "Shared Heritage" (I). Kolonialzeitliche Sammlungen und die Zukunft einer europäischen Idee, in: *Merkur* 829 (2018), 30–44.

infrastructure to provide appropriate custody for the returned objects as a neo-colonial myth of alleged African incapacity. Amongst others, they refer to the "ultra-modern" Museum of Black Civilizations in Dakar to contest this myth. Above all, Sarr and Savoy propose concrete criteria and a timeline for action that is oriented along the five-year frame set by the Macron moment but seek to establish structures that prevent the "historical window" opened by Macron from ever being shut again.[30] The foremost criterion for determining which objects qualify for restitution is not provenance or the concrete historical context but the time of acquisition. A first group comprises all those objects that are to be restituted in a swift and wholesale manner without any further research into their provenance, because they were "taken by force or presumed to be acquired through inequitable conditions" within the decades defined as colonial period between 1885 and 1960. This pertains to everything acquired in the context of French military aggression or scientific expeditions, through collection by military personnel or colonial administrators but also to objects that were once loaned by African institutions and never returned. A second category foresees previous research into the provenance of objects that probably stem from colonial contexts but were acquired post-1960 or presented to the museum as a gift e.g. by later generations of families involved with the Empire. A final category consists of objects that should remain within French collections, provided their transaction rested upon documentable and agreed consent or followed the rules concerning illicit trafficking of cultural objects established by UNESCO since 1970.

Apart from defining the colonial period between 1885 and 1960 as a general context of injustice, the Sarr/Savoy-report applies to the colonial context the principle of reversing the burden of proof that was laid down in the 1995 UNIDROIT convention on stolen or illegally exported cultural objects. No longer shall the claimaint have to prove that a certain object was illegally taken; instead, the possessing institution must produce, as Sarr and Savoy put it, "explicit evidence or information witnessing to the full consent on the part of the owners or initial guardians of the objects under question.[31] This is a very important step to put the historically asymmetrical relationship between claimants and museums on a more equal footing. And given the fact that thousands of colonial objects in European museums lack sufficient documentation as to their provenance and acquisition, the reversal of proof challenges the established

---

30 On the following, see Sarr/Savoy: Restitution of African Cultural Heritage, 61–69.
31 Sarr/Savoy: Restitution of African cultural Heritage, 58. For a similar demand within the German debate, see Jürgen Zimmerer: Kulturgut aus der Kolonialzeit – ein schwieriges Erbe?, in: *Museumskunde* 80/2 (2015), 22–25.

practice that objects, if in doubt of their origin, should remain in their current location. To be sure, Sarr and Savoy did not propose an automatism of proactive restitution once French law has been changed accordingly. Such proactive restitution is only suggested for an attached list of carefully selected objects – including 26 bronzes looted from the Palaces of Abomey in 1892, which Macron promised to return immediately to the state of Benin from the holdings of the Musée Quai Branly. In all other cases, restitution or research into their provenance should only be undertaken after a demand for restitution was actively put forward from an African party.[32]

In a recent critical and mildly polemical, yet close and insightful, reading of the Sarr-Savoy-report, German journalist Patrick Bahners put special emphasis on the bureaucratic and political character of the document.[33] Although authored by an art historian and an economist affiliated with various academic institutions, the report is not a scholarly but rather a political enquiry. Facsimilated letters of mission accompanied the published report, testifying to everyone that it was mandated by the President of France. The report draws repeatedly and directly upon the Ouagadougou speech and tries to provide an authoritative and definitive exegesis of they key terms deployed in Macron's pledge. Sarr and Savoy do not question the limitations of the mandate: Since Macron only touched upon the dispersal of Africa's cultural heritage, the report is not concerned with the similar or different fate of objects acquired in other territories under French imperial domination. Disregarding the Middle Eastern, Asian and Oceanian parts of the French Empire,[34] albeit for pragmatic reasons, runs the risk, however, of entrenching once more the image of Africa as the plundered continent. Sarr and Savoy also tailor the restitution of Africa's cultural heritage as a specifically French problem. Although they repeatedly draw upon examples from Belgian, British and German overseas imperialism to underline the magnitude and European dimension of the problem, they emphasize the specific history and "particular responsibilities of France" in the world region of Africa that are, in their eyes, "much different than those left by Great Britain, Belgium, Germany, or Italy".[35] This intentional nationalization is supposed to block the political escape

---

32 Sarr/Savoy: Restitution of African Cultural Heritage, 61.
33 Patrick Bahners: Französisches Ausleerungsgeschäft. Der "Bericht über die Restitution afrikanischen Kulturerbes", in: *Merkur* 838 (2019), 5–17, here 6 and 9.
34 See e.g. Christine Howald: The Power of Provenance. Marketing and Pricing of Chinese Looted Art on the European Market (1860–1862), in: Bénédicte Savoy, Charlotte Guichard, and Christine Howald (eds.): *Acquiring Cultures. Histories of World Art on Western Markets*, Berlin 2018, 241–259.
35 Sarr/Savoy: Restitution of African Cultural Heritage, 3.

route into a strategic Europeanization or internationalization of the problem. Yet, it frames imperialism as essentially a nationalist project and tends to underestimate the transimperial and entangled character of the historical phenomenon under discussion, as embodied e.g. in the existence of international markets for African ethnographica and artefacts.

The authors regard Macron's personal commitment as a unique chance to achieve a breakthrough in the decades-long stalemate concerning the restitution of Africa's displaced cultural heritage. This can be gleaned from the report's immediate and unpolished publication as a pdf-file, suggesting that Sarr and Savoy regarded their analysis and recommendations as too urgent to tolerate any further delay through regular publication. But the impact of the Macron moment is perhaps best discernible in Bénédicte Savoy's public contributions to the debate. In her inaugural lecture presented to the Collège de France in March 2017, Savoy sketched the outlines of the daunting intellectual project to reconnect the artefacts and artwork in Europe's museums to the places, people and cultures of their origin. The adequate mode in which this "provenance of culture" needed to be approached was, in her recommendation, "introspection". Such introspection included, amongst others, a critical reflection of the language of heritage, the analysis of the historical provenance of objects and the reconnection to present-day descendants of historical source communities. Savoy also addressed openly what introspection did not mean: "self-flagellation, or the hurried and muddled restitution of objects of whom some outside Europe, too, think they are better preserved in Europe, at least for the moment."[36] In early 2017, research into the provenance of ethnographic collections was just about to become established as a progressive venture in the museum world.[37] The possible future of heritage seemed best approached through reconstructing the history of how objects came to "us". Then came Macron, whom Savoy welcomed as the herald of a "restitution revolution".[38] The Macron moment was an

---

36 Bénédicte Savoy: *Die Provenienz der Kultur. Von der Trauer des Verlusts zum universalen Menschheitserbe*. Berlin 2017, 54.

37 See Bernhard Gissibl: Raubkunst, die nächste Debatte, in: *Frankfurter Allgemeine Zeitung*, 24 April 2017, URL: https://www.faz.net/aktuell/feuilleton/voelkerkundemuseen-beginnen-mit-pro venienzforschung-14984217.html (30 May 2019); Larissa Förster: Plea for a more systematic, comparative, international and long-term approach to restitution, provenance research and the historiography of collections, in: *Museumskunde* 81/1 (2016), 49–54; Larissa Förster et al. (eds.): *Provenienzforschung zu ethnografischen Sammlungen der Kolonialzeit. Positionen in der aktuellen Debatte*. Berlin 2017.

38 Bénédicte Savoy: The restitution revolution begins. President Macron is ushering in a new era for the return of displaced heritage (16 February 2018), URL: https://www.theartnewspa per.com/comment/the-restitution-revolution-begins (30 May 2019).

opportunity to be seized. It should not lose any of its momentum to the complexities of historical circumstance.

Historical Injustice, Historical Complexities

Indeed, the official and political character of the report shaped its genesis, content, aim and argument in decisive ways. Since time for travel and research was limited and the report's mandated aim was to facilitate restitution, the authors and their team only visited such African countries with experiences of or an ongoing debate about restitution, or with a receptive museographic or cultural landscape – in other words, states where the promise of restitution could reckon with resonance.[39] Since the mandated aim was to facilitate restitution, the report subordinated complex past historical engagements to the achievement of the laudable goal to right historical injustices. The intellectual endeavour of analysing and explaining human diversity that also found expression in ethnographic collecting and the disciplines of anthropology and ethnology does not feature in the report. These disciplines, their practices and their intentions are shorn of their ambiguities[40]: They were "born from an era of violence", capitalized on the opportunities provided by European colonialism and realised their scientific value in the services they rendered to colonial rule.

Since the report's main recommendation is swift and thorough restitution "without any supplementary research" regarding the provenance of objects obtained from Africa between 1885 and 1960, Sarr and Savoy have no need to question or distinguish their provenance. Neither the various ways in which they became art or ethnographic objects nor their changing and often disputed

---

39 The states visited were Benin, Senegal, Mali and Cameroon, see Sarr/Savoy: Restitution of African Cultural Heritage, 4, fn. 6.
40 For critical and nuanced readings see e.g. Hugh Glenn Penny: *Objects of Culture. Ethnology and Ethnographic Museums in Imperial Germany*. Chapel Hill 2002; Andrew Zimmerman: *Anthropology and Antihumanism in Imperial Germany*. Chicago 2001; Andrew Zimmerman: Bewegliche Objekte und globales Wissen. Die Kolonialsammlungen des Königlichen Museums für Völkerkunde in Berlin, in: Rebekka Habermas and Alexandra Przyrembel (eds.): *Von Käfern, Märkten und Menschen. Kolonialismus und Wissen in der Moderne*. Göttingen 2013, 247–258; Hugh Glenn Penny and Matti Bunzl (eds): *Worldly Provincialism. German anthropology in the age of empire*. Ann Arbor 2003; Anja Laukötter: *Von der „Kultur" zur „Rasse" – vom Objekt zum Körper? Völkerkundemuseen und ihre Wissenschaften zu Beginn des 20. Jahrhunderts*. Bielefeld 2007; Han F. Vermeulen: *Before Boas. The Genesis of Ethnography and Ethnology in the German Enlightenment*. Lincoln 2015; Benoît de L'Estoile: From the Colonial Exhibition to the Museum of Man. An alternative genealogy of French anthropology, in: *Social Anthropology* 11 (2003), 341–361.

ontological status before and after transfer and integration into European collections matters. The varying intentions of collectors are also considered irrelevant. All this may indeed be negligible, for looting, even with the honest intention of salvage collecting in the interest of mankind, still remains looting. The report is also not interested in the strategies, experiences, or agencies of those who were deprived of their material culture. Restitution without accompanying research into provenances runs the risk of effacing historical African agency in the confrontation with colonial asymmetries, violence and racism. It glosses over the results of years of historical research into the weaknesses of the colonial state, the regionally varying reach of its claim to power, its makeshift alliances, and the widespread use of material culture not to acknowledge the asymmetries of colonial rule but to assert claims and establish coevalness. While in 2017 Savoy was still interested if and "how much blood stained the objects kept in European museums",[41] these bloodstains were taken for granted in the report one year later. Thousands of different and differently acquired objects are qualified wholesale in homogenizing and politically charged categories such as "looted", "art", and "heritage". The scholarly debate and literature on "entangled objects", conquest and collecting, captured heritage, or trans-imperial cultural flows does not feature in the report, nor is it necessary for the report's foremost aims.[42]

Instead, Sarr and Savoy situate French imperialism in Africa within a deep history of warfare, conquest and looting since Greek and Roman antiquity. They emphasize the intellectual, aesthetic and economic appropriation of cultural heritage as a "natural correlate",[43] if not tool of empire. Indeed, their approach is predicated upon a homology or a structural dependency between the asymmetries of imperial conquest and rule and the transfer of material culture. The latter has no agency or rationality of its own but is conceived of as an effect of empire. With looting declared as the standard mode of acquisition, it is of minor importance to query e.g. the prevalent ideas and conceptions of justice or legitimate trade and exchange that were relevant in concrete historical

---

41 Ein unlösbarer Widerspruch, in: *Süddeutsche Zeitung*, 20 July 2017, URL: https://www.sued deutsche.de/kultur/benedicte-savoy-ueber-das-humboldt-forum-das-humboldt-forum-ist-wie-tschernobyl-1.3596423?reduced=true (30 May 2019).

42 See e.g. Nicholas Thomas: *Entangled Objects. Exchange, Material Culture, and Colonialism in the Pacific*. Cambridge/Mass., London 2001; Maja Jasanoff: *Edge of Empire. Conquest and Collecting in the East, 1750–1850*. New York 2006; Zachary Kingdon: *Ethnographic Collecting and African Agency in Early Colonial West Africa: A Study of Trans-Imperial Cultural Flows*. London 2019; Douglas Cole: *Captured Heritage. The Scramble for Northwest Coast Artefacts*. Vancouver 1985; Tom Flynn and Tim Barringer (eds.): *Colonialism and the Object. Empire, Material Culture and the Museum*. London 1998.

43 Sarr/Savoy: Restitution of African Cultural Heritage, 10.

situations.[44] Likewise, the variety of contact zones in which colonial encounters took place, the local and regional micro- and mesocontexts with their instabilities and often shifting asymmetries are rendered less relevant,[45] respectively they are subordinated epistemologically to a totalizing macrostructure of imperial colonialism as an all-determining context of violence, injustice, and racism. The framing categories are not analytical ones, applied with the intention to capture the multiplicity of object biographies and trajectories. They are political categories applied in order to facilitate a political decision. The restitution report shows little interest in historical ambiguities or the existence of historical contact zones or common grounds, their workings and dynamics.

Afrotopia

If the restitution report is less interested in the possible pasts of the objects, this is because its prime interest lies with their possible futures. The relative eclipse of the entangled colonial history of the objects is perhaps necessary to realize their Afrotopian potential and purpose. Set free from their imprisonment in Western museums, the re-placed cultural heritage has to fulfil an at least twofold task: First, it has to serve as a foundation for a new "relational ethics" between Africa, Europe and the rest of the world. After return and re-appropriation, Africa's cultural heritage should not inspire their communities or regions of origin alone. As sources of human creativity and ingenuity, the objects are supposed to circulate "within a temporality, a rhythm and a meaning, placed on them by their legitimate owners"[46] as well as "within both a continental and global geography".[47] Sarr and Savoy insist that the objects, having for decades served as markers of primitivism, backwardness, primeval originality, natural art, or authentic expressions of static "cultures" in European collections, will not be resigned to new forms of "enslavement to a cultural identity" again after their return. Therefore, the "freedom", newfound mobility and creative potential of the objects is underlined again and again

44 See Larissa Förster: Wer fühlte sich beraubt? In: Frankfurter Allgemeine Einspruch, URL: https://einspruch.faz.net/recht-des-tages/2018-11-24/wer-fuehlte-sich-beraubt/172449.html (30 May 2019).

45 For the broad analytical canvas of the diversity of cultural encounters in European expansion see Jürgen Osterhammel: Kulturelle Grenzen in der Expansion Europas, in: id.: *Geschichtswissenschaft jenseits des Nationalstaats. Studien zu Beziehungsgeschichte und Zivilisationsvergleich.* Göttingen 2001, 203–239.

46 Sarr/Savoy: Restitution of African Cultural Heritage, 38.

47 Sarr/Savoy: Restitution of African Cultural Heritage, 39.

throughout the report, probably to dispel the impression that the reappropriation of the objects by their communities of origin could result in another freezing and immobility of the objects. This reappropriation is the second main task assigned to the objects, and Sarr and Savoy cannot emphasize enough that such putting back into their legitimate place has nothing to do with re-essentialisation or the cultural provincialization of once universally acknowledged art. The report abounds with a vocabulary of dynamism, departure, and possibility. Restitution does not mean dispersal but a "spatial explosion of cultural heritage"; they emphasize the objects' "power of germination" and their capacity to both reveal hitherto obscured epistemogonies as well as to give rise to new forms of meaning and knowledge.[48] Sarr and Savoy leave no doubt that objects that have been exposed to a "plurality of semantic, symbolic, and epistemological dispositives" over the last century do not allow for easy re-integration and re-appropriation. They return as a "different same". Yet, depending on the respective social contexts in which they are re-inserted, they have vital tasks to fulfil: they are supposed to serve as materializations that crystallize lost memories, give recourse to past creativity and ingenuity for young generations, and generally help with the "self-reinvention" of social entities.[49] Indeed, the restituted objects are fraught with expectations: as "operators of a relational and plastical identity",[50] they "could help to re-draw transnational territorial borders thereby reoccupying spaces of the circulation of communities, but also so as to help expand the circulation of these objects on a more continental and global scale. Furthermore, reappropriating for *oneself*, as a culture, allows for a toppling of colonial categories, thereby helping to re-fluidify fixed geographies and to invert the colonial hegemonic relationship in place that was instituted by a fixed location of the cultural objects along with monopoly of the discourse concerning them".[51] The passages on the manifold functions of restituted objects within African societies resonate heavily with Felwine Sarr's programme for cultural reinvention as laid down in his manifesto published under the title *Afrotopia* in French in 2016. The displaced cultural heritage counts among the many sources envisioned by Sarr to help overcome externally-imposed identifications and guide Africa to retrieve its identity.[52]

It is not difficult to point out the homogenizing, "continentalist" implications of this Afrotopian agenda, question the enormous and partially contradictory expectations burdened upon the returning heritage, or counter the

48 Sarr/Savoy: Restitution of African Cultural Heritage, 33, 35, 44.
49 Sarr/Savoy: Restitution of African Cultural Heritage, 32.
50 Sarr/Savoy: Restitution of African Cultural Heritage, 35.
51 Sarr/Savoy: Restitution of African Cultural Heritage, 38.
52 Felwine Sarr: *Afrotopia*. Paris 2016.

optimistic future programme of restitution with a more pessimistic scenario. It may well be the case that the re-integration into African contexts will not result in peaceful circulation across borders and the irenic scrambling of static social identities. Like any other form of heritage, the cultural variety will also be subject to contestation, rival epistemologies, perilous commoditization, and confrontative claims on objects whose significance, after, all, not only stems from their social and cultural functions but also from their often enormous economic value on art and touristic markets.[53] Indeed, it remains an open question how the transcending of boundaries and re-fluidifying of fixed geographies will be reconciled with the claims and rationalities of nation states who are key actors when restitution is conceived of as bilateral negotiation, as the report does. There is also a tension between the Afrocentric and Afropolitan assignments to Africa's cultural heritage. Still, the epistemic remobilization of thousands of objects that have for decades been rendered immobile and invisible in the storerooms of European museums and their reinvention as ambassadors of a new Afropolitanism is a timely and fascinating vision, and one can only support and admire the optimistic spirit in which the report is written.

Reverberations across the World Museum World

As yet, the world still waits to see how much of this optimistic spirit has permeated the Palais de l'Élysée. While the main addressee of the report has remained silent for months: and appears to withdraw, at least partially, from his earlier commitment.[54] Sarr and Savoy's recommendations caused a tremendous stir within the museum world, in the relevant academic disciplines, among postcolonial activists, on social media, and in newspapers and other news outlets.[55] The spectrum of

---

53 The economic dimension of African heritage is obvious, but remains glaringly unaddressed in the current debate, see Thomas Thiemeyer: Kulturerbe als "Shared Heritage" (II). Anerkennungsfragen, in: *Merkur* 830 (2018), 85–92.

54 See Vincent Noce: France retreats from report recommending automatic restitution of looted African artefacts, in: The Art Newspaper, 5 July 2019, URL: https://www.theartnewspaper.com/news/france-buries-restitution-report (25 July 2019).

55 For a comprehensive survey of reactions across academia, media, politics and the museum world see Margareta von Oswald: The "Restitution Report". First Reactions in Academia, Museums, and Politics (15 January 2019), URL: http://www.carmah.berlin/reflections/restitution-report_first-reactions/ (30 May 2019). The debate is closely monitored by the Cologne-based blog "Wie weiter mit Humboldts Erbe?" URL: https://boasblogs.org/humboldt/ and in the reflections-section of the Berlin-based Centre for Anthropological Research on Museums and Heritage, URL: http://www.carmah.berlin/reflections/.

reactions included everything from scathing indictment[56] to diplomatic and depo-liticizing differentiation, strategic embracement,[57] polite acknowledgement, and enthusiastic praise. Self-proclaimed "global thought leader in international arts and culture" Adrian Ellis regarded the report as more than just another salvo but even as the opening of "a new and possibly decisive battle in the long war" be-tween Western museums and those critics who regard them as treasure houses of largely looted non-European holdings.[58] Similarly, Jörg Häntzschel of Germany's quality daily *Süddeutsche Zeitung*, a journalistic proponent of the report, com-mended its authors for having elevated the debate over the adequate treatment of colonial objects to a new level.[59]

In any case, the report provoked reverberations beyond words and rhetori-cal declarations across Europe. This was perhaps the least so in Britain, where the directors of the most important museums reacted quickly, cautiously and, so far, defensively.[60] The British Museum, engulfed for decades in debates about the restitution of some of its most valuable holdings, launched a monthly gallery talk on "collecting histories" in autumn 2018. While these talks convey the diverse and often non-violent provenance of the collections, British Museum director Hartwig Fischer has, so far, only been quoted with statements that confirm his determination to preserve the integrity and universal claim of its collections. Colleagues like Tristram Hunt of the Victoria & Albert Museum were slightly more accommodating in that they acknowledged the need for transparency about their collections and promised increased cooperation and the long-term loan of artefacts. At the same time, Hunt called for more

---

56 Erhard Schüttpelz: Everything must go: Looting the Museum as Compensation for Looting the World. Raubkunstforschung als angewandte Wissenschaft, URL: https://boasblogs.org/humboldt/everything-must-go-looting-the-museum-as-compensation-for-looting-the-world/ (25 July 2019).

57 See e.g. Tristram Hunt, Hartmut Dorgerloh, Nicholas Thomas, "Restitution Report: museum directors respond", *The Art Newspaper*, 27 November 2018, https://www.theartnewspaper.com/comment/restitution-report-museums-directors-respond (30 May 2019).

58 Adrian Ellis: Museums in the changing world order: Restitution to Africa reaches tipping point (5 April 2019), URL: https://www.theartnewspaper.com/comment/museums-in-the-changing-world-order-restitution-to-africa-reaches-tipping-point (30 May 2019).

59 Jörg Häntzschel: Gebt sie zurück!, in: *Süddeutsche Zeitung*, 21 November 2018, URL: https://www.sueddeutsche.de/kultur/restitution-von-raubkunst-gebt-sie-zurueck-1.4220674 (30 May 2019).

60 See Oswald, Restitution Report; Ruth Maclean: Bronzes to Benin, gold to Ghana ... muse-ums under fire on looted art, in: *The Observer*, 2 December 2018, URL: https://www.theguardian.com/culture/2018/dec/02/british-museums-pressure-give-back–looted-african-art-treasures (30 May 2019).

development aid to create a satisfactory cultural infrastructure in the global South and cautioned against making museums the "instruments of government".[61]

Hunt's concern over state interference in museum affairs is probably widely shared across the European museum world.[62] Museums in the Netherlands used the absence of a national policy on restitution to take proactive steps themselves. In March 2019, the *Nationaal Museum van Wereldculturen* (NMVW) issued a catalogue of rules and principles under which claimants can request the return of cultural objects from the museum's holdings.[63] Just a few days later, the Amsterdam Rijksmuseum, an institution with substantial collections from Sri Lanka and Indonesia, came forth with an initiative intended to surpass the setting of conditions by the NMVW. Announcing that merely waiting for claimants is not enough and that the Netherlands started embarrassingly late with the return of colonial objects, the museum sent a senior official to Sri Lanka to discuss the return of objects looted from the island in the colonial era. These initiatives show that, in the Netherlands as anywhere else, strategic considerations prevail. The *Principles and Process for Addressing Claims for the Return of Cultural Objects* set up by the NMVW, for example, have been criticized for shifting the onus of proof once more onto the claimants who, for example, could be asked to provide evidence for a "persistence of belief" or "culture" as proof that an object is truly theirs. Such dictating of conditions does not signal a wholehearted embrace of restitution but must be regarded as a pre-emptive step to retain control and agency with a view to official state policies and the development of criteria for restitution on a national level. The same is true for the Rijksmuseum, which used its relative latecoming as the second mover among Dutch institutions to claim the morally higher ground vis-à-vis the NMWV, at least for the time being. However, as strategic and awkwardly phrased as the provisions of the NMWV principles may be, they do alert us to the unresolved tensions inherent in the much celebrated reversal of the burden of proof. What obligations does it precisely entail, and how is agency

---

61 Tristram Hunt, Hartmut Dorgerloh, Nicholas Thomas, "Restitution Report: museum directors respond", *The Art Newspaper*, 27 November 2018, https://www.theartnewspaper.com/comment/restitution-report-museums-directors-respond (30 May 2019).

62 The President of the German Federation of Museums (Deutscher Museumsbund) Eckart Köhne, for example, warned against state interference in the internal policies of museums by arguing that, in Germany, this last happened during the Nazi regime between 1933 and 1945 (Statement as a member of a panel discussion on "sensitive objects", held at the Landesmuseum Mainz, 25 April 2019.)

63 See https://www.afrikamuseum.nl/nl/teruggave-van-culturele-objecten-principes-en-processen (30 May 2019).

distributed in the process of producing evidence for legitimate or illegitimate ownership?[64] And can museums be expected to enter into in-depth provenance research of any object claimed without somehow previously establishing the claimant's entitlement to do so? Such questions concerning the legitimate heir will inevitably come up as soon as the "Africa" of intellectual debate falls apart into individuals, groups, communities and states who actively start reclaiming objects as "their" heritage.

The Macron Moment in the Federalized German World Museum World

In Germany, Macron's initiative and the Sarr/Savoy-report were received in the context of an already vitriolic and polarized debate about the country's adequate addressing of its colonial past. One strand of this debate has focussed on the question of a formal apology and the official recognition as genocide of Germany's brutal war of annihilation waged in its Namibian colony between 1904 and 1907, a protracted diplomatic process that has burdened German-Namibian relations at least since the centenary commemorations of the war's outbreak in 2004.[65] A second strand consisted of a number of local initiatives, driven by academic projects, postcolonial activist groups or both together, who addressed aspects and traces of Germany's colonial past in concrete urban contexts. Frequently taking up the critical "think global, act local"-spirit of older forms of Third World activism, these initiatives retrieved local historical

---

64 Also the North American Graves Protection and Repatriation Act (NAGPRA), often lauded as a model for handling restitution in the European colonial debate, is struggling with these issues, see e.g. Helen A. Robbins: In Consideration of Restitution. Understanding and Transcending the Limits of Repatriation under the Native American Graves Protection and Repatriation Act (NAGPRA), in: Louise Tythacott and Kostas Arvanitis (eds.): *Museums and Restitution. New Practices, New Approaches.* London, New York 2014, 105–121.

65 For a survey see Henning Melber and Reinhart Kößler: *Völkermord und was dann? Die Politik deutsch-namibischer Vergangenheitsbearbeitung.* Frankfurt/M. 2017; for the historiographical dimension of the debate over genocide see Christiane Bürger: *Deutsche Kolonialgeschichte(n). Der Genozid in Namibia und die Geschichtsschreibung der DDR und BRD.* Bielefeld 2017; Jürgen Zimmerer and Joachim Zeller (eds.): *Völkermord in Deutsch-Südwestafrika – Der Kolonialkrieg (1904–1908) in Namibia und seine Folgen.* Berlin 2003; Isabel Hull: *Absolute Destruction. Military Culture and the Practices of War in Imperial Germany.* Ithaca 2006; on the divergent memorialization in Germany and Namibia Larissa Förster: *Postkoloniale Erinnerungslandschaften. Wie Deutsche und Herero in Namibia des Kriegs von 1904 gedenken.* Frankfurt/M. 2010.

connections to overseas colonialism and addressed a variety of practices, attitudes and institutions that still awaited adequate decolonization. Among these were e.g. street names that glorified brutal colonial militaries and officials but also the local and provincial legacies of ethnographic collecting in the state capitals of a federally organized Germany.

In many cities, museums actively cooperated with such initiatives in the investigation of their colonial histories by making their archives accessible.[66] But certainly the most significant strand has crystallized around the flagship cultural project of reconstructing the former Hohenzollern palace in the heart of Berlin and opening it as a grand cultural institution named the *Humboldt-Forum*, supposed to showcase globalized Germany's cosmopolitanism by, amongst others, displaying items from the ethnographic collections of the Prussian and German state.[67] These collections comprise tens of thousands of objects from all over the world since the early modern period and include artefacts collected in non-German colonial contexts, such as a substantial number of the famous Benin Bronzes, the most notorious example of looted yet not restituted art from Africa. But above all, the Berlin ethnographic museum owns considerable holdings from the decades of German colonial rule in Africa, Asia and Oceania between 1884 and 1918. After 1889, the Berlin ethnographic museum functioned as the central institution collecting all objects acquired in the official colonial contexts of conquest, administrative duty, or military and state-sponsored expeditions. This monopoly resulted in a skyrocketing increase of colonial objects during these years, particularly from Africa.[68] Obviously, this official role constitutes a special and particularly deep involvement of the Berlin collections into Germany's overseas colonialism. The responsibility arising from this involvement, however, needs yet

---

66 From a flourishing field of initiatives, websites and publications see e.g. the websites of Berlin, Hamburg, Heidelberg, or Freiburg postkolonial, further Bernd-Stefan Grewe, et al.: *Freiburg und der Kolonialismus. Vom Kaiserreich bis zum Nationalsozialismus*. Freiburg 2018; Eva Bahl et al. (eds.): *Decolonize München*. München 2015; Felix Brahm and Bettina Brockmeyer (eds.): *Koloniale Spurensuche in Bielefeld und Umgebung*. Bielefeld 2014; Marianne Bechhaus-Gerst and Anne-Kathrin Horstmann (eds.): *Köln und der deutsche Kolonialismus. Eine Spurensuche*. Köln, Weimar, Wien 2013.

67 See Peter-Klaus Schuster and Horst Bredekamp (eds.): *Das Berliner Humboldt-Forum. Die Wiedergewinnung der Idee*. Berlin 2016; AfricAvenir (ed.): *No Humboldt 21! Dekoloniale Einwände gegen das Humboldt-Forum*. Berlin 2017; Friedrich von Bose: *Das Humboldt-Forum. Eine Ethnografie seiner Planung*. Berlin 2016; Karl-Heinz Kohl et al.: *Das Humboldt-Forum und die Ethnologie. Ein Gespräch zwischen Karl-Heinz Kohl, Fritz Kramer, Johann Michael Möller, Gereon Sievernich, Gisela Völger*. Frankfurt/M. 2019.

68 Christine Stelzig: *Afrika am Museum für Völkerkunde in Berlin 1873–1919. Aneignung, Darstellung und Konstruktion eines Kontinents*. Herbolzheim 2004, 15.

to be fully and explicitly admitted and addressed by the Forum's managers, who have long engaged in outright denial of or circumstantial whataboutism with regard to problem.[69] More recently, they have taken to weighing up a long history of benign, enlightened and cosmopolitan interest in the "Other" against a short, imperialist and violent aberration of colonial collecting, without acknowledging that one was implicated in the other.[70]

These years-long attempts at evading, eluding, belittling and obscuring the colonial problem of the Humboldt-Forum have not only contributed to an unprecedented media attention to colonial topics and fuelled the criticism raised by Berlin-based postcolonial initiatives and academics. They also provided a peculiarly fertile ground for the urgency and radicalism of the Macron moment. After all, the Humboldt-Forum faces even greater time pressures than does Macron, as it is due to open in late 2019. If this resulted in a doubling of urgencies in the German case, the Sarr/Savoy-report was also received with special attention, for it could be read as a comment on the Humboldt-Forum by a former member of its scientific advisory board. Bénédicte Savoy's spectacular resignation in July 2017 was accompanied by public accusations of fundamental misconceptions and a strategic unwillingness to address the problematic provenance of the Berlin ethnographic collections. The refusal of Berlin officials to sufficiently acknowledge the problem of colonial provenances has surely contributed its share to the uncompromising character of the report's recommendation. Moreover, Savoy's scathing criticism has tainted the substantial efforts at cooperative provenance research undertaken by the Berlin ethnological museum since 2016.[71] They appear, perhaps unjustified, as first and foremost strategic concession to the ever-mounting public criticism.

---

69 Hermann Parzinger: Konzept zur Präsentation der außereuropäischen Sammlungen im Humboldt-Forum 2008, in: *Baessler-Archiv* 59 (2011), 113–184, esp. 122.

70 See e.g. "Ich lehne diese Argumentation der Gleichsetzerei ab". Interview with Horst Bredekamp in Deutschlandfunk Kultur, 26 November 2018, URL: https://www.deutschland funkkultur.de/bredekamp-widerspricht-savoys-empfehlungen-ich-lehne-diese.1013.de.html? dram:article_id=434280 (30 May 2019).

71 These efforts at unveiling "shared histories of objects" have dealt with, above all, collections acquired during warfare in colonial Tanzania and are intended to develop a "framework concept" for colonial provenance research, see Pilotprojekt: Tansania–Deutschland: Geteilte Objektgeschichten?, URL: https://www.smb.museum/museen-und-einrichtungen/ethnolo gisches-museum/sammeln-forschen/forschung/tansania-deutschland-geteilte-objektge schichten.html (30 May 2019), and Lily Reyels, Paola Ivanov, Kristin Weber Sinn (eds.): *Humboldt Lab Tanzania. Objekte aus kolonialen Kriegen im Ethnologischen Museum Berlin. Deutsch-tansanische Perspektiven*. Berlin 2018.

Unsurprisingly, the Sarr/Savoy-report met with reserved and diplomatic public reactions from the directors in charge of the Humboldt-Forum. The Forum's manager Hartmut Dorgerloh welcomed an "overdue" debate and promised to increase provenance research in order to establish if "injustice was done in the process", for "looted art must always be returned".[72] His colleague Hermann Parzinger, the President of the Prussian Cultural Heritage Foundation, reacted by what has been characterized as "rejection through overembracing"[73]: he has not directly commented on Sarr and Savoy, but has praised Macron's first statement after the handing-over of the report. On this occasion, Macron once more presented the exchange and circulation of objects as possible forms of cooperation with African states alongside restitution. Sidelining the report itself in favor of Macron enables Parzinger to emphasize the fundamental congruence between Macron's initiative and the cooperative approach to determining the provenance and deciding upon the possible return of colonial objects as practiced by German institutions and their partners. Urging the necessity of dialogue, cooperation, and exchange with formerly colonized societies, he then questioned the juridical feasibility of retroactive restitution. Instead of a legal solution, Parzinger proposed the formation of an international commission to develop ethical standards similar to the Washington Principles on Nazi-Confiscated Art agreed upon in 1998.[74] Above all, museums must be put in a position to digitize and make accessible their object-related documentation, to conduct provenance research and extend their world-wide networks with other museums and source communities. His contribution concluded with a statement that human remains must by all means be restituted[75] – a declaration that signals determination and

---

72 Tristram Hunt, Hartmut Dorgerloh, Nicholas Thomas, "Restitution Report: museum directors respond", *The Art Newspaper*, 27 November 2018, https://www.theartnewspaper.com/comment/restitution-report-museums-directors-respond (30 May 2019).

73 Margareta von Oswald: The "Restitution Report". First Reactions in Academia, Museums, and Politics (15 January 2019), URL: http://www.carmah.berlin/reflections/restitution-report_first-reactions/ (30 May 2019).

74 These proposals are, however, non-binding. For a model of principles on dealing with colonial cultural and historical objects based upon the Washington Principles see Jos van Beurden: *Treasures in Trusted Hands. Negotiating the future of colonial cultural objects.* Leiden 2016.

75 Hermann Parzinger: Zeitenwende oder Ablasshandel?, in: *Frankfurter Allgemeine Zeitung* 29 November 2018, URL: https://www.faz.net/aktuell/feuilleton/debatten/wie-sollte-man-mit-kolonialen-kulturguetern-umgehen-15914615-p2.html?printPagedArticle=true#pageIndex_1 (30 May 2019).

moral rigour but only states an obvious principle that is already a widely shared ethical consensus across the museum world.[76]

Of course, reactions in Germany have not been restricted to the embracing rejection by the managers of Germany's soon-to-be most egregious cultural institution. Forty years after director-general of UNESCO Amadou-Mahtar M'Bow called upon media "to arouse worldwide a mighty and intense movement of public opinion so that respect for works of art leads, wherever necessary, to their return to their homeland",[77] journalists sympathetic to the cause of restitution immediately popularized the report's recommendation in equally radical headlines (*"Gebt alles zurück!"*). The report resulted in a further increase of academic workshops and panel discussions on colonial collections. Well over a hundred scholars from history, ethnology and other humanities disciplines published a public appeal in the quality weekly *Die Zeit* in December 2018 to sympathize with the appeal for restitution and call for a deep and broad societal engagement with German colonialism and the manifold legacies and entanglements it forged across continents.[78] Just a few days later, high-ranking cultural politicians Michelle Müntefering and Monika Grütters acknowledged the need for a thorough engagement of German society with its colonial past. In an article that was published simultaneously in the quality daily *Frankfurter Allgemeine Zeitung* and on the website of the German Foreign Office, they appealed to museums to ensure a maximum of transparency about their

---

76 See e.g. the *Recommendations for the Care of Human Remains in Museums and Collections*, issued by the German Museums' Association in 2013 (URL: https://www.museumsbund.de/wp-content/uploads/2017/04/2013-recommendations-for-the-care-of-human-remains.pdf); Larissa Förster and Sarah Fründt (eds.): Human Remains in Museums and Collections. A Critical Engagement with the "Recommendations" of the German Museums' Association (2013), in: *H-Soz-Kult* (03 February 2017), URL: <www.hsozkult.de/debate/id/diskussionen-3902> (27 May 2019); and, from a vast literature, Friedemann Schrenk, Anke Kuper, Anne Marie Rahn, Isabel Eiser: Menschen in Sammlungen. Geschichte verpflichtet, in: Anna-Maria Brandstetter and Vera Hierholzer (eds.): *Nicht nur Raubkunst! Sensible Dinge in Museen und universitären Sammlungen.* Göttingen 2018, 45–61; Holger Stoecker, Thomas Schnalke, and Andreas Winkelmann (eds.): *Sammeln, Erforschen, Zurückgeben? Menschliche Gebeine aus der Kolonialzeit in akademischen und musealen Sammlungen.* Berlin 2013.
77 An Appeal by Mr. Amadou-Mahtar M'Bow, Director-General of UNESCO. A Plea for the Return of an Irreplaceable Cultural Heritage to Those Who Created It, in: *The Unesco Courier*, 31, July 1978, 4.
78 Was wir jetzt brauchen: Für Restitutionen und einen neuen Umgang mit der Kolonialgeschichte. Ein Appell von Wissenschaftlern aus der ganzen Welt, in: *Die Zeit*, 12 December 2018, URL: https://www.zeit.de/2018/52/kolonialgeschichte-umgang-kunstwerke-restitution (30 May 2019); Rebekka Habermas and Ulrike Lindner: Rückgabe – und mehr!, in: *Die Zeit*, 12 December 2018, URL: https://www.zeit.de/2018/52/kunst-kolonialzeit-rueckgabe-restitution-geschichtspolitik (30 May 2019).

collections and to openly engage with the return of colonial objects to their societies of origin.[79] Thereby, they increased the pressure on an institution that had already sought to develop a uniform position on the matter. For example, half a year earlier, in May 2018 and preceding the Sarr/Savoy-report, the German Museums' Association had published preliminary "Guidelines on Dealing with Collections from Colonial Contexts" which has just been republished in summer 2019 after discussion with experts from selected source communities.[80] While the first edition was characterized by a cautious approach to the "return" of colonial objects, the revised version is marked by a far greater sensitivity to non-European perspectives on the matter. The guidelines do not assume a determinism between colonial context and illegal acquisition, as Sarr and Savoy do. Rather, provenance from a colonial context obliges museums to act with particular sensitivity and meticulous examination.[81]

The guidelines of the German Museums' Association originated from debates that well antedated the Macron moment[82] and show that we should be careful not to attribute too much impact to the Macron momentum. The same is true for the recent restitution of a whip and a bible from the holdings of the Linden-Museum Stuttgart to Namibia.[83] The museum received these items as a gift from a colonial official in 1902. Originally, bible and whip had belonged to Hendrik Witbooi, a Nama leader who fought against the Germans and who is counted among the national heroes of Namibia. In February 2019, his belongings were transferred in a solemn official state ceremony that conveyed a powerful impression of the cultural importance of such objects for the deprived communities and, indeed, the potential to initiate the new relational ethics that

---

79 Monika Grütters and Michelle Müntefering: Eine Lücke in unserem Gedächtnis, in: *Frankfurter Allgemeine Zeitung*, 15 December 2018, URL: https://www.bundesregierung.de/breg-de/bundesregierung/staatsministerin-fuer-kultur-und-medien/eine-luecke-in-unserem-ge daechtnis-1561942 (30 May 2019),

80 Deutscher Museumsbund: *Leitfaden zum Umgang mit Sammlungsgut aus kolonialen Kontexten*. 2. Fassung, Berlin 2019.

81 Ibid., 6.

82 See e.g. the contributions in *Museumskunde* 81/2016, vol. 1, Positioning Ethnological Museums in the 21st century.

83 See Reinhart Kössler: *The Bible and the Whip – Entanglements around the Restitution of robbed Heirlooms*. ABI Working Paper No. 12, Freiburg 2019, URL: https://www.arnold-berg straesser.de/sites/default/files/field/pub-download/kossler_the_bible_the_whip_final_0.pdf (30 May 2019). Thomas Thiemeyer and Jochen von Bernstorff: Südwestdeutsch trifft Deutsch-Südwest. Baden-Württemberg gibt zwei kolonialzeitliche Objekte an Namibia zurück, in: *Merkur* 840 (2019), 17–29.

Sarr and Savoy invoke. At the same time, this restitution was accompanied by severe frictions between subnational groups and the Namibian state, who both laid claim to ownership and disposal of the restituted items, thereby exposing, as Reinhart Kössler has argued, that restitution can not only not undo colonialism and its consequences, it can even cause old colonial frictions to "become re-articulated in fresh conflicts on the ground."[84] The initiative to restitute whip and bible antedated the Macron moment by a few years, originating in negotiations between the Namibian Embassy and the owning state of Baden-Württemberg that started in 2013. Like the proactive move by the Amsterdam Rijksmuseum, this restitution must also be seen as a form of strategic cultural diplomacy by both the museum and the government of Baden-Württemberg as the legal owner of the museum collections. The Linden-Museum, already a pioneer of provenance research among Germany's ethnographic museums,[85] established itself among the institutions working proactively for restitution. The Green government of Baden-Württemberg accrued the symbolic capital of a progressive leader in the moral politics of coming to terms with the country's colonial legacy, in contrast to the hesitant stand of the Grand Coalition in the federal government in Berlin.

The list of examples and reactions across the German political, academic, museal and cultural landscape could be extended, e.g. by an important memorandum drawn up by a consortium of ministers and politicians responsible for cultural affairs on the federal, state and communal level in March 2019.[86]

---

84 Kössler, The Bible and the Whip, 1.

85 See Gesa Grimme: Annäherungen an ein "Schwieriges Erbe". Provenienzforschung im Linden-Museum Stuttgart, in: Larissa Förster et al. (Hg.): *Provenienzforschung zu ethnografischen Sammlungen der Kolonialzeit. Positionen in der aktuellen Debatte*. Berlin 2017, 157–170 (http://edoc.hu-berlin.de/18452/19800); Claudia Andratschke: Provenienzforschung in ethnographischen Sammlungen, in: Alexis von Poser and Bianca Baumann (eds): Heikles Erbe: Koloniale Spuren bis in die Gegenwart. Dresden 2016, 304–309.

86 The consortium defined the appropriate dealing with colonial collections as a central aspect of cultural policies and an important contribution to a shared postcolonial cultural memory. Apart from a pledge to transparency, accessibility and digitalization, the memorandum once more entrenched provenance research as the German approach to the problem, declaring it the indispensable basis for "determining the provenance and the circumstances of acquisition" of questionable objects: see Erste Eckpunkte zum Umgang mit Sammlungsgut aus kolonialen Kontexten der Staatsministerin des Bundes für Kultur und Medien, der Staatsministerin im Auswärtigen Amt für internationale Kulturpolitik, der Kulturministerinnen und Kulturminister der Länder und der kommunalen Spitzenverbände (13 March 2019), URL: https://www.kmk.org/aktuelles/artikelansicht/eckpunkte-zum-umgang-mit-sammlungsgut-aus-kolonialen-kontexten.html (20 May 2019).

This shows that the restitution debate is ongoing and liable to sudden changes. Still, there are three aspects that stand out as distinctive in Germany's take on displaced cultural heritage. First, and contrary to Sarr and Savoy's proposal, most decision-makers in German museum and cultural policies do not follow the report's automatism of colonial context leading to restitution. Rather, they take colonial contexts as an automatism that necessitates sensitive handling and thorough research. This procedure tries to do justice to historical accuracy and individual objects but remains unsatisfactory from the perspective of those who were historically deprived of their cultural heritage. They are, despite all pledges to dialogue, once more reduced to supplicants who are told to wait and play by the rules set by the privileged inheritors of an asymmetrical history, as Sarr and Savoy put it. This said, the report's emphasis on restitution has created media-fanned expectations of immediate action that has made the research on provenances already underway seem dilatory rather than progressive. Therefore, it should be particularly emphasized that those German museums that hold ethnographic collections have adopted a clear stand on the restitution of objects acquired under unjust conditions in their recent Heidelberg Declaration in May 2019. And while thorough provenance research takes time and thus tends to postpone restitution, it is a cooperative effort. Wherever it is practiced, it brings German institutions and curators into conversation with institutions, communities and individuals from the "source" regions. Thus, provenance research already puts into practice the new relational ethic demanded by the report.

Second, if regulating the problem through the highest authority of the state stands in the continuity of French centralism, the same is true for the federal approach that becomes visible in the varying German ways of addressing the legacies of the colonial past. The politics of culture and museums are predominantly federal affairs. The need to coordinate a far greater number of federal and communal actors and institutions than in the case of France or the Netherlands takes time and opens manoeuvring space for the self-positioning of individual states and museums. While some museums remain silent and hope to be overlooked until the storm might calm again, like it did so many times before, individual states, like Bremen or Hamburg, or museums, as in Hannover or Stuttgart, take the lead and accrue the symbolic capital of a progressive stand towards restitution and the confrontation with the colonial past. In doing so, they forge new networks with source communities, make themselves attractive for externally-funded provenance research, exert pressure on institutions in a similar situation, and try to wield influence in the overall debate about displaced cultural heritage. The regional and municipal competition that is becoming visible today is an interesting equivalent of the "worldly provincialism" that drove museums (and the proud urban bourgeoisie supporting them) into an intra-German municipal competition for the biggest and most significant ethnographic collections.[87]

The third characteristic peculiarity of the German debates is their framing first and foremost in categories and institutions developed with a view to identify art looted during the Nazi regime. For example, in January 2019 the funding of colonial provenance research was entrusted to the German Lost Art Foundation (one of the members of the funding committee being Bénédicte Savoy),[88] an institution for the restitution of displaced cultural property that traces its history back to the early 1990s. Established formally as a foundation in 2015, its main task consisted of facilitating the restitution of Jewish property confiscated under the Nazi regime, with an ever greater emphasis on formalized provenance research. Before taking up the funding of research into colonial provenances, the Foundation was also entrusted with research into the confiscation of cultural assets in the former GDR or the Soviet Occupation Zone. The path dependency of doing colonial provenance research using the terms and infrastructure of Nazi-related provenance research reflects the historical course of German expansionism but also the established way for German politics and society to come to terms with a problematic past. It makes good sense to draw upon existing databases and the already accumulated knowledge of art dealers and art markets. The treatment of colonial rule as another historical "context of injustice" alongside acknowledged dictatorial regimes also has the potential to weaken the principle of intertemporality and to enable, as in the case of Nazi Germany, the retrospective application of law. Undeniably, the restoration of historical colonial victimhood benefits from a coeval moral standing alongside acknowledged crimes against humanity. Yet, it remains a challenge to adequately reflect both contextual similarities and differences between centuries of asymmetric cultural encounter with their conjunctures of violence and racism and the systematic deprivation of existing rights, persecution and annihilation practiced under National Socialism.

Conclusions

Did the Sarr-Savoy report effect a "sea change" in the relationship between global North and global South, taking the debate on displaced cultural objects

---

87 Penny and Bunzl (eds.), Worldly Provincialism.
88 So far, however, its guidelines for application have not provided a mechanism, e.g., for scholars or source communities from the Global South to have the provenance of certain collections investigated.

to new levels, as Jörg Häntzschel would have it? As yet, there has been much discussion and many ideas: we witness a museum world in motion and the forging of many new and promising networks between Western museums and source societies. Still, there has been far greater movement in discourse than of actual objects. In the light of decades of ebbs and flows in the international debate about displaced heritage, it remains to be seen whether we are currently experiencing just one more conjuncture, as in the early and late 1970s, or, indeed, the beginning of an "age of restitution" (Ciraj Rassool) or a "restitution revolution" (Bénédicte Savoy).

While a revolution may or may not be under way, the Sarr/Savoy-report has definitely shifted the moral parameters of debate. As a document consciously placed in the political arena, it contains elements similar to strategic litigation. Whatever Macron will decide, the report has established once more that the restitution of objects acquired under unjust conditions is the necessary and right thing to do. By privileging restitution over provenance research the report elevated those who supported immediate restitution to the moral high ground. Those arguing for historical complexity or those who deemed provenance research and cooperation with source communities the cutting edge of progressive work in museums, could suddenly find themselves on the wrong side of the moral equation. Doing or defending provenance research can seem like playing for time and an almost neo-colonial perpetuation of an untenable, unjust status quo. This said, the report also forces European audiences to approach the problem of displaced cultural heritage from a first and foremost African perspective. For those deprived of core objects of their cultural identity, any further deferral is, indeed, the perpetuation of historical injustice. However, the "African" perspective, as currently represented in European debates, so far consists mainly of contributions by public intellectuals like Felwine Sarr or Achille Mbembe, who have access to Western academia and publishing outlets. Other voices from "Africa" or indigenous communities are not missing, but they remain woefully underrepresented, despite the best efforts by journalists to dig up relevant voices and new perspectives[89] or by the organizers of panel discussions to feature experts from Africa or at least with an African background. Tight budgets, language requirements and the multiplicity of possible source communities all combine to make the aim of coeval representation of African voices in European debates a challenging and partially random affair. Here, it would help if museums made their existing cooperations with source

---

[89] See e.g. Jörg Häntzschel: Der Geist eines Kontinents, in: *Süddeutsche Zeitung*, 24 April 2019, URL: https://projekte.sueddeutsche.de/artikel/kultur/raubkunst-der-geist-eines-konti nents-e890780/?reduced=true (20 May 2019).

communities more transparent and converted the silent expert knowledge of these partners at least partially into publicly audible voices.

For a historian whose academic socialization took place in the late 1990s and early 2000s, many of the arguments of the Sarr/Savoy-report read like a blast from the past of the late 1970s. My generation has been trained to question claims to fixed identities and think that nations are constructed, imagined communities created by elites who dexterously invent traditions and manipulate historical myths. Progressive historiography, as I have learned to understand it, is about transcending narrow containers of identity and a postcolonial approach to colonial history is about overcoming the inherited and powerful binary oppositions of black and white, colonizers and colonized, modern and traditional, centre and periphery, victims and perpetrators. For all the asymmetries and racism of the colonial encounter, the colonial situation was marked by subversion, mimicry, sly deception and the agency of the colonized, who limited the grand designs and all-powerful fantasies of the colonizers in decisive ways. Orientalist binaries were to be deconstructed, hybridity was the concept of the day. Sarr and Savoy, however, argue for cultural nation-building and cultural sovereignty as progressive instruments for African cultural decolonization when they present the "return of emblematic objects" as essential for the "construction of a political community" and the "reconstruction of the identity of subjects and communities".[90] Such essentialism may in part be strategic, but one is left to wonder how the political postcolonialism of restitution, with its emphasis on historical victimhood and future-oriented identity-building, can be reconciled with the epistemological postcolonialism practiced by Western academia during the last quarter of the century. It seems that practical agency in the present based upon a position of victimhood is preferred by many to a merely discursive agency in the past generously granted by Western historians.

In their relative disinterest for provenance, Sarr and Savoy privilege the African reclamation of history through the objects over the epistemological status of the objects as documents for an entangled history between Europe and Africa in the past. The future epistemologies of the objects are to be decidedly African, not so much entangled, and certainly not European. One is left to wonder, however, if it is entirely unavoidable or necessary to privilege restitution over provenance, to set ethics against law and history, and to play the future off against the past and Africa against Europe.

---

90 Sarr/Savoy: Restitution of African Cultural Heritage, 35. For an analytical notion of cultural sovereignty see Gregor Feindt, Bernhard Gissibl, Johannes Paulmann (eds.): *Kulturelle Souveränität. Politische Deutungs- und Handlungsmacht jenseits des Staates im 20. Jahrhundert.* Göttingen 2017, esp. 40–44, 227–283.

Perhaps it would already help to unpack such loaded and homogenizing terms like "looted art" or "heritage" so as to differentiate the plurality of things lumped together in these categories. Thereby options could be recovered that are more flexible than the automatism of colonial context/restitution. The majority of objects are not art but material culture of everyday life. While they may still have significance for African societies, they are less likely to qualify as relevant heritage than, for example, ritual objects. The appropriate questions concerning such objects are not only about the circumstances of their acquisition but why and for what purposes they should remain hidden away in the storage rooms of European museums. Other objects are so obviously looted that there is simply no need for in-depth provenance research. The restitution of human remains has become an acknowledged ethical norm, although the practice of identification and return remains severely wanting. In such cases, museums should achieve the legal capacity to restitute, especially if one wants to avoid state actors using restitution as a tool for cultural diplomacy. Claimants, on the other hand, ought to be put in a legal position that ensures that the return of objects is more than a mere supplication granted by museums. It must evolve into an entitlement to be claimed, and return should also be a viable option for objects of cultural significance whose historical acquisition has been legitimate. There are fascinating suggestions in the debate about how to deal flexibly with objects that, for one reason or another, cannot yet be returned, such as immediately restoring ownership and then loaning them back until the best suited future place for these objects is negotiated.[91] This is, indeed, the fourth dimension of the introspection Bénédicte Savoy demanded in her lecture at the Collège de France. Introspection, she wrote, must entail dreaming, the conjuring up of creative solutions for the future of cultural heritage, unprecedented legal constructions, new forms of partnership, flexible models adapted to the realities of different regions.[92]

There is one final and Eurocentric argument why it seems necessary that provenance research is not replaced by swift restitution, the entangled past of colonial objects not entirely eclipsed through their potential future after restitution. Historians Rebekka Habermas and Ulrike Lindner have pointed to the hitherto untold and unacknowledged histories of colonial artefacts and their constitutive role for the development of European arts and identities.[93] Sarr and

---

91 This point has repeatedly been made by Jürgen Zimmerer, most recently in ZEIT Geschichte 4/19: Die Deutschen und ihre Kolonien. Hamburg 2019, 96.

92 Savoy: Provenienz der Kultur, 58.

93 Rebekka Habermas and Ulrike Lindner: Rückgabe – und mehr!, in: *Die Zeit*, 12 December 2018, URL: https://www.zeit.de/2018/52/kunst-kolonialzeit-rueckgabe-restitution-geschichtspolitik (30 May 2019).

Savoy have argued that being in the presence and spell of these objects should no longer be reserved to the beneficiaries of privilege and asymmetrical mobility. The inconvenient truth is that European societies have made far too little of this privilege during the last century. Indeed, while some egregious pieces have been elevated to the status of art, the vast majority of objects has hardly ever been systematically dealt with. Museum curators have been hopelessly unable to cope with the sheer amount of objects, the majority of which had been stored away in magazines for decades. Not only do we know far too little about their concrete provenance but also about their histories and changing epistemologies after they were integrated into European collections. Not only African societies have a displaced heritage to rediscover. European publics, too, hardly know what riches have been acquired from faraway places, often bought and cared for with public money. The rediscovery of these objects in the current debate and an unprecedented transparency of museums about their collections is a unique opportunity for European societies to unlearn what these objects have told them about the colonized world in the past and to use them to learn about the deep involvement of their cities and societies in overseas colonialism. Indeed, every single object has the potential to teach European citizens about past colonial entanglements. Hence, Sarr and Savoy are to be credited for their report for yet another reason. Like no text, book, or statement before, the restitution report has thrown up the very real threat that European museums could really lose these objects whose presence has so long been taken for granted. We have finally started to attend to them. This opportunity should not be missed so that the acknowledgment of historical injustice can be based upon a profound and widespread societal knowledge of what colonialism was, in fact, about.

List of Contributors

Cornelia Aust is a historian of early modern Jewish history at Bielefeld University. She studied in Leipzig, Jerusalem, Berlin, and Warsaw and received her PhD from the University of Pennsylvania. She has been a postdoctoral fellow at the Martin Buber Society of Fellows at the Hebrew University in Jerusalem and a Research Fellow at the Leibniz Institute of European History in Mainz. Her research interests include Jewish social, cultural, and economic history in German-speaking lands and Poland and in its European and global dimensions. She has published on Jewish economic history and commercial networks, including her first book, *The Jewish Economy Elite. Making Modern Europe* (Bloomington 2018). She is currently working on a project on Jewish dress and outward appearance and its perceptions by Christians and Jews.

Beata Biedrońska-Słota is an art historian and certified curator, and she headed the Textile Department of the National Museum in Cracow until 2011. She was the curator of numerous exhibitions, among them "Orient in Polish Art" (1992), "Fashion throughout the Centuries" (2003), and "The Golden Age of the Rzeczpospolita" (2011). She has published widely in the field of textile history: alongside many articles and a monograph on Persian carpets (1985), she has edited several volumes, such as *Crossroads of Costume and Textiles in Poland* (Cracow 2005) and *Samartism. A Dream of Power* (Cracow 2010; in Polish).

Giulia Calvi was Professor of Early Modern History at the University of Siena and from 2004 to 2012 held the Chair of "Gender History in Europe and the World (XVI–XIX)" in the Department of History and Civilization at the European University Institute in Florence. She is Senior Researcher in the ERC project *Luxury, Fashion and Social Status in Early Modern South-Eastern Europe* (http://luxfass.nec.ro). In 2012 she was appointed to the Chair of Italian Culture in the Italian Studies Department at the University of California (Berkeley). Her main publications and research interests are in the field of early modern cultural and social history. She has written on medical practice in times of epidemics; family relations; women's writings and autobiographies; and court culture and female courts. Her recent research investigates the circulation of images, texts, and material culture in and beyond Europe: "Across Three Empires: Balkan Costumes in XVI Century Europe", in: Constanţa Vintilă-Ghiţulescu (ed.), *From Traditional Attire to Modern Dress: Modes of Identification, Modes of Recognition in the Balkans (XVI–XX)* (Cambridge 2011), 29–51; "Cultures of Space. Costume Books, Maps and Clothing between Italy and Japan (Sixteenth to Nineteenth Centuries)", in: *I Tatti Studies* 2 (2017): 331–363.

Flora Cassen is Associate Professor of Jewish, Islamic, and Middle Eastern Studies, and of History at Washington University in St. Louis. She was previously Associate Professor of History and Van Der Horst Fellow of Jewish History and Culture at the University of North Carolina at Chapel Hill. Her research interests focus on early modern Jewish history in Italy and the Mediterranean and on the history of antisemitism. Her publications include *Marking the Jews in Renaissance Italy. Politics, Religion, and the Power of Symbols* (Cambridge 2017) and articles on a variety of topics such as Jewish spies, Jewish food, and new historiographic trends in Jewish studies. She currently is working on Joseph Ha-Kohen's books on the discovery of the Americas and the conquest of Mexico.

Bernhard Gissibl is a permanent Research Fellow at the Leibniz Institute of European History in Mainz. His doctoral thesis explored the political ecology of hunting and wildlife conservation in Tanzania during the German colonial period and was awarded the Young Scholars' Prize of the African Studies Association Germany (VAD). His research interests include environmental history and the history of conservation, transnational communication and media during the Cold War, and the history of European imperialism, especially in its local repercussions and entanglements.

Gabriel Guarino is Lecturer in Early Modern History at Ulster University. His main research interests are: Italian and Spanish early modern history (1500–1800) and the cultural history of the royal courts of Europe (1600–1800). These are reflected in numerous publications, including articles in such journals as *The Historical Journal*, *The Sixteenth Century Journal*, and *Historical Research*, as well as in a monograph titled *Representing the King's Splendour. Communication and Reception of Symbolic Forms of Power in Viceregal Naples* (Manchester 2010). He is presently working on a book manuscript, provisionally titled *Between Habsburgs and Bourbons. Dynastic Change, Political Communication and Diplomatic Relations in the Court of Naples, 1700–1799*.

Maria Hayward is Professor of Early Modern History at the University of Southampton, and her research interests cover clothing and textiles in the sixteenth and seventeenth centuries. Her publications include *Dress at the Court of King Henry VIII* (Leeds 2007), *Rich Apparel. Clothing and the Law in Henry VIII's England* (Aldershot 2009), *The First Book of Fashion* (London 2015) with Ulinka Rublack, and *Stuart Style. Monarchy, Dress and the Scottish Male Elite 1566–1701* (forthcoming, 2020).

Denise Klein is a historian of the Middle East and a Research Fellow at the Leibniz Institute of European History in Mainz. She has published on the social and cultural history of the Ottoman world in the period between the sixteenth and the eighteenth centuries, including *The Ottoman Ulema of the 17th Century. A Closed Society?* (Berlin 2007; in German) and ed., *The Crimean Khanate between East and West (15th–18th Century)* (Wiesbaden 2012). She is currently revising her book manuscript, *Narrating the Past in Tatar Crimea, 1550–1750*, and has started working on a new project, which investigates the experiences of immigrants in Istanbul between 1500 and 1800.

Maria Molenda is a historian, costume historian, and designer. She is a history graduate of the Jagiellonian University in Cracow, where she also completed a PhD. She is an independent researcher and author of papers on the history of clothing and of the book *Splendide vestitus. The Meaning of Clothing at the Royal Court of the Jagiellon Dynasty in the Years 1447–1572* (Cracow 2019; in Polish). Her research interests include Polish fashion of the late Middle Ages, the Renaissance, and the nineteenth century. Since 2004, she has been the president of the Nomina Rosae Foundation, an NGO dedicated to popularizing historical knowledge through a wide spectrum of educational and artistic projects (http://www.nomina.pl).

Constanţa Vintilă-Ghiţulescu is Principal Investigator for the ERC project *Luxury, Fashion and Social Status in Early Modern South-Eastern Europe* (http://luxfass.nec.ro), hosted by New Europe College, Bucharest, and Senior Researcher at the "Nicolae Iorga" Institute of History, Bucharest. She is the author of many books, including *Liebesglut: Liebe und Sexualität in der* *rumänischen Gesellschaft 1750–1830* (Berlin 2011); *Im Schalwar und mit Baschlik. Kirche, Sexualität, Ehe und Scheidung in der Walachei im 18. Jahrhundert* (Berlin 2013) and has edited volumes on *Women, Consumption, and the Circulation of Ideas in South-Eastern Europe, 17th–19th Centuries* (Leiden 2017) and *From Traditional Attire to Modern Dress: Modes of Identification, Modes of Recognition in the Balkans (XVIth-XXth Centuries)* (Cambridge 2011).

Thomas Weller is a permanent Research Fellow at the Leibniz Institute of European History in Mainz. He has published widely on the social, political, and cultural history of the Holy Roman Empire and the Spanish-speaking world in the early modern period. Among his recent publications related to the topic of this volume is "'Von ihrer schändlichen und teuffelischen Hoffart sich nicht abwenden lassen wollen . . . '. Kleider- und Aufwandsordnungen als Spiegel 'guter Ordnung'", in: Irene Dingel and Armin Kohnle (eds.): *Gute Ordnung. Ordnungsmodelle und Ordnungsvorstellungen im Zeitalter der Reformation* (Leipzig 2014), 203–219.